*A London Life
in the
Brazen Age*

A London Life
in the
Brazen Age

FRANCIS LANGLEY
1548-1602

William Ingram

HARVARD UNIVERSITY PRESS

Cambridge, Massachusetts, and London, England   1978

Library of Congress Cataloging in Publication Data

Ingram, William.
    A London life in the brazen Age.

    Includes bibliographical references and index.
    1. Langley, Francis, 1548–1602.   2. London.
Swan theatre.   3. Theatrical managers—England—
London—Biography.   I. Title.
PN2598.L22I5   338.7'61'7920924   [B]   77-28573
ISBN 0-674-53842-0

Publication of this book has been aided by a grant
from the Andrew W. Mellon Foundation

For Herbert Berry

e come sare' io sanza lui corso?
chi m'avrìa tratto su per la montagna?
PURGATORIO

Preface

In the presentation of my materials I have followed conventional practice. All dates reflect the historical year, which I take to begin on January 1, regardless of the mixed customs observed in the documents. All notices of christenings, marriages, and burials are from the Harleian Society Registers unless otherwise noted. All such data from St. Saviour's parish come from the register book of that parish, the property of the Corporation of Wardens of St. Saviour's but currently on deposit, along with a great many other parochial documents, with the Archivist of the Greater London Council in County Hall at Lambeth.

I have, albeit reluctantly, modernized the spelling and punctuation of the many passages that I quote from original documents. The chief advantage of modernization is that it makes for easier reading, unhampered by orthographic technicalities. Where the interpretation of a passage may be at issue, the literal and unamended text is provided in the notes. My one concession to readability in these latter passages has been to expand certain suspensions, the supplied letters in such cases being indicated by italics. In all cases, however, both in the text and in the notes, the wording of the documents is faithfully reproduced.

Portions of this work appeared, in somewhat different form, as journal articles. " 'Neere the playe howse'; the Swan Theater and Community Blight" first appeared in *Renaissance Drama*, new series IV (copyright 1972 Northwestern University Press); "The Closing of the Theatres in 1597," in *Modern Philology* 69:2 (copyright 1971 by the University of Chicago; all rights reserved). I thank the editors of these journals for permission to use this material. Quotations from Ellesmere MSS 2334 and 2468 appear by permission of the Huntington Library, San Marino, California. Transcripts of records in the Public Record Office appear by permission of the Controller of Her Majesty's Stationery Office. The drawings by H. W. Brewer are reproduced from *Old London Illustrated* (London, The Builder Ltd., 9th edition, 1962) by permission of George Godwin Ltd.

I owe numerous acknowedgments for assistance and advice in the writing of this book. The University of Michigan was generous in support from its Faculty Research Fund, making possible extended research in London. The American Council of Learned Societies supported me with a grant in the spring of 1973. The officers and staffs of the Public Record Office, the Department of Manuscripts of the British Library, the National Register of Archives, the Society of Genealogists, the Corporation of London Record Office, the Greater London Record Office, the Minet Library, the Inner Temple Library, the Middle Temple Library, and the Corporation of Wardens of Southwark Cathedral were all most helpful.

I am grateful to the Marquess of Salisbury for allowing me to consult his library at Hatfield House, and also to the archivists, librarians, and clerks of the following organizations: the Hampshire Records Office, the Lincolnshire Archives Office, the Surrey Record Office, and the worshipful companies of Goldsmiths, Dyers, Saddlers, Haberdashers, Weavers, Vintners, and Girdlers. I am indebted to the staffs of the Newberry

Library, the Henry E. Huntington Library, and the Folger Shakespeare Library for numerous courtesies and unfailing assistance.

Mildred Wretts-Smith was indispensable to me in ferreting out documents when I was not in London. Clifford Leech kindly offered criticisms of an early draft, and Sam Schoenbaum and Norman Rabkin made helpful comments at later stages. Betty Masters, Deputy Keeper of the Records in the Corporation of London Record Office, and Susan Hare, Librarian of the Company of Goldsmiths, have been helpful beyond all reasonable expectation. I am, finally, grateful to Christopher Corkery for editorial assistance on all points, to Joseph Lau for the maps, and to William Goodman of Harvard University Press for encouragement of the best sort.

But my primary obligation is to Herbert Berry, who first suggested to me that there were documents in the Public Record Office about Francis Langley that ought to be pursued. He had already seen many of them in the course of his research on the Boar's Head playhouse, and rightly sensed that there were many more. He gave me free access to his notes and references concerning Langley's role in the Boar's Head, with no restrictions on my use thereof; this generosity, coupled with his constant readiness to furnish help and counsel when I was in difficulty with my own research, taught me something about the nature of the true scholarly spirit.

Contents

The Ages in their growth wax worse & worse . . .
This is the Brazen Age.
THOMAS·HEYWOOD

I

The Youth

I do commit his youth to your direction.
KING JOHN

Francis Langley was an Elizabethan and a Londoner, in every way a creature of his time and place. His life neatly embraced the second half of the sixteenth century—he was born just before 1550 and died just after 1600—and all but the first eight years of his life were spent in or near London. Among his London contemporaries during portions of the same period were such diverse types as Christopher Marlowe, Nicholas Hilliard, William Byrd, Inigo Jones, and Francis Bacon. But unlike these more famous figures, Langley was a perfectly ordinary Londoner, with no gifts of creativity or perception to distinguish and memorialize him beyond his immediate time and place, or even to attract a following while there. As a compensation, perhaps, Langley was imbued instead with that spirit of enthusiasm and expansion, or perhaps more accurately the spirit of ostentation and aggrandizement, that lent itself so readily to the pens of the social satirists of the period.

Langley hungered for the benefits that attended affluence and power, and in his pursuit of wealth and position he was undeterred by what a later age was to call Higher Feelings. Nature had framed him of the four

1

elements and taught him to have an aspiring mind; but in his scramble to the top he manifested not the mastery of a Tamburlaine but rather, by turns, the honor of a Quomodo, the scruples of an Overreach, the proclivities of a Mammon, the contrivances of a Security, the heart of a Bobadil. Nor were his real successes any more lasting than their imaginary ones.

But even as these theatrical types, with all their quirks and foibles, can no longer be properly grasped without some elucidation of the social contexts from which they sprang, so Francis Langley cannot come to life without a fairly circumstantial understanding of his time and place. To that end I feel obligated to do more than simply recite in sequence the events of his life; one might merely reproduce the available documents in chronological order if no more than that were required. The facts themselves are not difficult to master.

But even after we have the facts, we cannot know what they mean if we do not have the context. For Langley, as for Shakespeare, life in London meant a series of daily strains and pressures that sooner or later had their effect. In this book I will speculate, albeit sketchily, on the influence of London life on Langley's own life; as a result, this study may appear to be unnecessarily discursive, straying time and again from the plain biographical narrative that is its central theme. But to me this discursiveness is essential. Francis Langley was born on a farm in Lincolnshire and lived there until he was eight; when he came to London he had to learn a great many things about City life, and we must learn those same things if we are to understand how the City shaped him, and how he came to be involved in the multitude of activities that occupied his time and energies. Historians of the theatre are accustomed to describing Francis Langley as the builder of the Swan playhouse, and they discuss him only in that context. This is like thinking of Henry Clay Folger or Henry E. Huntington only as the found-

ers of libraries. I like to reflect on Langley's own possible reaction if he could know what odd thing we have
chosen to remember him for. His life was multifarious,
and the Swan was but one part of it; to understand the
man, we must know what else was on his mind.

Of Langley's physical appearance I have been able to
learn nothing. No portraits seem to have survived; perhaps none were ever made. Any information about his
height, weight, coloring, or possible deformities has
passed into oblivion. His contemporaries were far more
interested in describing his actions, and even in specu-
lating on his motives for action, than in limning his
likeness. This is just as well, for it enables us instead to
reconstruct a reasonable picture of the coloring and
possible deformities of the inner Langley, what we
might wish to call—and I use this overworked term
with reluctance—his personality. As my narrative proceeds, the reader will not fail to notice the emergence
of certain basic characteristics. It will be clear that
Langley early developed a kind of haughtiness or disdain of those around him, perhaps in emulation of the
social postures adopted by the Londoners of rank and
position whom he knew as a youth. For he was indeed
privileged, as a young man, to know several aldermen
and sheriffs of the City, and more than one Lord
Mayor, all of them men who required—and got—their
due of deference. Langley early determined to require
the same kind of deference for himself, and the tenac-
ity with which he demanded it is perhaps matched
only by his apparent inability to inspire it naturally in
those who had dealings with him.

He also developed a kind of arrogant ruthlessness,
akin to the proud man's contumely and the insolence of
office that Hamlet later pinpointed for his London audience as two of life's insufferable pains. In Langley's
case the behavior manifested itself in a deliberate refusal of compassion for the plight of inferiors, coupled
with a readiness to take advantage of them whenever
the opportunity might present itself. In this he pur-

sued a mode of conduct that he might easily have observed around him. London was never devoid of exemplars for this sort of behavior, and they could be found at all levels of society. Robert Greene's cony-catching tracts describe, at one end of the social scale, a variety of ways in which the unscrupulous might ensnare the innocent. One of my own favorite instances, however, is from the opposite end of the social spectrum, and is almost Dickensian in its description of a confrontation between a timid shopboy and a powerful noble.

In the summer of 1588 the Earl of Lincoln, passing by a goldsmith's shop in Cheapside, saw "two ropes of pearls hanging on papers in a glass [case]" which took his fancy. The goldsmith was absent; only a young and inexperienced apprentice was in the shop. The Earl demanded the price of the smaller rope, and the boy, "being newly come and having no skill, nor yet admitted to make any price," quoted an absurdly low figure. The Earl, seeing his opportunity, immediately told the boy "to take them out, saying he would have them"; but the boy, now frightened that he had given the wrong price, tried to evade the demand by claiming "he had not the key and could not open it." The Earl then "sware great oaths he would have them" and threatened "he would break the glass"; at this the boy, thoroughly cowed, opened the case, and the Earl took not only the smaller rope but the larger as well, giving the terrified boy only a few shillings for them. The goldsmith, Hannibal Gammon (a friend of Langley's), later sought redress in the Court of Chancery, but with scant success, the court finding it difficult to determine how the Earl had been at fault. I cite this instance not only because the behavior it portrays was not unusual, but also because such behavior, when conspicuously flaunted by one's betters and when attended by such demonstrable success, must have commended itself irresistibly to the emulous.[1]

I do not mean to suggest that Francis Langley was still seeking role models as late as 1588, the year of this incident. Quite the contrary; his priorities had been quite firmly arranged many years earlier. Indeed, with his increasing confidence and security in the power of his arrogance to intimidate others, he soon came to recognize a kind of satisfaction in violent physical behavior and began to indulge more and more frequently in simple acts of mayhem. This is a curious aspect of the man, and I wish I understood it more fully. I have resisted the urge to engage in facile psychoanalysis; but as one reads the descriptions of his activities in his later years, one cannot fail to sense a kind of deep-seated pleasure in violence for its own sake, or to notice that Langley often went out of his way to provoke physical confrontations.

Langley died at the age of fifty-four, not a particularly advanced age for the times, but a curious kind of senility seems to have overtaken him during the last year or two of his life. The urge to tyrannize and bully stayed with him, but his shrewdness and clarity of comprehension frequently deserted him. He became careless about business details, or embarked on foolish ventures that he would have shunned as a younger man. I do not know what brought about his death, but I suspect that the gradual deterioration of his last two years must be seen as related to it. He declined to make a will, perhaps refusing, with a touch of the old arrogance, to believe that his illness was terminal. His legacy to his wife was a swarm of lawsuits with which she was quite unprepared to cope.

One can find analogues for this capsule biography as near to hand as the *Mirror for Magistrates*. Indeed, there is a kind of *de casibus* symmetry about the pattern of Langley's life, and his more godly neighbors in the parish of St. Saviour's in Southwark no doubt moralized on his fall with commendable gravity. If his life served their turn thus, well and good; but our present age will ask for more than the mere affirmation of platitudes in a historical biography. We want to know why people behaved as they did, and what their normal expecta-

5

tions were about the behavior of others; and we are prepared to acknowledge that these matters cannot be resolved by recourse to dusty archives, any more than our own lives can be explained by examining our safe-deposit boxes.

And yet it is unfortunately the case that for the Tudor period the biographer often has little else to go on. Langley in particular is a difficult butterfly to pin down. I have been pursuing him for several summers, and while it would be foolhardy of me to suggest that I have exhausted the possibilities of discovery, a few observations are probably in order. To begin with, I believe no artifacts remain; there seems to be no surviving correspondence, nor any household items or books that may once have been his. He is, to be sure, quoted from time to time by his contemporaries, but only when they are trying to make some legal point; no Boswells they. It would be pleasant to report that I had discovered an account book to rival Henslowe's so-called *Diary*, but this distinction has not fallen to my lot, though one day such a book may yet be unearthed. The evidence upon which the present biography rests is found chiefly in various law suits, always a hazardous source because of the special pleading that is their nature. I have tried to assemble a connected narrative, based on these generally unpublished documents, and I trust the reader will not grow weary of my repetitive perhapses and possiblys; I feel one cannot be too cautious with this sort of material, and we know from the example of theatre historians before us that today's unhedged conjecture becomes tomorrow's hardened fact.

Despite these limitations it is important for us to understand Francis Langley, or to try to, if only to gain a sense of the sort of person Shakespeare must have had to do business with. Laurence Olivier is said to have contrived his demeanor and even his facial makeup for the cinema version of *Richard III* to resemble the person of Jed Harris, a theatrical entrepreneur whom he loathed; who is to say what effect Francis Langley may

6

have had on the players or playwrights of his own day, those abstracts and brief chronicles about whom we know so pitifully little? My own belief, of course, is that Langley is quite worth knowing on his own account, and not simply as a source of information for theatre historians. His life is important precisely because of what it tells us about his social milieu. He was in many ways the embodiment of his times: not of the aspirations of the times, like Sir Philip Sidney, but of the actualities.

Langley's story begins in Lincolnshire, where his father farmed for a livelihood. Thomas Langley leased two fields in Didthorpe, one from Roger Castleforth and another from Thomas Garland, and in August 1556 he was no doubt tending these two pieces of ground, fattening his livestock, and making preparations for the autumn harvest. He was in his middle forties and little expected that another sort of reaper was coming to his house. But the coming was swift; Thomas Langley sickened and weakened, and his estate had suddenly to be looked to. From his deathbed the ailing man made a cautious distribution of the cattle, carts, ploughs, brass pans, and beds among his wife and seven children as he dictated his will to Robert Staynton, the parish curate. The leases for the two fields were left to the two eldest boys, Richard and William, one to each, along with the equipment and animals necessary to continue farming. The house was left to the three eldest boys and to the mother "jointly to occupy together so long as they can agree together"; the younger children, as was usual, shared neither field nor house but would be expected to shift for themselves once they reached maturity. Young Francis Langley, only eight years old, was given a cow, a heifer, twenty shillings, and his father's blessing. His younger brothers Philip and John fared about as well.[2]

The lot of the non-firstborn is traditionally difficult, but Thomas Langley was nevertheless discontent with the meager legacies he had left to his younger boys and was not too proud to ask for help in such an extremity. He himself had a younger brother, John, who (perhaps for want of a similar legacy from *his* father) had left Didthorpe as a youth to try his fortunes in London. This John Langley still lived in London, and it was to him that Thomas now addressed his thoughts. "I will that my children and their parts shall be at the ordering of my brother John Langley, who I trust will be good to my poor children."

Thomas Langley was buried in his parish church, St. Oswald's, in nearby Althorp. Possibly John Langley came down to Lincolnshire from London to assist in the settling of his dead brother's affairs. If so, it would have been a notable visit, despite the solemnity of the occasion, for John Langley had been a successful man in the City. It had been some thirty years since he left Didthorpe, a boy barely in his teens, going up to London to make his fortune. But even as a youth John Langley apparently possessed all the necessary mercantile virtues; he managed to indenture himself to a wealthy goldsmith, and seems to have been so exemplary an apprentice that he was "set through" to his freedom early, with his master's approval, despite the "two years and a half service" still owing.[3]

The apprentice years had been eventful and fast moving ones in the realm as well. During the term of John Langley's indenture, King Henry had declared himself the head of the Church in England and had divorced his queen and married Anne Boleyn; Thomas Wolsey had fallen; Thomas More had risen and fallen; and Princess Elizabeth was born. John Langley's own master, Robert Trappes, had been chosen an alderman of the City of London, and the increased activity in the Trappes household during young Langley's last year there must have seemed quite in keeping with the accelerating tempo of the times. And then in 1535 John Langley was free, a yeoman goldsmith, able to work gainfully in his chosen trade. He proved himself, and prospered. In 1546 he was called to the livery. He began to have apprentices of his own. He was chosen Renter Warden of his company in 1550 and Fourth Warden in 1555; he was on the ladder, and his prospects were bright. This was the man to whom Thomas Langley, from his deathbed in August 1556, entrusted the care of his "poor children."[4]

And John Langley did not fail in his duty. Had he come to Lincolnshire after the funeral he would have seen that the widow Agnes Langley had been made tolerably comfortable for the remainder of her widowhood by the terms of her husband's will, and that Richard and William, the two eldest boys, had a house to live in and fields to work; these arrangements would require little additional attention. The daughter, Isabel, could be placed locally when she was old enough, and the two smallest boys, Philip and John, would probably stay with their mother. Thomas, the third son, was old enough to have been given a share of the house but had been left no land to farm, so like his uncle before him he would probably be thinking of trying his fortunes elsewhere. And Francis was too young to make his own way while too old to have to stay at home. These two boys must have seemed the most in need of assistance, and it was forthcoming; we may imagine that John Langley's wife, Joan, did what was necessary to make a home for Francis and Thomas when they came to her house in London.

Joan Langley had no children of her own, but her husband's home, like the home of many another well-to-do liveryman, was busy with servants, apprentices, and visitors. The arrival of the two Langley nephews need not have signified any undue change in her normal routine. But it must indeed have been a change for the two boys. Neither of them was yet old enough to be indentured as an apprentice; Thomas would not be fourteen for three years, Francis for six. So they were free to absorb the sights and sounds of their new life in the City. If the two boys arrived early enough in the autumn of 1556 they would have seen the pageant that

9

attended the installation of Thomas Offley, merchant tailor, as Lord Mayor. On October 28 of that year Offley, who had been elected at Michaelmas, made his formal procession to Guildhall and took his oath; and the following morning he went by water to Westminster to attend upon Queen Mary, accompanied by the City waits and trumpets in their scarlet cloaks, in a pinnace "decked with streamers and guns and drums."[5]

No less imposing a spectacle, though of another sort, might have come to their notice a day or two later—the funeral of Sir John Gresham, uncle of the celebrated Sir Thomas. Henry Machyn, a purveyor of funeral trappings by trade, duly recorded the details of the funeral in his diary, for the ceremony was one befitting an alderman and former Lord Mayor. Such men are not buried with the simplicity that attends poor Lincolnshire farmers, and the contrast of this funeral with Thomas Langley's simple interment at Althorp two months earlier would not have gone unremarked. The funeral procession consisted of "a standard and a pennon of arms, coat-armour of damask, and four pennons of arms, a helmet, a target and a sword, mantles, and a goodly hearse of wax, and ten dozen of pensiles and twelve dozen of scutcheons, four dozen of great staff torches, and a dozen of long torches; and all the church hanged, and the street, with black and arms great store; and [on the] morrow three goodly masses sung, one of the Trinity, and another of our Lady, and the third of requiem, and a goodly sermon; master Harpfield did preach; and after, as great a dinner as has been seen for a fish-day, for all that came to dinner, for there lacked nothing dear."[6]

The passing of Sir John Gresham had its effect on John Langley too. Gresham had been an alderman for sixteen years, and at his death he was the alderman for the ward of Bassishaw. The freemen of that ward met after a decent interval to suggest likely candidates to succeed him, and one of the four persons whom they

nominated for the office was Francis Langley's uncle
John. The nomination tells us something about John
Langley, for nomination to the office of alderman pre-
supposed certain other qualifications. As the office was
for life, it was incumbent on each wardmote to nomi-
nate men of proven ability, and any aspirant to the office would be expected to have a record of prior service
in his ward, or more likely in his parish, as a constable
perhaps, or beadle, or scavenger. These lower offices
were unpaid (as were the offices of alderman and Lord
Mayor), and some were unpleasant or costly. One had
to manifest a zeal for them, however, if one expected to
go further. Timothy Tapwell, the alehouse keeper in *A
New Way to Pay Old Debts*, accepted the system: the
profit from his tavern "hath made me in my parish /
Thought worthy to be scavenger, and in time / May rise
to be overseer of the poor." But the necessity of start-
ing at the bottom was not to everyone's liking. To Seagull, the sea captain in *Eastward Ho*, life in Virginia
made more sense: "For your means to advancement
there, it is simple, and not preposterously mixed: you
may be an alderman there, and never be a scavenger."
An aspirant to the office of alderman was also required,
by an order of 1525, to be possessed of temporal goods
to the value of a thousand pounds, which would ensure
his competency to discharge his duties. An even older
ordinance (1413) required that he be native born and
the son of an Englishman.[7]

We may take the fact of John Langley's nomination
in 1556 as evidence that his contemporaries thought
him well-to-do and experienced. A man so qualified
needed only to wait for a vacancy to occur, and they
did occur with regularity; between 1556 and 1566
there were twenty-eight vacancies in the Court of Aldermen, or nearly three a year on the average. Vacancies were normally caused by the death or translation
of the incumbent. As the honor was held for life, an alderman might expect to die in office, as happened in
Bassishaw ward in October 1556, when old Sir John

Gresham passed on. The freemen of the ward traditionally had a wide latitude of choice when they assembled in a mote to draw up a list of candidates to be
his successor. By custom, any qualified freeman of the
City might have his name placed in nomination for any
aldermanic vacancy, no matter where he lived, and
even if he were at that moment the alderman for some
other ward. The only requisite was that all the names
put forward should be suitable, for once the wardmote
had settled on its four names, it then forwarded them
to the Court of Aldermen, who had the right to reject
the entire slate if even one of the candidates was
deemed unworthy. This prerogative was primarily to
ensure that the wardmote did not try to force the hand
of the Court of Aldermen by "packing" the names on
its list. If the slate was found acceptable, the aldermen
then selected from the four candidates the one person
who would be privileged to join their ranks as alderman for the unrepresented ward.

On this particular occasion the freemen of Bassishaw ward offered a varied roster. It included Sir
Thomas Offley, merchant tailor and former Lord
Mayor; George Alleyn, skinner; John Langley; and
John Machell, clothworker, currently the alderman for
Vintry ward. On November 26, 1556, the Court of Aldermen chose Machell to be the new alderman for Bassishaw ward. As the successful candidate, alderman
Machell was given the choice of remaining the alderman for Vintry ward, or being "translated" to Bassishaw ward, and in this instance he chose the newer
honor. His decision of course created a vacancy in
Vintry ward, and the proceedings of wardmote began
there as they had begun earlier in Bassishaw ward. In
this instance, the wardmote of Vintry ward offered the
requisite four names, and once again John Langley's
was among them. On December 1, 1556, the Court of
Aldermen selected one of the other candidates.[8]

No doubt it was exhilarating to be so nominated, and
depressing to fail in the election, but such initial fail-

ures were to be expected; the fact of nomination was the important consideration, and it was not to be doubted that John Langley would be named again by some future wardmote. In the meantime, life both in and out of the Langley household continued to advance and to prosper. When young Francis was still eight years old he might have seen, in the early spring of 1557, King Philip of Spain arriving to visit his wife. The royal procession through the City brought forth "the aldermen and the sheriffs and all the crafts of London in their liveries . . . and the trumpets blowing with other instruments with great joy and pleasure, and great shooting of guns at the Tower." (This is Henry Machyn again, taking his usual pleasure in pomp.) Less than two years later there was another royal procession, as the new Queen, Elizabeth, passed through the City from the Tower to Westminster for her coronation, "with all the lords and ladies in crimson velvet, and their horses trapped with the same, and trumpeters in red gowns blowing, and all the heralds in their coat-armour, and all the streets strewed with gravel; and at Gracious Street a goodly pageant of King Henry the Eighth . . . and in Cornhill another goodly pageant of King Henry . . . and beside Soper Lane in Cheap another goodly pageant . . . and at the little conduit another goodly pageant of a quick tree and a dead . . . and so to the Fleet Street to the conduit, and there was another goodly pageant of the two churches."

In the year of the Queen's coronation John Langley was chosen Second Warden of the Goldsmiths' Company, and two years later, on December 23, 1560, he was present with the other wardens of his company at the funeral of his former master Robert Trappes "in St. Leonard's in Foster lane," as Henry Machyn duly noted; afterwards they all attended the customary "great dinner." Langley had secured his freedom from Trappes in 1535; had Trappes lived three years longer he would have seen his former apprentice rise to the highest honor of his company, for in 1563 John Langley was elected Prime Warden. Perhaps Langley's wife, Joan, lived long enough to see him so honored; but she died during this period, still childless, leaving John Langley a widower with two nephews in his care.

Such a household could not remain long without a mistress. Even Thomas Langley's departure, on reaching the age of fourteen, to be apprenticed to Robert Brendholme, a haberdasher, would not have reduced the activity in John Langley's household, and a guiding hand was needed. On January 3, 1566, John Langley took as his second wife Ursula Beresford, the daughter of William Tilsworth, a fellow goldsmith, and the widow of George Beresford, leatherseller. She brought to John Langley two sons by her former marriage, and also two interesting brothers-in-law: her sister Joan was the wife of Rowland Hayward, clothworker, currently the alderman for Queenhithe ward, a former sheriff and future Lord Mayor of London (one of the few men to be Lord Mayor twice); her sister Elizabeth was married to Francis Bowyer, a future alderman, sheriff, auditor of the City, and master of the Grocers' Company. Hayward and Bowyer were men of John Langley's own temperament; if Langley did not already know them, they seem to have warmed to him readily on his marriage. Perhaps it was Hayward who introduced John Langley in turn to Lionel Duckett, the alderman for Aldersgate, past sheriff, present master of the Mercers' Company, and future Lord Mayor. Bowyer, Duckett and Hayward became close associates of Langley's, and they embarked on numerous business ventures together, evidence as much of their affluence as of their friendship.[9]

It is tempting to see a connection between Langley's marriage to Ursula Beresford and his return to public life, for he was nominated and chosen alderman on one of the first vacancies occurring after his wedding. On October 3, 1566, Richard Lambert, grocer, removed from Billingsgate ward to Bassishaw ward, and the subsequent wardmote in Billingsgate produced the names of Rowland Hayward, Thomas Ramsey, William Bond, and John Langley. On October 8 the Court of Aldermen chose Langley.[10]

"When I go to Guildhall in my scarlet gown," says Thomas Dekker's madcap shoemaker Simon Eyre, "I'll look as demurely as a saint, and speak as gravely as a Justice of Peace." Whether such a sense of mission descended upon John Langley in his new dignity has not been recorded, but his accomplishment was a solid one. With an assured seat in the Court of Aldermen he was now securely placed in the political life of the City. It was just ten years since his elder brother Thomas had died in Didthorpe. During those ten years John Langley's young nephew Francis had grown from eight to eighteen, but he was perhaps not the model young man that his uncle had been at the same age. When he first came to London Francis was too young to be indentured, but there had been no question that the future would hold such service for him. Unfortunately, it is difficult to be certain about the nature or term of Francis Langley's apprenticeship. One would like to know, for example, why his uncle did not take him on as an apprentice goldsmith. He was, instead, apprenticed to William Hobbes, a draper of some affluence and standing. One reason for choosing Hobbes may have been proximity; Hobbes lived in St. Michael Bassishaw parish, and John Langley lived nearby in the section of St. Lawrence Jewry that was in Cripplegate ward. Hobbes was also well-to-do, though not so wealthy as John Langley; in the lay subsidy for 1571 Hobbes was rated at £100, while John Langley, like his neighbor and brother-in-law Rowland Hayward, was rated at £400.[11]

John Langley may have had some purpose in mind when he apprenticed his nephews to cloth merchants, Thomas to a haberdasher and Francis to a draper. Both of these guilds were, like his own, among the so-called Great Twelve companies, and the uncertainties of the cloth trade in the sixteenth century, which seem so clear to us by hindsight, may not have been visible to him. After all, his friend Rowland Hayward was a clothworker, and he and Hayward were the two richest men in Cripplegate ward; and the third richest man was his new friend Lionel Duckett, a mercer.

But though Rowland Hayward may have seemed a latter-day Jack of Newbury to his friends, the cloth trade was nevertheless a chancy one at this period. The history of Francis's own guild, the Company of Drapers, illustrates the point. In earlier times the Drapers had been broadly involved in many aspects of the manufacture and marketing of cloth, and in their variety of activities they had come into regular contact, and often conflict, with other guilds claiming the same prerogatives. The Taylors, the Shearmen, the Fullers, the Dyers, and many another group all claimed rights of monopoly, inspection, and control of the whole of the cloth trade, and tactfully accommodated themselves to one another while they jockeyed for position. By the early sixteenth century the Taylors had reincorporated (and claimed further privileges) as the Merchant Tailors, and the Fullers and the Shearmen had united to form the Clothworkers. The Haberdashers began at this time to compete as well. Under these pressures the Drapers were forced to rethink their position, and they soon found themselves abandoning what part they had taken in the making of cloth and devoting themselves more and more to the business of buying cloth made by others, preparing it for the market, and selling it. Their sense of the profitability of selling over manufacturing seems to have been confirmed in this period by the emergence of the Merchant Adventurers as a mercantile power, so much so that by the time of Francis Langley's apprenticeship the Drapers had almost, if not entirely, abandoned even the work of finishing cloth, and were almost exclusively engaged in wholesale or retail selling. These maneuvers may appear at first glance to be judicious accommodations to a changing business climate, but we now know that they were signs of a steadily worsening trouble in the cloth trade.[12]

Francis Langley probably found little to attract him in such a life, but he nevertheless began his training as a future seller of cloth sometime in the 1560s. He might have begun his term of apprenticeship as early as 1562, when he would have been the appropriate age, though he may not have begun it until some seven years later. The earlier date is far more likely, though the facts are scanty. His master Hobbes was a sound businessman, and had many strings to his bow. He was a merchant adventurer as well as a draper, and a freeman in Flanders as well as in London. For an aggressive apprentice, eager to learn the secrets of successful merchandising and exporting, and willing to work at his trade, Hobbes would probably have been an ideal master.

But Francis may not have cared for such merchant-venturing. "What are these ships but tennis balls, for the winds to play withal? Tossed from one wave to another; now under-line; now over the house; sometimes brick-wall'd against a rock, so that the guts fly out again: sometimes struck under the wide hazard, and farewell, Master Merchant." The words are those of Francis Quicksilver, the errant apprentice in *Eastward Ho*. His master's reaction is equally blunt: "Thou shameless varlet, dost thou jest at thy lawful master contrary to thy indentures?" No excess of affection there; that a similar uneasy relationship obtained between Francis Langley and his master is clear, for on January 18, 1570, Francis was brought before the Court of the Drapers' Company for a formal punishment, an event of some moment. A. H. Johnson, in his history of the Drapers' Company, tells us that during the whole of Elizabeth's reign only ten such ceremonies are recorded among the Drapers' records.[13]

"This day in the afternoon the Correction of this house was ministered to Francis Langley, the apprentice of William Hobbes, for divers his offenses against his master." The Master and three of the Wardens of were present, and so were "Mr Alderman Langley, uncle of the said Francis," and "Mr Metcalfe, goldsmith, brought hither by Mr Alderman Langley." The occasion was clearly intended to chasten Francis, and the clerk of the company soberly concluded his entry: "I pray God this small charitable correction may be to him such a warning as thereby he may avoid a greater."[14]

Though we might wish to know more precisely what the offences were, the records will not tell us. Absenteeism may have been one. A year or so earlier Francis seems to have gone off on a trip with his friend Thomas Peacock, a carpenter, to Molesey, in Surrey, to see Peacock's newborn son. Peacock was on his way to participate in the christening, and Francis Langley may have stood as a witness. In his later recollection of this event, Langley described himself as a "stripling" of sixteen or seventeen, though in truth he was nearer to twenty. Perhaps he chafed at the monotony of being a draper's apprentice, and took such holidays periodically to relieve the tedium.[15]

A second notice occurs in the Drapers' records a year or so after the public correction, and absenteeism again seems to have been the cause. Young Francis had apparently taken an extended leave from his duties, and William Hobbes in exasperation had refused to receive him again. The matter was brought before the Court of the Drapers' Company on June 25, 1571, and the Court allowed Hobbes one month to determine "whether he will take again into his service" the young absentee who had "gone out of his service without his leave." Hobbes may have refused; his decision is not recorded. Francis Langley appears no further in the records of apprentices until September 25, 1577 when, only a year or so short of being thirty years old, he took up his freedom. He is described on that occasion as "Francis

Langley, sometime the apprentice of William Hobbes."
The locution is unusual.[16]

Several explanations are possible. One is that
Francis Langley began his apprenticeship at the normal age, completed it on time despite his disciplinary
infractions, and then neglected to claim his freedom
until several years later. Though possible, this explanation seems unlikely. Alternatively, he may have
begun his apprenticeship at the last possible moment,
and claimed his freedom immediately on its completion; but this would be unusual in many respects, and
the description of him as Hobbes's "sometime" apprentice casts further doubt. Either way, he would
have been an apprentice in 1570 and 1571, the dates of
the two known references. It is more likely that his servitude was early and sporadic, and his unauthorized
leaves frequent and extended. Had Langley planned to
make his living as a draper, he would have been entering on his trade at an advanced age, being nearly thirty
when he claimed his freedom; but as he disappears
completely from the records of the company after 1577,
it is likely that he never seriously intended to pursue such a calling. My own interpretation is that he
began his apprenticeship on time, and was nearly at
the end of his term of indenture when Hobbes turned
him out in 1571. That he should have managed, despite this, to claim and receive the freedom of the
company six years later will require explanation, and
for this we must return to the career of his uncle,
John Langley.

In 1566, the year in which John Langley was elevated
to the dignity of alderman, the two sheriffs of London
were Ambrose Nicholas, salter, and Richard Lambert,
grocer. Sheriffs were normally county or shire officials,
though certain towns had them as well. The shire office was a royal appointment, for a term of one year, and
in each county the sheriff was the chief officer of the
Crown, though during the reign of Elizabeth the office

of Lord Lieutenant came to intervene between the sheriff and his monarch. A number of larger towns, however, had the privilege by charter of electing their own sheriffs. From the time of Henry I the City of London had the privilege of choosing its own men to fill this royal office. The City had also been granted the right by charter "to hold Middlesex to farm for three hundred pounds" and consequently had the right to "place as Sheriff [of Middlesex] whom they will of themselves." Thus, though the City of London and the shire of Middlesex were defined as one sheriffwick, there were traditionally two sheriffs in office at all times, in conformity with the charter. The sheriffs of London and Middlesex, like other sheriffs, served in office for one year; one of them was chosen each summer by the commonalty of the City in Common Hall, and the other was appointed by the Lord Mayor.

Though it was not necessary that the two sheriffs be aldermen, no alderman could anticipate a successful political career without passing through the office of sheriff, for an act of Common Council from the time of Richard II had declared "that no person shall from henceforth be mayor of [London] if he have not first been sheriff of the said city, to the end that he may be tried in governance and bounty [*governance et bountee*] before he attains such estate of the mayoralty." This act was consonant with the policy, described earlier, of expecting ward or parochial service of all who aspired to aldermancy. If John Langley coveted a higher dignity than alderman, he would have to begin by seeking the office of sheriff. As luck would have it, he did not have to wait long. Richard Lambert, one of the incumbent sheriffs in the year of John Langley's election, died only a few months before the expiration of his term of office. A replacement was needed for those few months, and John Langley was chosen. It was an odd coincidence: Lambert's removal as alderman from Billingsgate to Bassishaw in October 1566 had created the opening that allowed John Langley to become an alderman; now his death allowed John Langley to become a sheriff.[17]

If a man were disposed to covet the highest political office in the City, the shrievalty would be his final hurdle. When Dekker's shoemaker Simon Eyre is chosen by the commonalty, his man Firk recognizes the importance of the achievement: "Run, good Hans, O Hodge, O mistress! Hodge, heave up thine ears; mistress, smug up your looks; on with your best apparel! My master is chosen, my master is called, nay condemned by the cry of the country to be sheriff of the City, for this famous year now to come: and time now being, a great many men in black gowns were asked for their voices, and their hands, and my master had all their fists about his ears presently, and they cried Ay, Ay, Ay, Ay, and so I came away: wherefore without all other grieve, I do salute you: Mistress Shrieve."[18]

The news may not have come to Ursula Langley in quite this fashion, but she might have said, like Margery Eyre, "welcome home master shrieve, I pray God continue you in health and wealth." Such at any rate was John Langley's fortune in this period, to be continued in prosperity. In 1568 he was chosen for the second time to be Prime Warden of the Goldsmiths. In 1570 (the year of his nephew's "correction" before the Drapers' Court, at which he must have felt compelled to be present) he removed his aldermancy to Queenhithe ward, and early in 1572 removed again to Langbourn ward, having been successfully nominated by both those wardmotes. At each fresh honor he must have felt more keenly the disparity between his own performance and the lackluster record of his nephew. If Francis was indeed turned out by his master Hobbes, as I suspect, he may well have been living once again with his uncle John after 1571. This would be further embarrassment; the sons of the gentry might well be idle in this fashion, but not the nephew of a prominent goldsmith and sheriff of London.

Nor would John Langley's house be any longer the

exciting place that it was to the young boy from Didthorpe. The house would of course still be full, for John
Langley was earnest in his training of apprentices, and
would always have a few under his care. But these
would be boys in their late teens, or at most in their
early twenties, and Francis would perhaps be feeling
the pangs of age along with a general disdain of apprentice life. But there was one older apprentice, who had
come to John Langley probably in 1566; this was Hannibal Gammon, the son of Richard Gammon of Cray-
ford in Kent. In 1571 Hannibal would have been
twenty-five, two or three years older than Francis, and
their similar sense of superannuation may have been
one of the considerations that drew them together.
They became close friends. Hannibal Gammon's arrangement with John Langley may have been informal
at first, for Langley neglected to certify him officially
to the company as his apprentice until 1573, when he
was nearly at the end of his term of indenture. No
harm seems to have come of this, however, and late in
January 1575 Langley formally presented Gammon,
who took his oath and was made free of the Goldsmiths.[19]

Hannibal Gammon remained serious about his craft.
Francis did not infect him with irresponsibility, but
neither did he infect Francis with industry. They
managed to respect one another despite their contrast-
ing attitudes. Gammon went to work as a goldsmith as
soon as he gained his freedom. He attached himself to
the shop of Thomas Metcalfe, the friend whom John
Langley had brought to Drapers' Hall to witness the
"correction" of his nephew. In that very year, even as
Gammon was setting out on his career in the City,
Francis Langley was learning about City life the hard
way. His friend John Griffith was clapped into prison
for debt, and two dubious acquaintances, Matthew
Tomlinson and Richard Porter, persuaded Francis to
join them in signing a bond for £10 as security to free

Griffith. Langley did so, and like so many innocent men of that age, later found himself being sued for default of payment. His rage at being thus duped must have overmastered his reason, for he confronted the man who was suing him "with very furious and hot speeches" and threatened that for every shilling the man should recover against him at the common law, Francis "would have as much of [his] blood." This threat was accompanied by "other unseemly speeches." Perhaps Francis began to see at this time how his station in life, as a drifting ex-apprentice without a regular income, was untenable. As he seemed determined not to be a draper, some other means of livelihood had to be found. Both he and his uncle must have agreed on that; and his uncle was the first to find a way.[20]

In September 1576, as the time for the annual election of the Lord Mayor drew near, alderman John Langley stood tenth in order of seniority in the Court of Aldermen. The nine men whose years of service exceeded his own had all served in the office of Lord Mayor (or "passed the chair"), and John Langley was the senior alderman below the chair. Elevations to the dignity of Lord Mayor had proceeded almost routinely on the basis of seniority during John Langley's career, so that he could not have been surprised to find himself nominated for the honor, or more than decorously overwhelmed when he was duly elected to the office on September 29, 1576. His election was the occasion of great festivity in the Goldsmiths' Company, for not since the mayoralty of Martin Bowes in 1545 had a goldsmith been Lord Mayor. Indeed, for nine of his ten years as alderman, John Langley had been the only goldsmith in the Court of Aldermen; fifty years earlier, a fifth of the aldermen had been goldsmiths.[21]

Langley entered upon his duties on October 28, 1576, succeeding Sir Ambrose Nicholas. His term of office seems to have passed without major incident, though certain difficulties suggest that Langley's administration was not without controversy. For example, twice during his mayoralty the Privy Council found it necessary to instruct him about the disposition of certain lawsuits in his own Lord Mayor's Court.[22]

There were further difficulties. The summer of 1577 was a plague summer, and John Langley's management of the City's affairs during this crisis was found by the Privy Council to be unsatisfactory. In addition, the new phenomenon of public playhouses had burgeoned during his mayoralty: the Theater, the Curtain, and the playhouse at Newington Butts were all in operation, and in late summer the Council was constrained for the first time in its history to order that they be closed. The Lord Mayor was directed to suppress all stage-playing within the City. The City's own plague measures for other public gatherings and for sanitation and burial were set in motion by the Court of Aldermen without prompting from Whitehall. But in the late summer the plague became unexpectedly virulent, and the Council, presuming that bureaucratic inefficiency was the cause of the worsening, saw fit to intervene in the City's procedures.[23]

In late August 1577 the Privy Council wrote sternly to Lord Mayor Langley that he was neglecting his duty in the matter of the plague. Though the Secretary had written him to shut up sick houses, he had not done so, which "their Lordships cannot but greatly mislike, considering that he [is] the head officer of the principal city of this realm . . . it should not be needful for others to put [him] in remembrance of [his] duties." Langley was "required and in her Majesty's name straightly commanded" to set about his business.

On the last day of September the Council wrote again, the plague having worsened. The Queen's commandment had been delivered to Langley, but "her Majesty, finding it carelessly observed to her great misliking, doth hereby again require the said Lord Mayor and the rest of the Commissioners above named to see the former commandment duly executed"; and, that the negligent parties might be identified and punished, all those responsible for the plague orders were to be examined and certified, "to the end that upon consideration of the same, there may be some order taken for the punishment of such as shall be found to have been offenders."

Langley was not alone in being censured at this time. William Fleetwood, the Recorder of London, was at dinner with the Lord Mayor when he learned of his own fall from estimation in the eyes of Lord Burghley over the way he had managed the plague arrangements in the Duchy of Lancaster. It may, indeed, have been a season of general mismanagement; certainly the plague was more severe than had been anticipated. The Lord Mayor's social life seemed to proceed undisturbed, however; Fleetwood wrote Burghley after his dinner that "at my Lord Mayor's there dined the Master of the Rolls, Justice Southcote, Sir William Damsel, Mr Lieutenant, Sir Rowland Hayward, Mr Justice Randoll, Alderman Pullyson and myself; and after dinner we heard a brabble between John Wotton and the Lieutenant's son of the one part, and certain freeholders of Shoreditch, for a matter at the Theater."[24]

John Langley received honors as well as admonitions during his year as Lord Mayor. Among other things, he found himself chosen yet again to be Prime Warden of the Company of Goldsmiths. Near the midpoint of his mayoralty, on March 15, 1577, he was knighted; a routine matter for a Lord Mayor. Hard upon the heels of this honor came the royal request for reciprocity: the Queen would be pleased if Mr. John Hubbard, servant to the Groom of her Privy Chamber, should have the office of Seacoal Meter or Salt Meter, or the next reversion to either of those offices. One of the prerogatives of the Court of Aldermen was the appointment to such City offices, from garbler and gauger to water bailiff, common hunt, and secondary, and one of the characteristics of Elizabeth's reign was the mounting of a determined assault on this prerogative by continual bombardment of the Court of Aldermen with requests for special appointments. In this case Sir John Langley, with his knighthood freshly upon him, wrote to the Privy Council on March 21, 1577, to explain that by the laws of the City such offices and reversions could be granted only to freemen by birth or servitude, all other grants being void.[25]

A reversion to a City office would be a comfortable possession, for one would then be assured, on the death of the incumbent—assuming there were no prior reversions—of an income-producing position. It was natural that men should seek to purchase reversions to the more remunerative posts, and perhaps the idea of a reversion for his nephew Francis first occurred to Sir John at about this time. Francis had, however, the same difficulty that the Queen's candidate Hubbard had; namely, that he was not a freeman of the City. If Sir John were to provide for his nephew in this way, it would be necessary first to make him free. There is no record of the accommodation that may have taken place between Sir John, Francis, and the Company of Drapers, but it is duly noted in the Company's records that Francis Langley, the "sometime apprentice" of William Hobbes, was made free of the Drapers on September 25, 1577.

The next step was to secure a reversion, and with dispatch, for Sir John had only a month left in office. As Francis needed to begin making his own way promptly, a post to which the succession seemed imminent would be the most desirable. On Tuesday, October 22, 1577, just a week before the end of Sir John's year as Lord Mayor, the clerk of the Court of Aldermen recorded that "at the request and desire of my Lord Mayor, the reversion and next avoidance of any one of the alnagers, searchers and sealers of woolen cloths, belonging unto Blackwell Hall of this City, which shall first and next happen to fall or become void, was freely and lovingly given and granted by the Court unto Francis Langley, draper, to have, hold, exercise and enjoy the same . . . upon condition that the said Francis Langley, at such time as he shall come to claim the benefit of this present grant, shall be found fit, apt and able for the execution thereof and not otherwise."[26]

There were at the time three alnagers in the City. Their chief function was to examine and certify all woolen cloths brought into the City for sale. The weekly market for woolen cloths was at Blackwell Hall, and there, on the days preceding each market, the alnagers (from the French *aulne*, an ell), with the help of their auditor, would measure and seal all incoming bolts of cloth to certify that they were a full measure between the lists or selvages, as wide in the middle as at the ends, and of full length and weight. These standards had been observed since they were first set forth in the "Assize of Cloth" in the time of Richard I. The alnagers charged a fee for each seal; bolts of cloth that did not measure to the full size or weight had the letter *F* pressed into the seal, and the dealers in such bolts were fined. The alnager's fees and fines were the chief perquisite of the office. Surprisingly, no one else seemed to hold a reversion to an alnagership, so Francis might properly expect that on the next vacancy he would be able to step into his post. It was a generous and provident action on Sir John's part to secure this opportunity for his nephew; of Francis Langley's gratitude there is no record.

At Michaelmas 1577 Thomas Ramsey, grocer, was chosen Lord Mayor, and on October 28 Sir John Langley formally relinquished the office to him. He put aside forever the calaber cloak of an alderman below the chair, and took up the grey cloak of an alderman who had passed the chair. He was not destined to enjoy this new dignity for long, however; before the year was out he became mortally sick. Two days after Christmas he made his will, on New Year's Day he added a codi-

cil, and on January 4, 1578, at about four in the morning, he died. He was in his early sixties. He had first
arrived in London nearly half a century earlier, the
younger son of a farmer from Didthorpe, Lincolnshire.
He had worked hard, and had been rewarded with the
City's honors, almost as though he were the hero of a
Deloney novel. He was buried in the church of St.
Lawrence Jewry on January 14 with full ceremonies as
befitted his rank. On January 25 his will was proved,
and Francis Langley was among the beneficiaries.[27]

II

The Heir

What treasure, uncle?
HENRY V

Both of John Langley's marriages had been childless, so his selection of heirs and the settlement of his estate were necessarily circumstantial. Thomas and Francis Langley, his two nephews, were the collateral descendants to whom he felt closest; but there were other claims on his attention, perhaps more than he could easily accommodate, and in the intensity of his illness it may have seemed easiest simply to do nothing. As he grew sicker his friends urged him to make a will, but, as Francis recalled, he "was very unwilling to make any."[1]

Finally on the night of December 26, 1577, the Lady Ursula called Francis into Sir John's counting house, and there, "in very mourning wise," told him that "both she and he and his brother Thomas were like to be greatly hindered if her husband would not make his will and set some order down of his lands." She told Francis that she herself and several of her friends had tried "very earnestly . . . at several times since his sickness" to get Sir John to make his will, but "by no persuasion of her or them he would do it." She told Francis that if Sir John "did not set down in writing some order for his lands, both she and [Francis] and

29

also his brother Thomas should have small or no benefit thereby, but that it must then descend and fall unto
their eldest brother in the country"; which event, she
observed, would be "great pity and small conscience,"
because Sir John had "promised to make me a jointure
and never did for all the substance I brought him."
Lady Ursula also reminded Francis that her husband
"hath done nothing for you and your brother Thomas
and specially for you, Francis, that so long hath served
him."

The last remark can hardly be true, but its exaggera-
tion is perhaps understandable when we note that
these are Francis Langley's own recollections of the
conversation with Lady Ursula. Francis recalled that
his immediate response, at any rate, was to go and
fetch his cousin Thomas Peacock, the carpenter,
"whom I know can persuade him more than any man,"
and bring him to Sir John's bedside. The visit was apparently successful, for on December 27 Sir John addressed himself to the making of a will. He sorted out
his desires and intentions in the presence of his wife
and his wife's cousin Henry Townsend of Lincoln's
Inn, "the lawyer," as Francis termed him. Lady Ursula
was to be the executor, and Sir John's three good
friends Sir Rowland Hayward, Sir Lionel Duckett, and
Francis Bowyer were to be overseers.

The disposition of the estate seemed straightforward
enough. Sir John held some lands in Lincolnshire, near
Didthorpe, where his aged sister Joan Whitefoot lived
with her grown children and grandchildren; he willed
that the tenancy of these lands should be given to Joan
for the remainder of her life without rent, and on her
death pass to his wife Lady Ursula. At Lady Ursula's
death the lands would descend finally to William Langley, the eldest brother of Francis and Thomas, who
still lived and farmed in Didthorpe where he now had
a wife and family.[2]

Sir John's holdings in London were varied. He held
some messuages—the common term for dwelling-

houses with grounds—near Whittington College, in St. Michael Paternoster parish; these were to be left to Lady Ursula to sell, that she might raise cash to meet some of Sir John's obligations. For indeed the expenses of his year as Lord Mayor had pretty well depleted his reserves, and Lady Ursula was heard to lament to friends that Sir John had left her poorer than he found her. One of Sir John's debts, for £440, was to Rowland Beresford, Lady Ursula's son, and this was met by leaving to Rowland a meadow in Hackney and some copyhold lands elsewhere near London. The Saracen's Head, a messuage in Cheapside leased to one Robert Wright, a goldsmith, was to be Lady Ursula's for the term of her life, and then pass to Francis Langley. Four other messuages or tenements, constituting the remainder of Sir John's freehold property in London, were to be Lady Ursula's for life, and then Thomas Langley's.

Various other personal bequests—£5 to the widow of Erasmus Clinkerdagger, the longtime Beadle of the Goldsmiths' Company who had died only the year before; £10 to sister Joan Whitefoot and £6 to her grandchildren; £6 to William Langley's children—and also various gifts of the sort that would be expected of an alderman and a former Lord Mayor with any consciousness of his station—£5 to St. Bartholomew's Hospital, £10 to the poor of Christ's Hospital—appear in profusion in the will. Lady Ursula, recalling the circumstances of the will's making, later noted that "the legacies contained in the said will amount to the sum of £324 20^d, being much more than the said Sir John Langley at the beginning of the said will determined to have bequeathed, and by sundry occasions increased, as the remembrance of his friends came to his mind."[3]

At last Sir John's string of remembered friends came to an end, however, and then Henry Townsend organized his notes and made a fair copy of the will; he read this copy to Sir John, who signed it. Townsend signed as a witness. Other witnesses being needed, Townsend left the bedchamber to find them. He found Christopher Hunt, merchant tailor, who was present elsewhere in the house; Hunt later recalled that he "was caused to put his hand to the same as a witness thereunto," although "he was never privy to the contents of the said will." Francis Langley said that he "and others of the said Sir John's house were caused to subscribe their names thereunto as witnesses of the same, but heard it not read nor understood the contents thereof till after his death." It is little wonder that some suspicions were aroused about the nature of the proceedings.

Nor were matters made easier when, a few days later, changes were made. When Sir Rowland Hayward learned that he had been named an overseer, he immediately had Townsend show him the will. Then he, Townsend, and Lady Ursula engaged in some calculations. They soon discovered that Sir John's resources were not equal to his bequests; furthermore, as Sir Rowland observed, Sir John had forgotten something: "namely . . . that he was to be buried according to his calling, which would grow to a great charge, estimated to three hundred pounds at the least, not before considered nor remembered." They were joined by Bowyer, who concurred that "the estate that [Sir John] stood in was not, without some other help, any way able to answer the said will and to bury him to his calling, leaving his wife according as he meant to do."

Sir Rowland therefore urged that Sir John try to release more capital for Lady Ursula's use, perhaps by calling back some of his earlier bequests. Hayward was seconded in his urgings by Townsend and Lady Ursula. Sir John's need to confront his own poverty must have been painful to him, for Sir Rowland recalled that Sir John ultimately capitulated, sighing "naked I came into the world, and naked I shall go out again." On New Year's Day, 1578, Henry Townsend appended a short memorandum or codicil to the will at Sir John's instance, "because I would not have all this my said will newly written again"; in the codicil Sir John bequeathed to his wife two houses or tenements in Cheapside currently let to John Ballett, a goldsmith. These two houses, adjoining the Horse Head, were a moiety of the estate that had originally been designated to go to Thomas Langley, whose inheritance would be halved by this action. But Sir Rowland reasoned that, if these two houses were sold, the proceeds would be sufficient to cover the funeral and the bequests. Sir John signed, and Hayward and Townsend witnessed.[4]

Francis Langley, who was still in the house on New Year's Day, knew that a secret conference was being held in Sir John's bedchamber because he and others had been asked to remove themselves from the room. He had left his pen and inkhorn in the room, closed up in their case on the cupboard. When he was again permitted into Sir John's chamber after the drawing-up of the codicil, he found "the pen lying upon the cupboard wet with ink and his inkhorn open," which raised his suspicions that the three counselors "had either altered the will or had written some new device."

Thomas and Francis Langley must have known about the legacies their uncle had in mind for them, and one may well imagine that when the will was probated and made public the two young men reacted indignantly, seeing in the codicil evidence of collusion on the part of Lady Ursula and her friends rather than of any considered change of heart by Sir John. In fact, Francis maintained that "Sir John, both before and after their coming unto him at that time, was not able to speak nor to subscribe his name to anything without help of one or other to hold his hand, the which this deponent did both mark and consider when he and others were bidden go out of the chamber."

In this recollection he was supported by others who were there. Christopher Hunt, the merchant tailor, recalled that Sir John was incapable of speech "sensibly uttered" for "his tongue so greatly failed him"; nor had

he the strength "to subscribe his name to anything."
Thomas Bradshaw, goldsmith, remembered Sir John as
being "scarce able . . . to speak [or] to command anything to be written . . . for as he was not well able to
utter his mind in words to be understand [*sic*]." Robert
Crowley, a Puritan preacher, said that "at no time
when he was with him he had the use of his speech."[5]

Against these views, Hayward and Townsend maintained that Sir John could indeed speak, though with
difficulty, that he was of perfect understanding, and
that he could and did sign his own name to the codicil.
The point is perhaps a technical one. Having seen the
need for an alteration in the will, Hayward, Townsend,
and Lady Ursula perceived that their task was primarily to convince Sir John of the necessity of such action. Sir John needed no more than the power to com-
prehend and to affirm, and these things he could do.
The charge of Francis and others that Sir John could
not have dictated the codicil is no doubt true, but it is
not the heart of the matter. That Thomas Langley's
legacy had shrunk by half in the process is undeniable,
but that it resulted from fraudulent purpose rather
than direct concern for the whole will is more difficult
to support.

Nevertheless, Thomas Langley was not slow to take
action. As Lady Ursula began to execute the will, with
Sir Rowland Hayward's help, she found Thomas seeking "all ways and means possibly that he can for to
overthrow the said true intent and meaning of the said
Sir John Langley" with regard to the two tenements.
Thomas Langley's insistence that the tenements were
rightfully his, and not Lady Ursula's, perhaps caused
prospective purchasers to hesitate, so that Lady Ursula
soon found herself "much hindered of the sale of the
said tenements, to the great hindrance of the performance of the said will, and the payment of the said testa-
tor's debts, and the title of the same tenements very
likely to come in question hereafter."[6]

Thomas Langley must not have been the only frustration Lady Ursula encountered as she attempted to execute her husband's will, but he may well have been the straw that broke the camel's back. Civil discourse having failed to dissuade him from his obstructionist path, Lady Ursula took him to court. In the spring of 1578 she swore out a bill of complaint to Sir Nicholas Bacon, lord keeper of the Great Seal, in which she set forth the grounds of her complaint. Thomas responded, and "put himself on the country," that is, claimed the right to have witnesses called in his behalf. Lists of interrogatories were duly drawn up by the attorneys, and the long process of taking depositions on both sides began in the early summer and lasted through the autumn. Sir Rowland Hayward, "knight, alderman of London, of the age of sixty years or thereabouts," deposed on July 5; Robert Crowley the preacher, on October 3; Francis Langley "of London, draper, of the age of thirty years or thereabouts," on October 18; Christopher Hunt on October 31, Thomas Bradshaw on November 10, and Henry Townsend the lawyer on November 20.[7]

During the course of these proceedings, however, Thomas Langley devised a plan that, in effect, disengaged him from anything more than a nominal interest in the progress of the suit. In August, while the litigation was still pending and most of the depositions were still to be made, Thomas and Francis Langley made an agreement whereby Thomas sold to Francis all his right in his inheritance. On the face of it the transaction seems curious, and we may properly suspect a mess of pottage hidden somewhere. In the indenture by which Thomas granted his rights to Francis, he speaks of his inheritance as the reversion of "all [the] freehold lands tenements and hereditaments and every part and parcel thereof" which Sir John had left to Lady Ursula for the remainder of her life. By the terms of the amended will, however, Thomas was not to have all of Sir John's freehold lands in London, but only those that Lady Ursula was not free to sell. Possibly Thomas and Francis thought to frustrate the course of the lawsuit by this purchase. They may have hoped to demonstrate that the property in question— the two messuages next to the Horse Head occupied by John Ballett—had in fact already been sold, and that a judgment in favor of Lady Ursula would result in legal complications.[8]

But the ruse was too simple to work. There is no record in Chancery Decrees and Orders of any resolution of this lawsuit, which suggests either that a settlement was reached out of court, or more likely that Thomas and Francis simply capitulated. Lady Ursula was, after all, simply trying to sell the two tenements, and her claim that Thomas was frustrating this purpose would weaken as soon as the tenements were in fact sold. In the event, the simplest and most obvious solution presented itself. To break the stalemate, Sir Rowland Hayward himself bought the two houses from Lady Ursula, and Francis Langley's claim to have bought them from his brother Thomas quickly evaporated.[9]

Sir John's estate was thus settled at last; and Francis Langley, having failed in his bid for his brother's lost Cheapside properties, might have paused to take stock of himself and his situation. He was in his early thirties. The passing of his uncle had deprived him of perhaps his most sympathetic and tolerant ally. Sir John had been avuncular in the best sense, and his death marked the end of patronage for Francis; any further advancement, so far as Sir John had provided for it, depended curiously on yet more deaths. Lady Ursula's death would bring Francis into his estate in the Saracen's Head in Cheap. On the death of one of the city alnagers he would move into that office. An odd sort of mortal dependency, but it had the virtue of being ultimately certain. There was less surety in the affections of the living: in the struggle over Sir John's legacy

Francis had alienated Lady Ursula, offended Sir Rowland Hayward, and ultimately disappointed his
brother. Though he was a draper, no respect accrued to
him in that company. He had prospects, but no assets;
connections, but no influence. Worst of all, he had no
money. Sir John in his providence had left him property and employment in the future, but no cash in the
present.

III

The Moneylender

Did you but know the city's usuries.
CYMBELINE

Ingenuity, however, might yet provide a solution to Francis's financial problems. "I have not lived amongst goldsmiths and goldmakers all this while, but I have learned something worthy of my time with 'em," says that wayward apprentice Francis Quicksilver in *Eastward Ho*; and we soon learn, as that play unfolds, that Quicksilver has been lending out his master's money to gamblers in taverns while still under the bond of his indenture. Thrown out in anger and exasperation by his master ("There, sir, there's your inden-ture . . . from this time my door is shut to you"), Quicksilver takes lodging with his middleman, a scriv-ener named Security ("I, and such other honest men as live by lending money, are content with moderate pro-fit; thirty or forty i'th' hundred: so we may have it with quietness"). The play is Jacobean, but the point of this sequence was not novel: a young man with no other visible prospects might find a living of sorts as a broker in the moneylending business. Francis Langley was not above such endeavors. He knew not only the value of money but also its pleasures, which exceeded those of drapery. Further, he had himself been the in-nocent victim of a defaulted bond, and the experience had advanced his education. Someone had made a profit on his discomfiture on that occasion; perhaps such profit lay open to his grasp as well.

The lending of money was a business in the London of Francis Langley's time, and the money broker, like other merchants in the City, bought his merchandise in one market and sold it in another. The broker was not expected to lend his own capital any more than the clothworker was expected to raise his own sheep. Some goldsmiths there were who made loans out of their own store—John Langley had done so on occasion—but most brokers merely represented persons of wealth and station who desired to make a profit on their cash reserves, and who did so through the agency of a scrivener or some other person acting as broker on their behalf.[1]

One such person was Cecily Cyoll, a well-to-do widow whose funds were not otherwise employed, but whose station in life made it quite improper for her to engage directly in moneylending. She was the daughter of Sir John Gresham; she had married a Spanish merchant named German or Jermyn Cyoll, who had grown rich and then gone bankrupt, and who was now dead. To bolster his widowed niece's diminished reserves, her uncle Sir Thomas Gresham had left her an additional £100 in his will, and the widow Cyoll now lived quietly in the parish of St. Helen's, Bishopsgate, lending out her money at interest. Her agent for these transactions was Thomas Chapman, a scrivener who lived in Soper Lane. Chapman arranged the loans, drew up the bonds, and shared in the profits.

Langley knew both Chapman and widow Cyoll. Further, he must have known that he could perform Chapman's function perfectly well. He needed only to find someone with funds whom he might represent. His friend Hannibal Gammon, who had been apprenticed to Sir John and who was now working as a yeoman goldsmith, had begun lending money fairly early in his career, and it may have been Gammon who provided Langley with his first contacts. Gammon's own resources were not large; in 1582, for example, his total assets were rated at £3, yet he made loans of £100 on at least one occasion that year. One would like to know whom he represented, and to whom he might have introduced Langley; but the records do not exist. It is perhaps more likely that Langley began by working on commission for someone like Chapman. "For the scrivener hath his agents abroad to entrap gentlemen . . . his brokers . . . who at ordinaries and other meetings lay baits to entrap such as either by easiness of nature or need have occasions to use money." So might the moralist sneer at the moneylender and his minions; such activity was, however, simply a fact of life.[2]

The lending of money at interest, or usury, had been illegal in England for centuries, and as late as 1552 an Act of Parliament had prohibited all taking of interest as "a vice most odious and detestable, as in divers places of the Holy Scripture it is evident to be seen." But the economic expansion of the realm in the sixteenth century had not been built on such unenforceable pieties, and legislation could not lag behind reality indefinitely. John Calvin might have reminded his followers that usury was contrary to God's will, but Sir Thomas Gresham had brought to his contemporaries a clearer notion of how money worked, and it may have been part of his legacy that the Parliament of 1571 repealed the medieval prohibition and acknowledged that interest up to ten percent might legally be charged for the use of capital. The effect was salutary. Before 1571, when interest had been prohibited, loans had required devious modes of repayment and had carried exorbitant interest rates in order to cover the risk run by the broker. After 1571, however, many more people engaged themselves in the business, borrowing became respectable, and the covert procedures of the underground moneylenders quickly surfaced as the standard practice of the newly legalized brokers.[3]

Chief among these practices was the device of formalizing a loan by the drawing up of a bond. Bonds of one sort or another had always been customary in such matters, but after 1571 the overt bonding of borrower to lender became a flourishing business in London, and nowhere more than at the church of St. Mary le Bow, also called St. Mary Arches. This church was one of thirteen parishes in the City under the direct jurisdiction of the Archbishop of Canterbury, and the so-called "Court of Arches," the highest of the ecclesiastical courts belonging to the Archbishop, sat regularly in its precincts. The services attendant on this court, its facilities for engrossing documents and for administering oaths, and its central location in Cheapside, soon made Bow Church the obligatory place for borrower and lender to ratify their agreements.

Let us follow a typical borrowing situation from beginning to end. Sir James Mervyn, a knight from Wiltshire who is in London and in straitened circumstances, casts about for a "scrivener" or "goldsmith" from whom to borrow a hundred pounds for half a year. (Those who made it a regular business to lend money often styled themselves "scrivener" or "goldsmith" and may in certain cases have been entitled to such designations, but these terms were also euphemisms that everyone recognized.) Someone puts Mervyn in touch with Francis Langley, "goldsmith," who agrees to arrange for the loan. Mervyn will of course need guarantors, so he persuades his friends John Chamberlain, Thomas Witton, and Lord Audley to second him. Langley in turn finds a source of funds, but to secure them he must deal with William Nicoll, scrivener. When all is in readiness Langley, Mervyn and the cosigners appear at St. Mary le Bow. It is the second of June. All covert haggling about the terms of the loan has been settled by this point, and the overt agreement is for the legally allowed ten percent. Mervyn wants a hundred pounds for six months, so his charges will be five pounds. He will owe Langley £105 in half a year, on the second of December.[4]

But Langley needs some sort of legally enforceable security to guarantee his efforts. The furnishing of such a guarantee is the function of the bond. In the bond, which will be drawn up by a clerk at St. Mary Arches on June 2, Mervyn will acknowledge that he owes Langley £200—that is, twice the amount of the loan. The bond is engrossed in Latin, and the formula is standard: *Jacobus Mervyn recognovit se debere Francisco Langley ducentas libras bone et legalis monete Anglie, solvendi eidem Francisco aut assignatis suis*, etc., embellished and particularized as necessary. This debt is of course a fiction on June 2, at the time of signing, but it will become legally enforceable on December 2 in the event of a default on the loan. This condition to the bond, which is a formal part of the agreement, is written in English on the dorse of the bond, in a formula of this sort: *The condition of this bond is that if James Mervyn, John Chamberlain, Thomas Witton or Lord Audley pays to Francis Langley one hundred and five pounds at the house of William Nicoll, scrivener, on 2 December next following, then this bond is to be void; otherwise to stand in full force and virtue.* The borrower and his seconds will then sign the bond, and Langley will take it for safekeeping.

If Mervyn repays the £105 at the time and place appointed, the bond will be returned to him and the negotiation will be at an end. Certain unscrupulous brokers would on occasion feign the device of having mislaid the bond, but would collect the debt nevertheless; borrowers who allowed themselves to be deceived in this manner would be confronted, sometimes years later, with the unreturned bond and a demand for payment of the penalty sum. Alternatively, if the borrower defaulted, the holder of the bond could then proceed against him at the common law. The bond, once it came into force on the failure of the condition, was a negotiable instrument, and might be passed from one creditor to the next, so that anyone might bring suit against the defaulter. In the case of the loan just described, Sir

James Mervyn did indeed default, and Francis Langley took him to court. The case did not proceed to a judgment, so presumably Mervyn paid Langley, perhaps by borrowing money from someone else. On the due date of December 2 Langley would have had to protect his own credit by returning the original £100 plus costs to Nicoll the scrivener; if he could find temporary funds to cover this repayment, or if he could pay the interest and extend the loan for another six months on his own initiative, he would still be ahead as soon as he recovered his penalty sum from Mervyn. One could, in fact, begin to make a reasonable living in this manner, if enough borrowers defaulted, and if one had the stomach for it.[5]

Unfortunately, the tracing of such a career in the surviving records is fraught with pitfalls. The evidence of the bonds themselves is slight, for they survive only by accident, usually as appendages to other business or as souvenirs. The contents of bonds are often rehearsed in the pleadings of law suits, but if a bond has gone to court it has already been defaulted, and one has no clear sense of the number of bonds that were paid on time and duly returned. Nor can one be entirely sure from the lawsuits themselves whether the plainant was legitimately suing for non-payment or whether the suit was part of a program of harassment. Civil suits arising from non-payment of debts will normally be found in the Court of Common Pleas, though on occasion. they may be found in King's (Queen's) Bench or Exchequer, or even in Requests. One could pursue Francis Langley at tedious length through the Court of Common Pleas alone, where numerous records of his lawsuits survive; but there is no need to analyze every brick in the structure. One or two instances from this period will make clear enough the kind of activity in which Langley came to be engaged.

One of the devices that he learned to exploit with a fair degree of success was to offer himself as a cosigner to persons who were borrowing money from other bro-

43

kers but who had no sureties of their own. The hazard of cosigning a bond was, of course, that in the event of default the creditor could proceed at law against all the named persons therein. Langley's services to needy borrowers in such circumstances carried a price; not in money, but in legal entanglement, for by his patience he hoped to catch larger fish. The instance of Christopher Percy is instructive. Percy signed a bond for Francis Langley which has survived because Langley required that it be enrolled in the Court of Chancery. From the enrollment we learn that Richard Renching, a goldsmith, was willing to lend Percy £100 for a year, and that Francis Langley was willing to serve as Percy's cosigner. The penalty clause in Percy's bond to Renching was for £200, the usual doubled sum. Langley's price for his services was the signing of another bond by Percy, to "save him harmless" in the event of a default. Percy's bond to Langley was to protect him against the default sum of £200, and it carried its own default sum of £400. On the dorse of this latter bond Langley carefully and explicitly spelled out its purpose: that "the said Christopher Percy, his heirs, executors, administrators, or assigns . . . do at all times hereafter . . . clearly acquit, exonerate and discharge the said Francis Langley . . . against the said Richard Renching . . . of, for and concerning the said obligation or writing obligatory before recited and the sum and sums of money therein contained."[6]

This is the purpose of the bond to Langley; but it is not the condition. The formal condition is that Percy's bond to Langley will be voided only if Percy or his assigns "do well and truly content and pay, or cause to be paid, unto the said Richard Renching, his executors, administrators, or assigns, the said sum of one hundred pounds on the day and at the place aforesaid." Langley's intent, though obfuscated by the language of the bond, thus becomes clear: if Percy fails to repay Renching on time, he defaults simultaneously on both bonds, and owes Renching £200 and Langley £400. Renching may sue Percy in court and collect his £200, but Percy will still owe £400 to Langley. Langley cannot lose; he can only win or be saved harmless. This is but one of several devices Langley exercised on Christopher Percy; how Percy finally became completely enmeshed in Langley's toils is made painfully evident in Percy's own plea for relief to Sir Christopher Hatton. The document is damaged; my emendations are in brackets. We can learn merely from the opening sentences how successful Langley's tactics were.

[In most humble wise complaining] sheweth unto your good Lordship your daily Orator Christopher Percy, esquire: That whereas one Francis Langley, citizen and draper of London, at the [request and instance of your] Lordship's said Orator and for his debt, together with your said Orator by divers obligations became bounden jointly and severally unto Robert Freke [of the City of London] esquire, for the payment of divers sums of money at certain days past, as by the said obligations and conditions thereupon at large appeareth; and [whereas also the said Francis] Langley, at the like request of your said Orator, together with the said Robert Freke by one other obligation stood bound unto one Robert Harvey of London, [esquire, in the sum of one] hundred pounds for the payment of three score pounds of lawful money of England on the first day of May last past, as by the said obligation and [condition thereupon at large] appeareth; and whereas also the said Fancis Langley at the further request of your said Orator became bail for your said Orator as well in the King's [Bench at Westminster as in the Spir]itual Court in London, and unto the Sheriffs of London and Middlesex, for the appearance of your said Orator in the same Courts the first day of Easter [term . . .][7]

One needs to read no further. In the remainder of his plea Percy describes more bonds and conditions in which Langley holds him fast, and Langley in his answer lists still more, and tells about imprisonments for debt to which Percy has been subjected. It is the stuff of melodrama. In his plea Percy voices a conviction that many of his contemporaries would come to share: "the said Francis Langley [is] of a covetous and greedy mind, being desirous to wrest something from your said Orator whereby to enrich himself."

On at least one occasion Langley tried the tactic of the misplaced bond. It began when one William Gresham wanted to borrow a hundred pounds for six months. Thomas Chapman, the scrivener in Soper Lane, later recalled that he and Francis Langley were able to secure money from "one William Rowe of Higham Bensted in the county of Essex, esquire, (for whom this deponent was a disposer of his stock of money) of the penalty of £200 with condition for the payment of £105." Chapman drew up the bond, Gresham signed, and Langley cosigned. Langley then demanded of Gresham the additional bond, with a penalty sum of £300, to save him harmless. At the end of six months Gresham could not pay, so both bonds were renewed, and in another six months they were renewed again, but Rowe refused to carry the loan beyond that point. Chapman recalled that he then found another source of funds, enabling Langley to settle Gresham's debt to Rowe by binding Gresham in a "bond of £200 to Cicely Cyoll of London, widow, (for whom this deponent was also a disposer of her stock of money) for the payment of £105." Again Langley demanded and got the second bond, with a penalty sum of £300. William Gresham, no doubt to everyone's surprise, paid the widow on the appointed date and retrieved his bond from her; but he neglected to retrieve Langley's bond as well. Several years later Langley sued, claiming that William Gresham owed him £300.

Langley of course maintained that the bond was a just debt. Henry Smith remembered that he had "divers and sundry times heard the said Francis Langley say that he knew not what was become of his bond which [Gresham] had made unto him as aforesaid, by the space of many years together, and that at length one Richard Langley his nephew brought him the said bond which, as it was said, was found in a trunk amongst divers other writings left at a house in Cheapside London when the said Francis Langley removed from thence." Smith also remembered hearing Langley say "he would not abate them one penny of the said debt of £300." Hannibal Gammon dutifully remembered "that the said Francis Langley did oftentimes . . . come to the shop of this deponent's then dwelling house in Cheapside and would tell this deponent that he missed a bond wherein [Gresham] stood bound unto him."

Against this, William Gresham and his brother maintained that Langley's attempt at collecting the bond was fraudulent. "The said Francis Langley, having still in his hands your said Orators' obligation of three hundred pounds, never made mention of the same unto your said Orators, but as much as in him was concealed the same, hoping that through driving of time either some parties might depart this life that might be able to testify the discharge thereof, or else matters might in length of time be so forgotten as that it should not appear neither upon what consideration your said Orators had entered the said obligation nor that the same was discharged."[8]

One may perhaps find satisfaction in learning that the Court awarded its judgment in this case to Gresham; but for our purposes the outcome of this suit, or of the Percy suit, is of less importance than their value as exempla. These suits, and others like them in which Francis Langley figures, show us in dim outline the operation of a network of money merchants who sold the use of capital to the needy or the naive, often in collusion with one another, and seldom to the detriment of anyone but their customers. In the ten years following the death of his uncle, Francis Langley engaged in money broking and its attendant services with ever increasing success. At one point he even attempted to defraud his own brother-in-law, Anthony Ashley. When

Langley first began his career as a money broker, Sir Francis Drake had just set out on his round-the-world voyage of plunder and the Queen was busily engaged in her double game of courtship with the Duc d'Alençon. Richard Topcliffe, Walsingham's interrogator, was perfecting the ingenious machines that he was later to use in extracting confessions from Jesuits and others suspected of plotting against the Crown. During that period William of Orange was assassinated, Sir Philip Sidney was shot, and Mary Stuart was beheaded. Throgmorton, Babington, and their associates hoped to do as much for Elizabeth, and Philip finally sent his Armada to finish the job. It was a decade that began with the *Shepheardes Calender* and *Euphues* and ended with Martin Marprelate and *Tamburlaine*. If one may speak of such a thing as the temper of the times, one might tentatively suggest that pragmatism was becoming the order of the day, and demonstrable victory the vindication of that order.[9]

Francis Langley's triumphs were not on the scale of the nation's triumphs, but he too settled an old score in 1588. Barely a month after Drake and Howard had driven the Spanish ships up the channel to defeat, Langley sat down with Sir Rowland Hayward and drew up an indenture by which Hayward sold to Langley two messuages in Cheapside next adjoining to the Horse Head. These two messuages, still occupied by John Ballett, goldsmith, had been the cause of the contention over Sir John's will ten years earlier. Francis had been balked in his first devious attempt at obtaining them, but now they would be his. Hayward's price was reasonable; £466 13^s 4^d "to him in hand paid before the ensealing hereof."[10]

These were the first of Francis Langley's properties in Cheapside. As his legacy from Sir John he held the reversion to the Saracen's Head, and had bought his brother's reversion to the Horse Head, so that on Lady Ursula's death both these messuages would be his as well. But to own the house in which John Ballett lived

Cheapside, looking westward. In the left foreground, the tower of St. Mary le Bow church. The near structure in the street is the Standard; the far one, the Eleanor Cross. Left of the Standard is Goldsmiths' Row. In the distance, the east end and tower of St. Paul's.

and kept his shop was no mean accomplishment. Ballett was one of the wealthier goldsmiths in Cheapside and would not live and work in inferior quarters. I know of no precise statement of annual income from these two messuages, but from the selling price, and the value of Ballett's goods, one might hazard a guess of twenty pounds per year. A man might live on that. Langley would later realize an annual income of eighty pounds from the Horse Head alone, but that was another matter. For the moment he was well placed. Much of his business as a broker was conducted in Cheapside because of the location of St. Mary Arches; for some years he had lived near Cheapside; now he held property in Cheapside. He must have felt confident about the future, and of his career as a money broker, a "goldsmith." But there was more to Langley than that; the picture is incomplete. Concurrent with his broking activity he had embarked on another career, which has been generally misrepresented to us. We ought not pass beyond 1588 without first considering this other aspect of his life.[11]

IV

The Alnager

'Tis in reversion that I do possess.
RICHARD II

Francis Langley's reversion to the office of alnager, secured for him by his uncle in 1577, was, according to the records of the Court of Aldermen, the only reversion outstanding for an alnagership at the time it was granted, and Langley therefore had every expectation of advancing into the office at the next vacancy. A vacancy appeared to be imminent as early as 1580, when William Parker stated that he intended to resign. But Parker's affairs were complicated by patronage. The aldermen had appointed him alnager several years earlier at the express insistence of Lord Burghley, the Lord Treasurer. Parker was constantly in monetary difficulties, and the City had seen fit to turn over to him, at Burghley's further request, the lease of one of the City's houses, valued at 100 marks. But even this seemed not to help; and in casting about for other means of succor, Parker had decided that he might try to sell his alnagership to the highest bidder. Sir Peter Osborne, who was seeking the advancement of his servant Robert Nicholls, offered to pay Parker £160 for the office, and Parker agreed. Osborne, who was Lord Treasurer's Remembrancer, was in the direct service of Lord Treasurer Burghley, who had originally sponsored Parker, and to the City it must have appeared

51

that a power play was being attempted, with Parker and Nicholls as pawns, in an effort to remove from their own control the matter of succession in the office of alnager.

It was not customary for alnagerships to be sold in this manner. The City might allow certain persons to purchase reversions, tenable when a vacancy occurred, but the prospect of an alnager selling his own office was disquieting. Besides, Francis Langley had held a reversion to the office since 1577, and if Parker indeed intended to resign, then the City was obligated to advance Langley's claims against Sir Peter Osborne's efforts on behalf of Nicholls.

This was but one skirmish in a continuing battle, for the aulnage of cloth was a privilege that had already become a cause of friction between the City and the Court, perhaps as a result of the slowly declining status of the English cloth industry in general. The Council would have liked to secure control of the alnagerships, and the City was determined not to allow them out of its grasp. In 1580 the Queen had granted a patent to Edward Stafford to have the profits of the fines levied for improper measures of kerseys, a perquisite properly belonging to the alnagers of the City. The Queen was at this time obligated to Stafford for his excellent service in the cause of the Alençon engagement, in which he served as the Queen's personal messenger and representative in the same way that Simier represented Alençon (Simier spoke of Stafford as "monsieur d'Estafort"). It would be ingenuous of us to believe that the Queen rewarded Stafford with this patent in ignorance that it conflicted with the ancient privileges of the City; but it was a gesture typical of her. It cost her nothing; it inflamed a quarrel that she may have wished to fan; and it enlisted Stafford on her side, as he would surely take steps to consolidate his privilege.

Stafford's attempts to exercise his patent brought him into almost immediate difficulties. Having fined certain clothiers for violations of the statutes, he was then troubled by them a second time when they returned to complain that the City alnagers were also fining them. Stafford wrote to the Lord Mayor and aldermen asking them to desist, as the patent for levying such fines belonged to him. He invited the Court of Aldermen to inspect his patent, issued under the Great Seal. The Lord Mayor responded, explaining that the ancient charter of the City, which antedated Stafford's patent, reserved the rights of aulnage to the City or its deputies, and that the City could not relinquish those rights. So the Queen's reward to Stafford, like many of her rewards to her loyal servants, proved in the event to be troublesome and ultimately evanescent; but it had also served notice to the City that the right of aulnage was to be one of the targets of Court pressure. It is against this background that the Court of Aldermen received Sir Peter Osborne's request that his servant Robert Nicholls be appointed alnager in place of William Parker.[1]

Meanwhile, Parker was having second thoughts. Perhaps someone had offered him more money; at any rate, he tried at the last minute to decline Sir Peter's offer, and to return the money to him, but Sir Peter refused. There is no record of what conference followed upon this development; but by the middle of September 1580 Parker had been induced to surrender to Nicholls, and the Court of Aldermen had seen fit to grant Parker an annuity of £30 out of the common charge. On September 27, 1580, the Court of Aldermen formally accepted the resignation of Parker, and Nicholls was sworn in as a new alnager. Francis Langley's reversion had been ignored in favor of an accommodation with Lord Treasurer Burghley, and no doubt the Court of Aldermen felt they had made the best of an unpleasant business. Francis Langley still held the only extant reversion to the office, and the aldermen no doubt salved their consciences by insisting that this reversion would be duly honored at the next vacancy. But events proved otherwise.[2]

In the following summer an unexpected bit of information was brought to the attention of the Court of Aldermen. They were reminded that during the mayoralty of Lionel Duckett, on October 27, 1573, a reversion to the office of alnager had been granted to William Packington, mercer, Duckett's "brother-in-law, sometime his servant and apprentice." This reversion seems to have been quite forgotten by everyone; for Packington had no sooner received it than he had gone off to be about his business in Wiltshire, presuming that the Lord Mayor would notify him when the appropriate time came to exercise his prerogative. There had been no notification. The Court of Aldermen was reminded on June 13, 1581, that Packington had "absented himself from this City, during which time of his absence divers persons, for special causes this Court moving, have been removed out of the said Office and others placed in their rooms, whose rights and interests thereunto began long since the said grant of this Court made to the said William Packington. Of which said displacing and admittance the said William Packington had no knowledge or understanding until now of late."[3]

If, as I suspect, the Court of Aldermen had agreed at the time of the Nicholls appointment that the next vacant alnagership would be filled by their own first reversioner regardless of the pressure from Court, then this peculiar turn of events meant that, in strict conscience, they would have to pass over Francis Langley yet again in order to honor the Packington grant. It is highly unlikely that Langley appreciated the subtle irony of the situation. The aldermen, on June 13, 1581, "after long debating and deliberate examination of the said cause, and minding as much as in them lieth to maintain the credit of their former grant, have ordered, determined, and fully decreed that the said William Packington shall have the next room, place, and admittance to any of the said Office of alnagers, searchers or sealers of woolen cloths, within this City or the liberties thereof . . . any act, decree, order or promise of this Court, at any time heretofore had or made, to any manner of person or persons to the contrary in any wise notwithstanding."[4]

In the early winter of 1582 John Sutton died, and the Court of Aldermen moved to confirm William Packington in his new office. Francis Langley protested, as he must have done with the Nicholls appointment two years earlier. It is probable that he took up the matter with his brother-in-law, Anthony Ashley, a follower of Sir Christopher Hatton who was at the time a member of the Privy Council. Ashley was Langley's most well-placed connection, in that he had the ear of a Privy Councillor; but where, two years earlier, a protest from Langley about Nicholls would have run counter to Burghley's wishes, now in the case of William Packington the interference of the Council on Langley's behalf might be possible. Not that Burghley or Walsingham, or even Hatton, had any special interest in Langley; but it would be another opportunity to interfere with the City in the matter of aulnage. So the Privy Council made Langley's cause its own. On December 3, 1582, Langley personally delivered a letter from the Council, then sitting at Windsor, to the Lord Mayor, to remind him that "the bearer hereof, Francis Langley," had long since been granted "the reversion and next avoidance of one of the alnagers," and that "by the death of one Sutton your late officer the same is now become void."

The Council also saw fit to inform the Lord Mayor and aldermen

that the said Francis is a very honest man and fit for your service in that place, and that this present vacancy of right belongeth (as it is said) unto him, the right of one Packington, which pretendeth some interest therein by a former grant, being extinct by reason he was disposed thereof at the last vacancy before this, for such commodity to himself as then best liked him; the man being also otherwise (as it is said to be well known unto you) insufficient, we have therefore thought good to pray your Lordship and the rest that the said Francis Langley, according to his grant of reversion, may be admitted to the execution of the said office; wherein, as you shall in equity perform your grant to one that is reported to be a very fit man, so shall you give us occasion to remember it as a favor done at our request in any your honest causes when occasion shall require.[5]

A full battery of signatures was brought to bear on this letter: Burghley signed first, and then the earls of Lincoln, Warwick, Bedford, and Leicester, and then Hatton and Walsingham. Less than a week later Walsingham sent off another letter over his own signature, reminding the Lord Mayor and aldermen that the Council "did by their late letters recommend unto you one Francis Langley," a man reported to be "very honest and sufficient for the place." Walsingham claimed to have "some more particular respects which move me to further his well doing," and chose to follow the Council's official letter "with these few lines of mine own." Walsingham expressed his confidence that the City would wish to advance Langley, and commended the Lord Mayor and his brethren "for that good you shall all like to do him," especially as "his honesty and sufficiency is great and well liked of you all." The orderly and good government of the City virtually required that "no other man's colorable or pretended title may be suffered to prevent or any ways prejudice [Langley] in his lawful causes," because the example of such a miscarriage would be "inconvenient." The implications of the letter were unmistakable.[6]

It must have amused the Privy Council to be in a position to plead for the appointment of the very man whom the City had insisted upon at the last vacancy in opposition to Nicholls. But this time the aldermen were in no mood to be pressured. Earlier in the autumn they had received an unpleasant letter from Hatton, intimating that the Queen was displeased with the

56

growing disorders in the cloth trade, and that she thought there should be more alnagers. This was probably a just observation, and one which the aldermen, under other circumstances, might well have acted favorably upon; but at this juncture they remained intransigent before the Council. When they met at Guildhall on December 11, 1582, just two days after Walsingham had written his letter in support of Langley, they took their stand: "this day William Packington, mercer, was admitted and sworn in open Court to be one of the alnagers, searchers and sealers of woolen cloth within this City and the freedoms and liberties of the same in the stead and place of John Sutton, draper, deceased." In response to Hatton's letter, they further affirmed "that there shall be no more appointed officers to have divident of the profits of that Office above the number of four."[7]

So Packington took his place with the other alnagers. There were indeed four of them, as the aldermen had decreed, but so constituted that the number included the auditor, who kept the books at the weekly cloth market at Blackwell Hall, as well as the three searchers. Packington joined company with Nicholas Spencer, merchant tailor, who held the office of auditor, and with the other two searchers, Peter Worlych, merchant tailor, and Robert Nicholls, cook. It is probably true that there was too much work for these men. The aldermen adjusted matters quietly. Having formally declared a limit of four alnagers, and having defined an alnager as one who shares in the dividing of the profits of the office, they then discreetly effected an increase in the number of alnagers by decreeing that "after the death or removing of Nicholas Spencer, the Auditor or Surveyor shall have only his fee and no divident of the profits as searcher of cloth."[8]

Nicholas Spencer was elderly, and his retirement as auditor could not be far off; in anticipation of that event, John Leake, a deputy alnager, was invited to begin assuming the duties of an alnager in his own right, so that the names of four searchers might appear in the records at the time of Spencer's removal. Leake was also needed for other reasons more immediate, for William Packington was apparently in ill health and discharging his duties with difficulty. Francis Langley, his grievances still fresh upon him, was partially appeased by the offer of the clerkship of Blackwell Hall, which enabled him to work under Spencer and to observe the activities of the searchers. He seems to have made himself useful in the office and agreeable to his colleagues, for two years after Packington's appointment the Court of Aldermen moved Langley gingerly into an alnagership.[9]

It was not quite a formal appointment. William Packington was "so sickly and infirm of body as he cannot execute his said office," and the aldermen had decided that "it shall and may be lawful . . . for the said William Packington presently to surcease and forbear the execution of his said Office, and at his pleasure to depart hence into the country." Packington was given license to stay there "until it shall please Almighty God to restore him to health." In the interim, however, his work had to be done. The Court of Aldermen was moved, "at the . . . suit and desire of all the said alnagers," to let Francis Langley supply the labor, "for his good experience therein." But Langley's assumption of duties was clearly delimited; he was to work in Packington's "room and office until [Packington's] return to the same without any prejudice or hurt in any wise to the said William Packington." Langley was to be no more than a substitute; but at least it was a step in the right direction.[10]

Packington went into the country, but the Wiltshire air was powerless against his senescence. He held out for the better part of a year, but was dead at the end of the following summer. On Thursday September 9, 1585, the Court of Aldermen recorded that "this day Francis Langley, draper, was admitted into the room

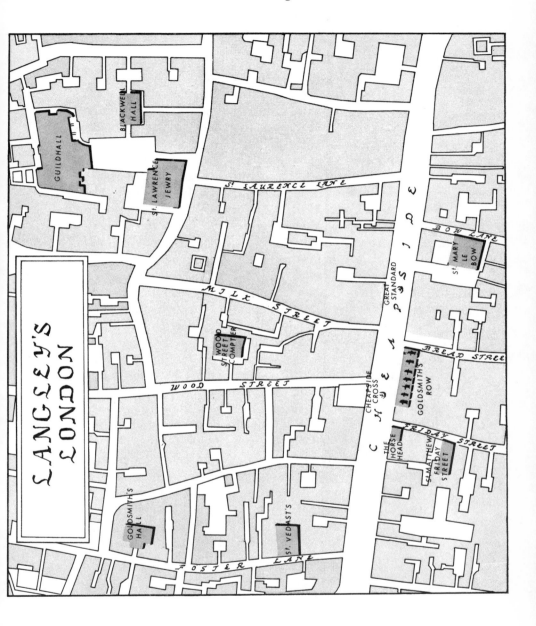

GUILDHALL

BLACKWELL HALL

St LAWRENCE JEWRY

St LAURENCE LANE

BOW LANE

St MARY LE BOW

GREAT STANDARD

CHEAPSIDE

LANGLEY'S LONDON

MILK STREET

WOOD STREET COMPTER

BREAD STREET

WOOD STREET

GOLDSMITHS ROW

CHEAPSIDE CROSS

FRIDAY STREET

THE HORSE HEAD

St MATTHEW FRIDAY STREET

GOLDSMITH'S HALL

St VEDAST'S

FOSTER LANE

and office of one of the alnagers, searchers and sealers of woolen cloths at Blackwell Hall, now being void by the death of William Packington, mercer."[11]

Langley was finally an alnager in his own right. It had taken eight years from the time Sir John purchased the reversion, and two frustrating setbacks with Nicholls and Packington, but it was bound to have happened eventually. And Langley had known that. In fact, he was so secure in his sense of ultimate office that he had begun, even while he was only the clerk in Blackwell Hall, to arrogate to himself certain of the functions of the searchers. He knew that the alnagers were expected to be on duty in Blackwell Hall both in and out of market time, searching and sealing cloth when the market was not open, and overseeing the market in operation. Each kind of cloth had its own standards for length and weight, and these figures were pressed into the lead seal, along with the word *searched*. Cloths that failed to meet the assize were forfeit; the seal was impressed with an *F*, the merchant was fined, and the cloth was confiscated. Because the search was elaborate, and controversy always possible, the alnagers were not supposed to search and seal cloth while the market was in session. Importunate merchants continued to abuse this understanding, however, until their demands were tempered by a parliamentary statute authorizing the alnagers to levy a fine of £5 per search on any clothmaker whose wares had to be sealed during market time "to the disturbance of the sale of such cloths in the Market there."[12]

Langley also knew that, because of this custom, clothmakers arriving in London during market time would not go directly to Blackwell Hall but would normally go first to their lodgings at some nearby inn, later bringing their bolts of cloth to Blackwell Hall for searching and sealing when the market was out, and then returning to their lodgings with their sealed cloths to await the following market day. Or they might return home; for the goods, once sealed by the alnagers in Blackwell Hall, could then be offered for sale in any market. The market inspector in Faversham, for example, would only need to satisfy himself that the cloth brought there for sale had been properly sealed, and the seller could then proceed unhindered. To assist the inspectors in smaller towns, various parliamentary statutes had given them the right to "visit and go into all or any house or houses, shops, or other rooms of any clothiers, drapers, clothworkers, or of any other person or persons whatsoever where any of the said cloth shall be, and there to make due search and view the same" to certify the presence of the seal.[13]

But the license to enter and search applied equally well to the alnagers in Blackwell Hall, though in practice it was seldom invoked. If the market inspector in Faversham found that a cloth merchant had arrived in town with unsealed cloths, he might become suspicious; but in London unsealed cloths were a commonplace, as the sellers awaited their time to go to Blackwell Hall. Nevertheless, Francis Langley, as clerk of Blackwell Hall, began to take upon himself the function of seeking out cloth in the lodgings of clothmakers and clothsellers. He would of course find unsealed bolts; he would then express horror at such flagrant breach of the law, and threaten confiscation. He might then allow himself to be mollified by the offer of a fee for his mercy; or, if he met with recalcitrance, he might impound the cloths and take them to Blackwell Hall for later redemption (which would require the offer of another fee) by the merchant.

Langley engaged in these extortionary practices from an early time. Not all clothmakers were appropriately awed by him, however; on one occasion he was sued. In January 1584, nearly two years before he was officially made an alnager, Langley tried these tactics on one John Thompson at Thompson's lodging in the parish of St. Michael Bassishaw. Thompson declined to offer any bribe, or offered an insufficient bribe, and Langley impounded his cloths. Thompson secured the services of John Ive, an attorney, and they filed a bill of complaint in the Court of Queen's Bench, charging Langley with trespass, in that he came "with force and arms" [*vi et armis*] and seized Thompson's goods to the value of 13^s. Langley was summoned to Court to reply, but did not appear; judgment went to Thompson. But as the Court was uncertain what damages ought to be awarded in the case, they impaneled a jury, which met at Guildhall, and the jury found that damages, costs, and charges ought to be levied against Langley to the extent of £3 6^s 8^d. The Court thereupon ordered Langley's arrest and imprisonment by the Marshal.[14]

Such experiences did not dampen Langley's ardor. In his extralegal activities as clerk he found an ally in John Leake, a deputy alnager who had been raised to alnager at the time of the Packington appointment. Leake was fourteen years Langley's senior, but their instincts about the potential of their offices must have been similar. I have found no evidence to impugn the credit of either Peter Worlych or Robert Nicholls, the other two alnagers, but of Leake and Langley there will be much to say later. Langley's formal appointment as alnager in 1585 simply reinforced the potential for pressure that he was able to bring to bear on the merchants with whom he came into contact. His ventures in this field, both before and immediately after his appointment, coincided with his experiments in the moneylending field; his financial engagements with Christopher Percy and William Gresham, described above, date from this same period. John Eden, a merchant tailor who was obliged by his trade to deal with the cloth market and with the alnagers, found such conduct intolerable, and wrote a letter to the Lord Mayor early in 1585 listing his complaints—that the alnagers were corrupt, that they improperly used their power to affix or withhold seals, and that there were complaints about their conduct even in Parliament—and suggesting suitable remedies, chief among which was the urging of his own fitness for such a post.

The letter of course elicited a response from the four alnagers. They observed to the Lord Mayor that "the said Eden is, and of long time hath been, a very troublesome and contentious person," and that his incessant litigiousness had made him "so poor and decayed" that he was obliged to live "partly by the charity of his Company" of merchant tailors. The alnagers also observed that his "old age and other disabilities" made Eden "every way very unfit" for their office. "We are more of us in office already than in truth is needful," they protested, insisting that "we use the Seals according to the laws" and denying that they were called in question in Parliament "for any abuse by us committed in the execution of our offices." The letter is signed by Leake, Worlych, Nicholls, and Langley, in that order; curiously, Langley's signature has been forged. This is probably of no consequence. Langley was no doubt elsewhere, perhaps in Cheapside, on the day or days when the letter was drawn up and signed. If the letter was required on a certain day, and Langley was not available, someone would have had to sign for him. But his very inability to be present on such an occasion lends force to Eden's complaint.[15]

Eden's letter may in fact have accomplished some good. One result was the awarding to Eden of a reversion of the office of alnager, though such an award was little likely to benefit him, for by that time three other people held prior reversions. A more likely benefit was the decision of the Court of Aldermen on April 12, 1586, to require the alnagers to be bound to the Chamberlain of the City, that is, to post bond for their good performance in their office. Perhaps the hope was that such bonding might protect the City from the consequences of an irresponsible discharge of duties by an alnager; further, it might keep the aldermen free from involvement in the disputes between the alnagers and the clothmakers. For the Court of Aldermen had other business to attend to. Throughout 1585 and 1586 the threat of armed invasion was in the air, and thousands of men were being mustered in London. In 1585 the Spanish king arrested all English trading ships on the Spanish coast, imprisoned their crews, confiscated their goods, and appropriated the ships and their armament for use in the Armada in preparation at Cadiz. To the merchants of London this was a severe blow. Ralegh's attempted settlement at Roanoke, a proposed economic alternative to Spanish trade that had financial support in the City, was known by 1586 to have failed. The City was at the same time committed to raising a subsidy of £4,000 to support the Queen's activities in the Low Countries, to which Leicester had gone off as commander of the English forces.[16]

The Parliament of 1584 was dissolved in 1586 and a new one summoned a month later. In both the old and the new Parliament three of the four members for London were from the Court of Aldermen, and the fourth was William Fleetwood, the Recorder of the City. The affairs of the nation intruded themselves into the consciousness of the City in more visible ways as well. Doctor Parry's execution in Palace Yard in the spring of 1585 for planning to kill the Queen was followed in the autumn of 1586 by the public execution at Holborn of Anthony Babington, John Ballard, Chidiock Tichbourne and their fellow conspirators, whose plotting had implicated both Philip II and Mary Stuart. The safety of the realm was clearly endangered, and at such a time Francis Langley's questionable conduct in his office, or reprehensible activity as a money broker, could hardly be ranked among the City's more pressing problems.

There is no need to rehearse the public history of the next two years, but it might be well to observe that the tenor of certain private lives continued undisturbed by the events at Fotheringay or Gravelines. Debtors continued to borrow, lenders to lend, the clever to outwit the foolish or imprudent. If, as some claim, the destruction of the Spanish fleet in 1588 helped to buoy the popular spirit, then perhaps we may presume that it had some small effect on Langley too; it may have made him more ambitious.

V

The Lord of the Manor

*This fellow might be in's time
a great buyer of land, with
his statutes, his recognizances, his fines,
his double vouchers, his recoveries.*
HAMLET

Francis Langley was forty years old in 1588, and an observer might, by viewing the evidence from a certain angle, detect a change of emphasis in his activities beginning at about that time. The misfortunes of John Goddard may serve as an illustration. Goddard was a London brewer who held some lands in Enfield, Middlesex, and when necessity compelled him to turn to one Thomas Hutton of London to borrow a hundred pounds he offered his deeds to these lands as security for the debt. Hutton accepted the deeds and advanced the money. Goddard's rather naive assumption was "that the said lands [were] conveyed to the said Hutton only upon trust and confidence" and that they would be given back to him without difficulty when he repaid his loan. He soon found otherwise. When Thomas Hutton in turn found himself short of funds, he did not scruple to pass on Goddard's deeds as security for his own borrowing. In 1588 Hutton borrowed £150 from Francis Langley, giving Langley the deeds to the Enfield lands.

Langley, as he later described the circumstances, said that at the time he did not have that much money readily at hand, and in order to accommodate Hutton he was forced to find it elsewhere. (The classic device of the moneylender will be recognized here.) Langley did find a source of funds, as he recalled, and he indentured himself, along with Hannibal Gammon and Thomas Covell, another goldsmith, in two bonds for a total amount of £150, which money he then passed on to Hutton. Langley could have continued the pattern of exchanges by giving the deeds as security for his own debt, but he apparently chose not to. He opted to hold the deeds, and instead to give bonds for the debt.[1]

Hutton eventually defaulted, as he may have intended to do all along, and Langley recalled that he found himself obligated to renew his two bonds at six-month intervals, paying some seven or eight pounds interest at each renewal. Ultimately Langley was constrained to sell a portion of the lands in Enfield to raise £150 and pay off his bonds. Perhaps such bonds truly existed; perhaps not. In any event, when John Goddard (with whom this episode began) repaid his loan and in his innocence asked Thomas Hutton for the return of his deeds, one can imagine his mounting horror at the tale of their peregrinations. Ultimately he found it necessary to go to law against both Hutton and Langley. The new element in this otherwise familiar tale is the matter of the deeds; from this dispute we learn that by 1588 Langley's acquisitiveness had broadened to include the getting of land as well as—or perhaps even in preference to—the getting of money. This change in Langley's desires may well have come about earlier, but it makes its first appearance in the records at this point. The timing is fortunate; for it possibly enables us to sense better the motives that underlay Langley's eagerness to acquire the manor of Paris Garden in 1589.[2]

For this story we must cross the river; for even as Hutton was disposing of Goddard's deeds in Middlesex, a similar scene was being enacted in Southwark, following hard on the death of Thomas Cure, sadler. Cure was a man of stature and substance: he had been

Master of the Company of Sadlers a remarkable five times, and was Sadler to King Edward VI, Queen Mary, and Queen Elizabeth. In 1570 he had moved to St. Saviour's parish in Southwark, and was almost immediately elected a vestryman, a post he held till his death. From 1572 he was one of the commissioners for sewers in Surrey. In 1579 he purchased Waverley House from Viscount Montague, and some property adjoining, and in 1584 he secured Letters Patent for the founding of a college for poor people there. He also acquired the title to many capital messuages in Southwark: the Red Lion, the Cross Keys, the Estridge Feather, the King's Head, the Vernacle, the Pewter Pot in the Hoop, and others.[3]

Thomas Cure was buried in St. Saviour's on May 30, 1588. He had drawn up his will less than a week earlier, and it would not be probated until June 22. But his two sons George and Thomas junior did not feel any need to wait. On June 15 they jointly sold to Richard Humble, vintner, their father's deeds to a capital messuage called the King's Head in the High Street in Southwark, and to three other messuages, all of them contiguous. The King's Head was an inn, and had been famous before the Reformation as the Pope's Head; Humble, as a vintner, no doubt intended to use it advantageously. The deeds to these properties might readily enough have been put up as collateral for loans, had the two sons been interested in such an arrangement; the speed with which they sold the deeds outright argues perhaps an immoderate need for fast cash.

The disposition of their father's estate may have been a part of the problem. Though the elder Cure's will was duly probated on June 22, and a register copy made (which may still be consulted in the Public Record Office), a curious set of circumstances surrounds it. Richard Humble, in a lawsuit filed many years later, described it aptly. He noted that Thomas Cure the elder "did make or cause his last will and testament to be made in writing; and having issue two sons, George his eldest son and Thomas his second son, did, in and by his said will and testament, devise and bequeath . . . his lands, messuages and tenements in Southwark aforesaid unto the said Thomas," but left the remainder of his estate, "the greatest part of his lands and inheritances, to descend unto his eldest son [George];" and then he died. "But the said will coming into the hands of the said George Cure and of Agnes Cure his mother, the said George Cure, combining and confederating with his said mother, refused to produce, enroll or prove the same; and they, or one of them with the consent of the other, suppressed and burnt the same, by means whereof great controversy grew betwixt the said George and the said Thomas his brother."[4]

This is surely strange. Nor are Richard Humble's recollections entirely in error, for there was indeed a dispute between the two sons over the respective portions of their inheritance, a dispute resolved only when the young men agreed to submit to arbitration. A panel of four arbiters was chosen; they were Owen Brereton, esquire, Arthur Langworth, gentleman, William Danby, gentleman, and Manasses Stockton, a goldsmith from the City. On February 3, 1589, the brothers George and Thomas each indentured himself to the other in a bond of £1,000 for the good performance of the arbitration, whatever the outcome. On February 5, two days later, the arbitrators made their written award. The decision was much as Humble remembered the legacies; Thomas was to have the many Southwark properties that his brother had claimed as his own. George Cure, having bound himself, was required to relinquish his claim on these messuages, and he duly transferred them to his brother Thomas by indenture on February 14, 1589.[5]

Thomas was thus finally given his rightful estate in the properties left by his father. But these properties were not a complete picture of the wealth of the elder Cure, for even during his lifetime he had settled valuable holdings on his two sons. The manor of Paris Garden was such a gift; the elder Cure bought it for his son Thomas eight years before his death. One would think that a prudent manager, someone like the elder Cure himself, would have been able to live and prosper quite comfortably with such an impressive list of holdings. But Thomas the younger was no more like his father than Francis Langley was like his uncle. Money and property seemed to slip through the fingers of the younger Thomas like water. George Cure may indeed have been trying to forestall the inevitable by claiming his brother's legacies as his own, but if that was his plan it did not work. Thomas needed money, and was not particularly careful or cautious about the kinds of entanglements which such a need engendered.

From John Savage, sadler, a man whom his father had remembered in his will, the younger Thomas Cure borrowed £50 and gave as security a lease of part of the manor of Paris Garden; he later borrowed another £50 from Savage, perhaps to cover the penalty on the default of the first loan, and for security gave him another lease to part of the manor. Cure also borrowed £50 from William Danby, a relative by marriage and one of the men called upon to be an arbitrator, and gave as security yet another lease to the manor. In 1589 Cure borrowed £100 from George Chute for an indefinite term, paying or offering to pay Chute a flat ten pounds per year for the use of the money—Chute spoke of it as his "annuity or yearly rent"—but soon found himself unable to make even these payments. He bound himself to Giles Simpson, goldsmith, in a £200 bond for the use of £100, and was unable to pay. He bound himself twice to Robert Peter, for two loans totaling £550, perhaps in a futile attempt to redeem some of his other indentures; the penalty sum on these two bonds alone was a staggering £1000.[6]

This is of course the familiar pattern of an inexperienced person entrapped by debts; one might almost predict by formula the ensuing troubles. When

Cure could not pay his £100 to Giles Simpson on the appointed day, Simpson refused to renew, but instead held out for the penalty sum of £200. He declined, in his generosity, to arrest Cure, but invited him rather to defer payment of the penalty by signing a bond for the £200. Such a bond would, of course, have its own penalty sum of £400. Cure assented, perhaps foolishly but perhaps unavoidably, and Simpson generously furnished a cosigner—one Nicholas Skeeres, possibly the same man who was with Christopher Marlowe in Deptford the day he was killed. Cure's debts were by now immoderate. It may have been Simpson who first suggested to Cure that Francis Langley would assist him; for Simpson was not only a money broker but also a legitimate goldsmith who kept a shop in Lombard Street, and he knew Langley and also his friend Gammon in both contexts. Langley's new interest in the acquisition of land may also have been a factor. If Cure would only sell the manor of Paris Garden to Langley, he would surely realize enough money to settle his debts.

Such a course could hardly have appealed to Cure, but by now his options were limited. An indenture was drawn up and enrolled, but not sealed, on May 24, 1589. Cure's asking price may have been too high, and Langley had nothing to lose by waiting. When the inevitable default on the bond for £200 occurred, in June 1589, Simpson swiftly had Cure thrown in prison. Cure appealed to Simpson from prison to show some compassion, and Simpson, in his generosity, allowed Cure to sign another bond, with a penalty clause of only £250, for the payment of the £200 plus charges of £11 14^s. Cure signed, and Francis Langley offered to be his cosigner, though no doubt certain understandings had to be reached about Paris Garden before Langley would set his name to parchment. Langley's terms for his proposed purchase were straightforward. He would pay £850 to Cure for the manor of Paris Garden; of that sum, £55 would be paid to Cure at the sealing of

the indentures. Within thirty days Langley would pay
£550 to Robert Peter and redeem Cure's two bonds; he
would pay £100 to John Savage and recover the two
leases; he would pay £50 to William Danby and recover
the third lease. And fourteen days after the sealing of
the indenture, he would pay Cure the balance of the
purchase price, or £95. Cure must have given in, for
the bond to Simpson was signed, to be due on December 20, 1589, and Cure was released from imprisonment. On November 18, 1589, the sale of Paris Garden
was formally sealed.[7]

This, in brief, is a summary of the circumstances by
which Francis Langley came to hold the manor of Paris
Garden. His relationship with Thomas Cure the younger was no different from his relationship with many
another needy Londoner; business is business, he
might have said, except that in this case the rewards
were greater, for the acquisition of Paris Garden was a
major achievement for Langley. Cure's bond to Simpson, due on December 20, was paid by Langley in installments; but as this final obligation was not an encumbrance on the title, Langley had already begun to
regard himself, and of course to style himself, as the
lord of the manor of Paris Garden. A certain dignity accrued to such an appellation, though perhaps not so
much as we might think. It may be useful, before proceeding further, to clarify the nature of Langley's purchase, so that we may better understand its real worth
to him.

The manor of Paris Garden lay to the south of the
City, its northern end stretching along the Thames op-
posite to Blackfriars and Bridewell. On its eastern
boundary it abutted on the manor or liberty of the
Bishop of Winchester, locally called the liberty of the
Clink. On its west lay Lambeth marsh and to the south
St. George's fields. The manor comprised somewhat
less than a hundred acres, and probably corresponded
to the medieval hide of ground called Wiðflete or
Wythiflete (that is, willow stream) and sometimes

Wylys. By 1420 its later name had come into use: some ordinances made in that year speak of "the privileged place called Parish Garden, otherwise called Wideflete or Wilys," and the earliest surviving court roll of the manor, from 1460, speaks of "Parisgarden alias Wylys." The origin of the name Paris Garden is unknown, despite various conjectures about one Robert de Paris or of a supposed parish. The manor belonged variously to Robert Marmion, to the Abbey of Bermondsey, to the Knights Templar, and to the Knights Hospitaller; and in 1536, as part of the dissolution, it passed to the Crown. It was made part of the dowry of Jane Seymour, but on her death in 1537 it returned to the King's hands and was passed on as a royal inheritance to his children. In 1578 it belonged to Queen Elizabeth.[8]

Paris Garden had been a manor for as long as anyone could remember. It had a number of tenants—about thirty-five in 1578—who held their lands of the lord "by custom of the manor," which custom had been, like the manor itself, in existence time out of mind. The rights and obligations of these tenants were documented by engrossment in the rolls of the manor court, a copy of which served as their evidence of title. Hence they were said to hold their estate "by copy of court roll," and came to be spoken of as the copyhold tenants or copyholders. The manor also had a few other tenants, who were not copyhold or customary tenants, but who had contracted with the lord of the manor to hold certain portions of the demesne lands at his pleasure. These were leasehold tenants, and their rights and privileges were different from those of the copyhold tenants. Their tenure was of a different kind—based on cash rather than on service—and so, therefore, at least in theory, was their relation to the lord, though by Langley's time all these relationships were undergoing change.[9]

The manor also had two courts which the lord traditionally maintained, one by right and one by franchise.

The court baron or lord's court was his by right, being a necessary part of any manor. Under its purview came the maintenance of services and duties owed to the lord by his tenants; the recording of surrenders of and admissions to customary tenure on the part of copyholders; and, in earlier times, certain actions of a personal nature in which the debt or damage did not nominally exceed forty shillings. This figure had been established by statute centuries earlier and was, by Elizabeth's reign, unrealistically low, the result being that the Paris Garden court rolls under the lordships of Cure and Langley show hardly any entries of this sort.

The other court held by the lord of the manor was the court leet. This court was not a personal court, but was the King's Court granted by franchise to the lord of the manor as a convenient means of extending royal justice locally. It was a court of record, and its original intent was to view the frankpledges, that is, the freemen within the manor who (according to the institution of King Alfred) were all mutually pledged for the good behavior of each other. This view of frankpledge was still a regular part of the business of the Paris Garden court leet in Elizabeth's day. The other general responsibility of the court leet was to present by jury any and all crimes that happened within its jurisdiction. If the crimes were trivial misdemeanors the court leet was empowered to punish, just as the court baron was empowered to recover trivial debts and damages. Presentments of a more serious nature, as for treason or murder, would of course be removed from the manor court to the royal court.

These, then, were the main features of the manorial structure of Paris Garden Manor, a structure in no way unusual. On July 10, 1578, at the request of her kinsman Henry Carey, Lord Hunsdon, the Queen granted the manor of Paris Garden, with its leasehold and copyhold tenants, its court baron and court leet, to Robert Newdigate and Arthur Fountayne. These two men are otherwise undistinguished in the period, and I do not know what arguments were urged on their behalf by Lord Hunsdon. The grant, in any event, was copious, consisting of several manors in Bedfordshire and Lincolnshire, and the lands of a number of dissolved religious houses, in addition to the manor of Paris Garden. All the former holdings were to be by common tenure which was free from wardship and other feudal dues; but Newdigate and Fountayne were to hold the manor of Paris Garden by knight service as tenants in chief, a form of tenure to which greater honor had traditionally been attached though in actual practice it was merely more burdensome.[10]

The grant to Newdigate and Fountayne conveyed the "lordship and manor" of Paris Garden, that is to say, not only the lands of the manor, but also the rents of the leasehold and copyhold tenants, the rights and profits of the court baron, court leet, and view of frankpledge, as well as other rights properly appertaining to the lordship of the manor. Lord Hunsdon's initiative in requesting this grant for Newdigate and Fountayne was soon rewarded, for on February 21, 1579, the two of them released to him by indenture the rights and profits of the customary lands, or copyhold portion, of the manor. A courteous gesture, but also a practical one: for Newdigate and Fountayne probably had no need for their copyholders. In an earlier age, the customary tenants would have been expected to work the demesne lands and tend their lord's crops, but by 1578 the lord of the manor was better served by the local City markets, and his demesne lands could more profitably be leased out than farmed for his own use. The service that was still technically owed him by the copyholders was by this time paid in cash rather than in days of labor, and the profits of the customary lands of Paris Garden manor represented, at best, less than a sixth of the total annual value of the manor. The copyholders may have been more trouble than they were worth. Indeed, this separating of the copyholders from the demesne lands made such good sense that the division was retained when Hunsdon, Newdigate and Fountayne, on April 1, 1580, divested themselves of their entire interest in Paris Garden.[11]

The copyhold tenants of the manor had for some time been interested in securing control of their own interests, and had chosen Thomas Taylor, gentleman, and Richard Platt, brewer, to negotiate as their agents toward this end. On April 1, 1580, they were finally successful, for on that date Hunsdon, Newdigate, and Fountayne affirmed by indenture that they had "demised, betaken, and to farm letten" to Taylor and Platt, on behalf of the copyholders, "all and singular the messuages, lands, tenements, meadows, leasows, pastures, and hereditaments whatsoever, being copyhold and customary, or demised or granted as customary or copyhold tenements, or by copy of Court Roll" of the manor of Paris Garden. The yearly rental value of the holdings is stated in the indenture to be £8 5^s 4^d, and the profits of these rents were also demised to Taylor and Platt, as were also "all and all manner of rents, services, duties, commodities, and demands whatsoever issuing out or payable, due or to be due, unto the Lord or Lords of the said Manor for the said copyhold lands and tenements, or any part and parcel thereof, and the Court Baron of the said Lordship or Manor and all profits and perquisites of the said Court Baron." For the grant of this lease the copyhold tenants, through their agents Taylor and Platt, paid £600 outright, and were obligated to renew the lease each year by paying, on the feast of St. Michael, one peppercorn rent if demanded. The lease was to become effective on Lady Day (March 25) 1580, and to last for two thousand years.[12]

To make clear their honorable intentions in the matter, Taylor and Platt affirmed in a separate indenture of the same date that the "lease and demise and other writings" related to the manor of Paris Garden "were had, obtained and purchased . . . at the costs and charges of all the copyholders of the Manor of Paris Garden aforesaid, every of them disbursing the[reto] according to the several rates of their several copyhold rents." Taylor and Platt formally disclaimed any intent to use the lease for their personal profit or benefit, "but to the use, behoof, avail and benefit of the said copyholders."[13]

On the same day, Hunsdon, Newdigate, and Fountayne sold to Thomas Cure the elder a lease to part of the demesne lands of the manor for the term of one thousand years, at a yearly rent of ten shillings. I have not been able to find this lease; one would like to know the nature and extent of the property described therein. Circumstantial evidence, to be discussed later, suggests that the manor house was involved. Having thus leased out the copyhold lands and parts of the demesne lands for fixed terms, Hunsdon, Newdigate, and Fountayne then sold the lordship of the manor in perpetuity to Cure, in the name of his son Thomas Cure the younger. For his good performance in both this indenture of sale to the younger Cure and the indenture of lease to the elder, Hunsdon bound himself in the sum of one thousand marks to both the Cures for the assurance of his conduct "according to the tenor and true meaning of the same several indentures." This bond was Hunsdon's guarantee that Fountayne, who for some unexplained reason was not present at the drawing up of the indentures, would acknowledge and seal them before May 1 next ensuing. There seems to have been no problem on this score; Hunsdon and Newdigate sealed the indentures on April 1 and Fountayne appeared in Chancery to seal them on April 26. Thereafter Thomas Cure was, through the efforts of his father, the lord of the manor of Paris Garden.[14]

Encumbered as it was with leases over which he had no control, young Cure cannot be said to have acquired much more than a titular lordship over the manor, but he did have a number of acres of meadow and pasture under his immediate control. His father may have intended to assign the thousand-year lease to his son at some later time, perhaps on evidence of maturity; but this never transpired, and the lease was still in the elder Cure's name when he died.

When Thomas Cure the younger accepted Francis Langley's offer of £850 for the lordship and manor of Paris Garden, Langley's first task was to find the money. In this instance he was fortunate, for he managed, as Hannibal Gammon remembered, to "take up upon interest out of the Orphans' Court in London eight hundred pounds in money or thereabouts upon bonds with sureties towards the purchase of the said manor of Paris Garden of the said Thomas Cure the younger." Richard Langley, haberdasher, nephew to Francis, recalled having "heard the said Francis Langley . . . say that he took up upon security out of the Court of Orphans in the Guildhall, London, the sum of eight hundred pounds or thereabouts for the purchasing of the said manor of Paris Garden." [15]

Both these recollections are correct. On April 22, 1589, even before Giles Simpson's dramatic arrest of Thomas Cure the younger, Langley had arranged to borrow £800 out of the Court of Orphans through the Chamberlain of London. He may have done this solely in anticipation of Cure's imprisonment and capitulation, or it may have been done initially in preparation for some other enterprise now lost to us, and later diverted. The money, in any event, was in Langley's hands before the end of April. It was part of the estate of Richard Walter, girdler, deceased, and properly belonged to his young son Nathaniel, an orphan and therefore the ward of the City. The Chamberlain, as custodian of Nathaniel's portion of the estate, made the money available to Langley by means of four separate indentures, each dated April 22, 1589, two for £300 and two for £100. Among those whom Langley brought with him as cosigners for the various indentures were John Holinshed, draper, John Bradshaw, mercer, Christopher Carey, scrivener, and Nicholas Herrick and James Pemberton, goldsmiths.[16]

It should not be surprising that Langley had to put himself in debt to raise the necessary money; he was already in debt in this period. His practice of cosigning bonds for defaulters in order to claim the penalty sum had made him a creditor to a number of his impecunious contemporaries, but the practice had not made him rich; for his defaulted bonds were simply negotiable instruments that he would then use to settle other obligations of his own. A great deal of parchment passed through Langley's hands in this fashion, but the process tended to impoverish those whom he served more than it enriched him. Nor was Langley himself the most astute of businessmen; early success had perhaps made him careless, for by the late 1580s we find others suing him for debt as often as we find him suing others. One of his creditors in this period was James Pemberton, one of the cosigners for the money from the Court of Orphans, and a gifted goldsmith who would in time become prime warden of his company, alderman, sheriff, and Lord Mayor.

From Christopher Wase, a goldsmith in Cheapside, we learn that in 1589 Langley was already in Pemberton's debt. Langley had cosigned a bond for Richard Walding for £200 for the use of £100 that Walding had borrowed from Wase. Walding defaulted, and Langley attempted to renew the bond while waiting to collect Walding's penalty sum to himself. Wase renewed, but required Langley's signature as principal. When Langley could not collect from Walding, he defaulted himself on the bond, and Wase went to law. Wase later recalled that the bond was finally paid in November 1589, but "by the hands of one Pemberton, a goldsmith," and not by Langley. Wase also received at the same time from Pemberton "the sum of 47^s 6^d or thereabouts for charges in law against the said Langley for the said money."[17]

I do not know in what fashion Langley compounded

with Pemberton for this relief, nor if this settlement, and the arrangement whereby Pemberton served as co-signer for some of the indentures from the Court of Orphans, represented the extent of their dealings in 1589. But Pemberton had enough of a claim on Langley that he was able successfully to insist on being party to the purchase of the manor. Hugh Browker recalled that the money that Francis Langley paid for Paris Garden was borrowed "upon interest and hard bonds and great sureties," and he may have had Pemberton in mind. Browker felt that hard terms were the only terms Langley was likely to get, for he thought "that the said Francis Langley had not any friend that would disburse any great sum of money for the good of the said Francis Langley." Pemberton was presumably not engaged in the transaction out of love; but he was engaged. The indentures were to be drawn "inter Franciscum Langley & Janam uxorem eius & Jacobum Pemberton . . . et Thomam Cure & Christianam uxorem eius," though the tenure in the manor was to descend only to Langley's heirs: "eisdem Francisco Jane & Jacobo ac heredibus ipsius Francisci imperpetuum."[18]

Nor do I have any record of the manner in which Langley cleared himself of encumbrance to Pemberton; but he seems to have accomplished it within the half year following the above transactions, for by the time the indentures were sealed in November Pemberton's name had been expunged, and the enrolled copy records a sale to Francis and Jane Langley alone. I regard this as further evidence of the importance Langley attached to his ownership of the manor: that he would satisfy an obligation so promptly, when his normal pattern was the opposite tactic of continual deferment and compounding.

Francis Langley was troubled by the younger Cure's apparent inability to convey his father's thousand-year lease along with the lordship of the manor. Some sort of agreement must have been reached between them on this matter before the sealing of the indentures, for

without control over the various leases to the lands of
the manor, Langley's lordship would have been as ineffectual as Cure's had been. Over the lease of the copyhold lands sold to Taylor and Platt, Cure had of course
no control at all, and if Langley wanted that lease he
would have to take other steps to try to secure it; but
the thousand-year lease he was determined to have.

The latter lease has a curious history; as with the
elder Cure's will, there are conflicting stories of its
whereabouts. In his will the elder Cure had named as
executors his wife Anne, his elder son George, and his
son-in-law Hugh Browker, husband of his daughter
Jane. Browker recalled that in his function as executor
he became persuaded that the widow Anne was not
likely to exercise her function with diligence; he felt
this for several reasons, "whereof amongst others, one
was for that the said Anne did possess herself of the
most part of the goods, and did not so effectually endeavour to perform the said legacies as [Browker]
thought she should have done." Browker was worried,
as Rowland Hayward had been earlier in another context, about having enough cash to pay Cure's legacies.
To raise some money, Browker on June 8, 1588 sold the
thousand-year lease to his friend Michael Smalpage.
Browker and Smalpage had been students together at
the Inner Temple, and George Cure had been one of
their fellowship there as well. I have found no record
of the price Smalpage paid to Browker for the lease;
but Richard Bury affirmed that the transaction did
take place, for Bury "was a witness to the said deed of
assignment [of the lease], and did subscribe his name
as a witness to the same."[19]

If these assertions are true, then the thousand-year
lease was held by Michael Smalpage at the time of
Francis Langley's negotiations with Thomas Cure.
And yet Cure seems to have arranged for his mother to
sell the lease to Gammon early in 1590. Gammon recalled that "Francis Langley did procure Anne Cure,
late wife and one of the executors of the said Thomas

81

Cure's father, to make a deed purporting that she did thereby grant and convey a lease of part of the said manor for the term of one thousand years unto this deponent . . . the said deed being under the hand or firm of the said Anne Cure and bearing date the fourth day of February" 1590. George Cure himself supported this view of the events: "Anne Cure, late wife and one of the executors of Thomas Cure deceased, this deponent's father, by the writing bearing date the fourth day of February [1590] . . . did assign and set over unto one Hannibal Gammon all her right and interest in a lease of the said manor or of part thereof, formerly made unto this deponent's said father, for the term of one thousand years; and this he knoweth to be true, for that he was present at the sealing and delivery of the said deed by his said mother unto the said Hannibal Gammon or to his use, and thereupon did endorse his name on the back of the said deed as a witness thereof."[20]

One of these stories must be in error. But as Browker and Langley each acted upon the conviction that the lease was under his control, it is possible that no outright deception was involved. Langley certainly proceeded on the assumption that Gammon held clear title to the lease. Smalpage surely thought it was his, for in his will he left it to his brother. The most generous explanation is that Hugh Browker, having little faith in his mother-in-law's competence as executor, did not trouble to inform her of his sale of the lease to Smalpage, thereby enabling her in all innocence to sell the lease to Gammon. It must be clear from the foregoing that the lease, the document itself, was not involved in any of these transactions; rather, deeds of sale are at issue, in which the seller conveys to the buyer "all his right, title and interest" in "a certain lease" whose whereabouts is never specified. Gammon and Smalpage each had his deed of sale. I do not know who had the lease. One would like to know why Langley was not able to buy the lease in his own name, as this was obviously his desire. Perhaps Langley owed Gammon money, and chose this way of settling the debt.

Thus Francis Langley became the lord of a manor, an honor rich in feudal associations, though the new economics had removed most of its traditional seigneurial prerogatives. As lord, Langley "held" the entire manor of Paris Garden, but the use or possession of large portions of it was out of his hands. The copyholders had become their own entrepreneurs; they were a local manifestation of the changes occurring across the country in the forms of manorial tenure. They held the rights and profits of their own lands, and of their court baron as well. To Langley they owed fealty, but little else. Various other parcels of the manor were out on leases as well, some, like William Brende's messuage, dating from the early years of the century, others issued by the younger Cure to cover his loans. What the new lord had immediate access to was some fifty or sixty acres of demesne lands, mostly meadow or pasture, which he might himself lease out or improve as he saw fit.

There was, of course, very little difference, other than houses, between the customary and demesne lands of the manor. Even in the settled portions held by the copyholders, Paris Garden was more rural than urban. It was heavily wooded in places, and the inhabitants valued their holdings as much for the gardens and orchards that they maintained as for the tenements or cottages in which they dwelt. The Auditors of Land Revenue had surveyed the manor for the Exchequer in 1546 as Crown property, and again in 1561. On these occasions they found, in addition to the manor house and the old water mill, some thirty-five dwellings, concentrated mostly along the Thames. This was by no means dense; nearly two decades later, at the time of the Queen's grant to Newdigate and Fountayne, the riverside portion of the manor was still heavily wooded, and was described as "so dark" even on a moonlit night, "being shadowed with trees, that one man cannot see another," and in places along the Thames "virgulta or eights of willows" had grown "exceeding thick" and were "a notable covert for confederates to shroud in." This is William Fleetwood, the Recorder of London, describing to Lord Burghley the site of some clandestine political meetings between the Bishop of Ross and the French ambassador in 1578. Fleetwood concluded that the grounds of the manor were "the bower of conspiracies" and "the college of mal-counsel."[21]

Such descriptions tell us perhaps more about Fleetwood than about the manor. Despite his vivid metaphors the landscape was not particularly Spenserian, though the willows were indeed notable. The drainage ditch that from earliest times surrounded and bounded the manor was lined with them, and hence called the Willows—the phrase "the ditch there called the Willows" or "fossa ibi vocatur le Wyllowes" figures in all descriptions of the property from this period, and the old name of the manor, Wioflete or willow stream, reflects the antiquity of this feature. The ditch was open to the Thames at the northwest corner of the manor, near Bargehouse stairs, and it ran from that point in a southerly, then an easterly, and then a northerly direction, tracing the boundary of the manor on those three sides until it returned to the river in the northeast corner of the manor.

On this ditch or stream at its eastern end a mill of one sort or another had stood for as long as anyone could remember. In Langley's day it was known as Pudding Mill, and it functioned as a tide mill with the rising and falling of the river; that is, its wheel turned in one direction as the tide rose and the ditch filled, and in the other as the ditch emptied. There was a large pond behind the mill, made by widening the ditch to some thirty or forty yards, in which the miller was able to store extra water at each high tide; but it

The South Bank. In the foreground is the Tower; just across the bridge, St. Saviour's church and the Borough; beyond it along the river, Clink liberty and Paris Garden, all together making up the parish of St. Saviour's. Beyond that, Lambeth marsh. In the far distance, Whitehall and Westminster.

regularly overfilled, and its faulty embankments and inadequate floodgates caused daily inundation of the surrounding area. Successive sewer commissions ordered the lord of the manor, or his tenant the miller, to board, pile, and cope the banks, especially "at the south end of Maid Lane where the water floweth over," or more precisely "at the farther end of Maid Lane, close unto the rail which parteth the highway and their wall." The miller was ordered not to "take any more water in at the said mill from the river of Thames but only to the nail which is fixed in the cucking stool there in the millpond," because the floodgates and groundwork of the mill were "very low" and the tidal water "oftentimes floweth over the same"; when this happened, the neighboring "lands, houses and grounds, and likewise the highways, are overflowed and surrounded, to the great annoyance and damage of the landholders."[22]

The mill, the millpond, and the whole of the mill-stream with its embankments all the way round the manor were held by copyhold, and the holder was responsible to the lord of the manor for their upkeep. The lord in turn was responsible to the sewer commission, which might fine him for unsatisfactory maintenance. Most of the periodic flooding occurred toward the end of Maid Lane where it abutted the manor a scant two hundred yards southeast of the millpond, though on occasion the water might go much further. The area threatened by flooding stretched an equal distance to the southwest of the pond, to the doors of Copt Hall, and to the west to the manor house itself. These two buildings were ditched about for further protection (the "mansion house" is described in the indentures as being "within the moat there"). Most of the demesne lands of the manor, in fact, lay several feet below high-water level, like Lambeth marsh immediately to the west. Only the copyhold lands along the Thames (called the Upper Ground) were safe from the threat of periodic inundation. For the rest, a series of ditches and reinforced embankments served as the area's chief protection against flooding. If the banks of the mill-stream gave way, even at the farthest end of the manor, several acres would be flooded at each high tide; but surface water from rain and snow had also to be carried off, and a series of interlocking ditches and floodgates was required. It had always been the responsibility of the lord of the manor to maintain these works, and if Langley expected to use his demesne lands profitably he would have to continue this maintenance.

Of the manor house itself little is known in this period. It was badly dilapidated in 1542 when William Baseley, the copyholder who held Copt Hall, secured a lease of the property for twenty-one years. The grounds were soggy from standing water. Baseley scoured the moat and repaired the house, turning the whole into a recreation area with bowling alleys out-of-doors and various kinds of table games—cards, dice, and the like—inside. The Auditors of Land Revenue inspected the house twice during Baseley's term of lease, but made no mention of it in their report. It is not to be confused with the "sporting house" they describe, for that was the property of William Hobson. Baseley's lease was not renewed, and it is not clear who was living in the mansion in 1589, or what its condition was. That it was itself a sporting house in 1630 under the direction of Susan Holland does not argue any continuity of function during the 1590s. It may have been standing empty. Thomas Cure at any rate was not living in it, for even before the sale of the manor to Langley, Cure was lodged in or adjacent to the Cross Keys in Southwark, one of his father's many holdings.[23]

The likeliest explanation is that the building was unoccupied, for Francis Langley and his family apparently moved into the manor house sometime in 1591. Francis and Jane Langley had lived in various places in Cheap ward for the previous several years, first in St. Matthew Friday Street parish, later in St.

Vedast Foster Lane. Their daughter Jane was christened in St. Vedast's on August 7, 1586, their son
Francis on July 5, 1590. Their move to the Bankside
may have been in the following year, for little Francis
was buried two years later, on August 29, 1592, in St.
Saviour's, the parish in which the manor of Paris Garden lay. He was buried in a crypt in the church, a sign
of his parents' consciousness of status; and, if the nota-
tions in the parish register are to be trusted, he seems
not to have died of the plague, though many other burials in that month are so noted.

Other evidence also places the Langleys on the
Bankside. Beginning in about 1592, the token collectors of St. Saviour's parish recorded the presence of
the Langley family in Paris Garden, somewhere between Copt Hall and Frith's Rents, which is a close
enough description of the locale of the mansion, though
the "manor house" as such is not mentioned in the
token books. All the adults in each household (all persons over sixteen) were counted each year for tokens,
and the Langley household was variously listed from
five to seven adults through the middle years of the
1590s. As the Langley children were far too young to
qualify on this score, the additional numbers must represent household servants. If the Langleys did not live
in the manor house they lived very near to it, and with
a household of such size their dwelling would have had
to be capacious. I know of no building in the vicinity of
the manor house that would be suitable, other than the
manor house itself.[24]

Finally, we have the recollection of Hugh Browker in
1604 that "Francis Langley did take the profits and use
the possession of the capital house and other things
part of the said manor"; and of Henry Smith, gentleman, who deposed in 1604 that some ten years earlier
he and Francis Langley had held a financial conversation "as they walked by the moatside of the said Mr
Langley's house called Old Paris Garden." The only
house between Copt Hall and Frith's Rents with a

moat was the manor house. I think it safe to assume that the Langleys lived there. But the particulars of their dwelling place are of secondary importance. It is more useful for us to note that such a move, from St. Vedast's parish across the river and into another county, argues a certain freedom by 1592 from the earlier constraints that had kept Langley physically present in Cheapside. His assumption of the manorial lordship did not in any way diminish his involvement in the various activities that constituted his livelihood, but in his continuing pursuit of these activities he apparently found himself able, by 1592, to rely to a considerable degree on the agency of others acting on his behalf. Chief among these agents was his own nephew, Richard.[25]

Richard Langley was one of the sons of Francis Langley's elder brother William, the Didthorpe farmer. William, like his father before him, recognized the value of having younger brothers in London, and did not fail to claim the advantages of such a situation for his own sons. One of these sons, another John Langley, followed his celebrated namesake by apprenticing himself to a goldsmith, one Richard Flint; but Richard Langley stayed closer to his kin. His uncle Thomas, who had come with Francis as a boy to London, took him as an apprentice haberdasher almost immediately on receiving his own freedom, and was able to make Richard free of the haberdashers in 1587. Richard then followed his uncle Thomas further in taking up the trade of a vintner. He also seems to have found favor in the eyes of his uncle Francis, for he was soon drawn into the latter's confidences.[26]

The move to the Bankside may have been further enabled by the death of Lady Ursula Langley in September 1590, which brought Francis Langley into his inheritance of the Saracen's Head in Cheap and also the Horse Head, the reversion to which he had purchased from his brother Thomas in 1578. The income from these two messuages, which would have been sufficient to maintain the life style of a manorial lord, may have been a deciding factor in the move. The Horse Head, which was just coming to be known colloquially as the Nag's Head, was a tavern of some repute. Langley leased it to his nephew Richard, thereby enabling the young man to continue plying his trade as a vintner, which in his case clearly meant a tavernkeeper rather than a merchant importer. By furnishing these premises to his nephew, Francis was able to keep him in Cheapside and also in a tavern, where he served with some success as a money broker on his uncle's behalf. The Saracen's Head, on the other hand, was occupied by goldsmiths' shops; Langley leased the premises to his friend Hannibal Gammon, and also to John Cornwall, John Terry, and Robert Howe. Terry and Howe, along with Gammon, figured actively in Langley's affairs from this point forward.[27]

Langley also acquired the income from another piece of property in 1590, although under different circumstances. By the terms of his purchase of Paris Garden he had undertaken to defend Thomas Cure the younger against the claims of certain named creditors by redeeming their bonds as part of the purchase price. This Langley had done. But one debt from which Langley did not protect Cure was the final bond to Giles Simpson. Langley had cosigned that bond, the reader will recall, and in his customary fashion had required another bond from Cure to save him harmless in the event of a default on the Simpson bond. Of the £850 that Langley had paid for the manor, £700 had gone to the redeeming of bonds and £150 had gone to Cure. Cure was supposed to pay Simpson's bond out of his own resources, but did not do so. When he defaulted, Langley paid the debt to Simpson by installments, as described above. He then collected the forfeit bond and proceeded to enforce his own claim against Cure for £400.

One of Cure's creditors was George Chute, and the Paris Garden settlement did not include provision for repaying Chute. Chute sued for payment of his bond, and got a judgment in his favor. He then "sued forth an Elegit to the sheriff of . . . Surrey," that is, got a writ out of Chancery directing the sheriff to make up the amount of the judgment by seizing the goods of the debtor. The sheriff, Herbert Pelham, seized three of Cure's holdings in Southwark and turned the earnings over to Chute until the debt of £100 was satisfied. As the properties so seized had been yielding between £18 and £19 annually, Chute could expect to hold them for somewhat more than five years. The messuages from which Chute was awarded the income were the Red Lion, the Falcon, and the Estridge Feather. But Cure, perhaps anticipating such a seizure, had in the meanwhile sold the Falcon to Richard Humble, the vintner who had earlier purchased the King's Head from George and Thomas Cure within a week after their father's death. The sale of the Falcon to Humble preceded by a matter of weeks the award of the Falcon to Chute. The matter had now become confused, with both Humble and Chute laying claim to the messuage. The situation was ripe. Langley, claiming that Cure owed him £400, "sued forth process of extent" in Chancery for recovery of his debt, and armed with this writ he seized the Falcon for himself, to hold until his claim was satisfied.

Chute and Humble both responded with lawsuits, Chute in Chancery and Humble in Requests. Each of them put forward his own title to the Falcon, and sued for redress. Humble's suit was against "Francis Langley, citizen and goldsmith of London," Chute's against "Francis Langley of London, goldsmith"; like many of their contemporaries, they both knew Langley primarily as a money broker. Chute knew about the bond to Simpson that Langley had cosigned, and also knew that Langley "either at that time or not long before or after did purchase of the said Thomas Cure the manor of Paris Garden in the county of Surrey for a far lesser sum than the same in truth was worth." He knew that

Cure had entered into "some other collateral assurance unto the said Francis Langley to discharge or otherwise save harmless the said Francis Langley against the said Giles Simpson."[28]

But Langley was not to be budged. He freely acknowledged that he "did and hath extended the said house" because Cure owed him £400 and would not pay. He maintained that "in all equity and good conscience he may yet hold and take the profits of the said house according to the said extent, until he be fully satisfied the said sum of four hundred pounds with his reasonable costs." Langley was in a strong position. Chute and Humble both laid claim to the Falcon; one of them was in error, and was therefore wasting time and money by going to law against Francis Langley. But which one? Chute and Humble both retreated to consider the matter.[29]

From this episode it will be seen that Langley had no intention of abandoning his earlier means of livelihood; his dignity as the lord of the manor did not seem to require any cessation of his other functions as "goldsmith" or as alnager. Indeed, on the acquisition of some free capital Langley might commence a further career as landlord by erecting some buildings on his demesne lands. His life, as Hugh Browker had observed in connection with his purchase of the manor, was not one that conduced to the formation of friendships. Langley seemed prepared to accept this, but in his new dignity he was determined at least to have respect. Perhaps in 1591 the new lord of the manor was unduly sensitive on this point, for the railings of one William Wood in May of that year proved too much for Langley to bear. He sued Wood for slander in the Court of Queen's Bench. The record has survived; it is in Latin, but a close English paraphrase will convey its tenor.

In the suit, Langley's attorney John Smythe described Langley as "a true and honest subject of the Queen and reputed to be without infamy or evil name of perfidy for the whole of his life, and of good estimation, and buying and selling for great sums of money with divers of the Queen's subjects; yet William Wood of malicious intent put it about in public that Francis was held in opprobrium, and on May 27 (1591) in the parish of St. Mary le Bow, Cheapside, in the presence of many of the Queen's subjects he spoke scandalous and opprobrious words in English, saying that Francis was *a rebellious knave and a traitorly knave* and that Francis was of bad reputation, to Francis' damage £500."[30]

Such a sum was of course excessive. Wood's attorney replied, explaining the nature of the quarrel, which involved the violation by Langley of a patent held by Wood. Wood's attorney explained that "Wood had said to Francis *what wilt thou have, thyself to be a rebellious and disordered person so as to contemn and despite her Majesty's letters patents in this sort as you do.* After this Wood said *thou art a rebellious knave and a traitorly knave,* and Wood maintains that this is true." The Clerk of the Court recorded that "Francis complained of the words," and a jury was ordered to be summoned; but there is no further record of the case, and it was presumably dropped.

Langley was also at law against a number of other people in this same period. The details tend to be repetitious. He brought suit for default of payment on bonds against Sir Walter Leveson, Avery Phillips, John Mabill, Richard Moore, and John Hampton, the last named being one of Hugh Browker's clerks. He sued William Mosyer over a disputed inheritance from Thomas Davies. He sued Francis Carpro for failing to pay for some jewels and pearls Langley had sold him. He sued Francis Wyatt for assault. At the same time, he was being sued by Thomas Mody, Gaius Newman, John Skeyton, and Richard Renching for his own defaults on bonds to them; by John Pasfield and Richard Veale over a disputed inheritance from Richard Walding; and by Thomas Godliff and William Moyerghe for assault. The particulars of these suits confirm certain patterns of conduct that are already sufficiently documented for our purposes.

A more curious matter, but none the more explicable for that, is found in the Privy Council minutes for the winter of 1591–92. At their meeting of January 16, 1592, at Whitehall, the minutekeeper noted that "a warrant was signed for the apprehension of [blank] Langley, a goldsmith; if he be sick to certify the same, otherwise to commit him to the Marshalsea." The effort at arrest was presumably unsuccessful, for a few weeks later the Council directed that another warrant be issued "for the apprehension of Francis Langley dwelling at Paris Garden in the county of Surrey, and to command him by virtue hereof to make personal appearance before their Lordships to answer to all such matters wherewith he standeth charged withal; and, in case of his refusal, [the arresting officer is] to crave in aid the next Justice of Peace and public officer near adjoining for the better performance of his service, whereof he is not to fail." Unfortunately the "matters wherewith he standeth charged" are nowhere specified. The matter must rest in obscurity, for the subject does not recur at any later meeting of the Council, nor do subsequent minutes record any appearance by Langley before their Lordships. It is tempting, but perhaps premature, to infer from the wording of the minute that Langley already had a reputation for refusing arrest.[31]

But even as this elusive confrontation was being arranged, and while Langley's other disputes were being put forward in the law courts, events were transpiring in the world at large that were to have important consequences for Langley, and that would ultimately involve him in more serious and better recorded difficulties with the Queen's Privy Council.

VI

The Carrack

We'll bring thee to our crews,
and show thee all the treasure we have got.
THE TWO GENTLEMEN OF VERONA

The most intriguing news from Court in the summer
of 1592 concerned Sir Walter Ralegh. Through most of
the early spring of that year Ralegh had been making
plans for a daring sea venture against the Spaniards.
He had secured financial support from various quarters, including the City, and the ships and crews were
to be ready in May. He was anxious to go to sea; for he
had been disappointed the year before. In the summer
of 1591 Ralegh was to have held a joint command with
Lord Thomas Howard of a small fleet fitted out to ha-
rass the Spaniards, but he was called back at the last
minute by the Queen, and Lord Howard left without
him. Sir Richard Grenville took his place, and sailed to
immortality on the *Revenge*. Ralegh wrote a stirring account of Grenville's last and finest fight and determined to be there himself the next time. By May 1592
he was ready again. This time he was to be in sole command of a squadron of thirteen ships, and his plan was
to sail to the Azores and lie in wait for the Spanish
treasure fleet. But again the Queen held him back, and
this time he was imprisoned in the Tower. The news of
his affair with Bess Throckmorton, and of their secret
marriage, had reached the Court and infuriated
Elizabeth.[1]

So once again his ships sailed without him, his command taken by Sir Martin Frobisher; the City and the

95

Court buzzed with gossip of the scandal. But the novelty of the intrigue had no sooner worn off than there was other news to engage everyone's attention; in the late summer of 1592 the nation learned of the capture off the Azores, by a part of Ralegh's fleet, of the wealthiest treasure ship of Elizabethan times, the great Portuguese carrack *Madre de Dios*. The capture was effected by Sir John Burroughs, sailing in Ralegh's flagship the *Roebuck*, and supported by the *Dainty* and the *Golden Dragon*. They were later joined by the ships of the Earl of Cumberland, the *Tiger*, the *Foresight*, the *Prudence*, and the *Samson*. Cumberland had been sailing with his ships far to windward, and as luck would have it he came upon Burroughs and the carrack in the midst of the fighting. They joined forces to overcome the carrack; but dissension began almost as soon as victory was assured, each captain claiming the right of capture and deprecating the assertions of the other. The two crews were quick to sense that there was a possibility of losing their rightful shares if their own captain's claim should not prevail; accordingly they began to plunder the carrack while it was still awash with the blood of its defenders.[2]

Nor was this plunder confined to the pilfering of petty trinkets by the ordinary seamen. Some of the crew reported seeing Robert Cross, captain of the *Foresight*, "go down and break up sundry chests," and on a number of occasions "send down the purser of the Portingales to bring up things of great value." Others claimed to have seen captain Newport of the *Golden Dragon* "break open chests and other things at his pleasure." Captain Caulfield was seen "divers and sundry times to go down into the hold" and bring up "such things as him pleased, which were of great value." It was reported by some of Cumberland's men that Sir John Burroughs "sent for his ship's boat to come aboard, and carried bags of cloves, cinnamon and other spices every day," and one day "the chests were so heavy that they could not be conveyed" by his small party.[3]

The captured ship was brought into Dartmouth on September 7. The Queen at once appointed Lord Burghley, the Lord Treasurer, and Sir John Fortescue, the Chancellor of the Exchequer, to oversee the proper distribution of shares among the many claimants, including the City of London, which had ventured £6,000 on the undertaking. The ship and its cargo were to be assessed by a special board of commissioners, among them Sir Francis Drake, William Killigrew, Richard Carmarden, and Henry Billingsley, the last named being the alderman for Candlewick ward and representing the City's interests. Thomas Middleton, a future Lord Mayor, was appointed secretary to the commission. To strengthen the commission's authority the Queen appointed the Secretary of the Privy Council, Sir Robert Cecil, to take charge of the proceedings and to oversee the unloading. Cecil went immediately to Exeter, and thence to Dartmouth and Plymouth, setting up local commissions of inquiry and dealing roughly with those suspected of pillage. He prudently took with him Walter Ralegh, released from imprisonment in the Tower at Cecil's request; Ralegh's presence at Cecil's side stood the young Secretary in good stead as he confronted the mariners and captains involved in the plunder. The carrack's bills of lading had disappeared, but the crew was able to report the theft of jewels, stones, pearls, musk, ambergris and other things to an estimated value of 114,150 crusados, or over £28,500.[4]

Cecil asked Middleton to make an estimate of the value of the surviving cargo, but Middleton found the task "very doubtful and intricate, so as the wisest man in England cannot make a guess so near but that he may be deceived twenty thousand pounds"; Middleton nevertheless hazarded a "wish and hope that the whole is worth a hundred and fifty thousand pounds, which is a great deal of money." His estimate was close; the bulky goods, pepper, spices, silks, and carpets, were valued at £141,200 and brought to Leadenhall in London for sale. But some reports estimated the original cargo to have been worth nearly a million in sterling, and such rumor could not but distress the commissioners; even if the true value of the lading were only a half or a third of that amount, it was still evident that a great deal had been lost by plunder. The greater part of the booty must have escaped the commissioners' hands, and in particular the precious stones, which alone were estimated variously from £100,000 to £250,000 above and beyond the rest of the cargo.[5]

Everyone concerned was interrogated. One deposition, that of seaman Thomas Favell, may serve as a representative example.

> I was one of the men that first came in Captain More's cabin. With me was Boatswain Wright; Thomas Johns, Trumpeter of the Golden Dragon; and Edward Tunkes, Corporal of the Tiger, and many more besides those. There was Captain Cross, a commander of the Queen's ship, and divers captains besides. To make it known what I had in that ship being thus taken, those jewels as followeth: first a chain of pearl orient, two rests of gold, four very great pearls of the bigness of a fair pea, four forks of crystal and four spoons of crystal set with gold and stones, two cuds of musk that I had given by Captain Caulfield; and all these things was stolen out of my trunk aboard of the Golden Dragon, saving the spoons and forks of crystal and a burclet, the which was taken from me by the Spaniard who had commandment to search my chest.[6]

In particular, there were persistent rumors that a great diamond had been aboard the ship. It was not found, of course, and some of the commissioners chose to disbelieve its existence. But Cecil had good reason to believe that it did exist, and he made it his special concern to trace it. Prestige as well as money was involved. Such a rumored "great diamond" would soon come to symbolize the whole of the plundered treasure; it would inspire countless stories and the rumors of its whereabouts would mock the efforts of the commissioners. But if Cecil could recover it, his own credit would be correspondingly enlarged.

There was no denying that the stone was of great

value. One of Cecil's informants, whom he labeled simply "the Frenchman," wrote to him promptly about the carrack and the diamond. The communiqué is in French; here is its essence.

> Being in the isle of Terceira I understood by Dom Jonay that the value of the vessel was some four millions [crusados, that is, about a million pounds] . . . without including an infinite number of gems [*vnne infynite de pierries*] in the ship which could not be saved which he estimated at a million [crusados] . . . The King has lost more than 700,000 ducats in stones . . . one stone costing 500,000 ducats [*vnne pierre . . . qui coustoyt au roy le somme de 500 mille ducatz*], and the whole loss did not grieve Dom Jonay or Captain More so much as the loss of this stone . . . There was a Portuguese in the vessel who came to the merchants giving them to understand that he was with the English by force, and that if they had any things they wished him to guard, to let him know, and said he was in good credit with the English; and I understand from Captain More that he gave him a bag of diamonds to guard which he valued at more than 120,000 ducats . . . if the man knew what he had bargained for he would be very rich.[7]

John Bedford, one of Burroughs's officers from the *Roebuck* who had been put in command of the *Madre de Dios* for its final voyage to Dartmouth, received independent corroboration of this story in a letter from Anthony Moon, which he passed on to Cecil. Moon claimed to have learned "by those which are come from the Terceira six days past that the great jewel which wanteth and is had in so high a price was delivered and given unto a Portingale that dwelleth in London and went in this action with your fleet or in my Lord's ships; this much the viceroy that was taken confessed to a merchantman there, and said that the Portingale promised him with fair words to restore it again, so that he had divers other jewels besides that. It is reported there at the Islands this jewel which he hath is worth 500,000 ducats."[8]

There was no difficulty in identifying the "Portingale"; he was Alonzo Gomez, one of the Earl of Cumberland's men, and had been interrogated in Exeter on the first of October by Sir Robert Cecil and Sir Francis Drake. Gomez was found to have on his person "three hundred and twenty sparks of diamonds, a collar of a threefold roll of pearl with six tags of crystal garnished with gold, a small string of pearl with a pelican of gold, one small round pearl garnished with gold, also two chains of twofold pearl with buttons of gold and two small jewels hanging unto the ends thereof." But of the "great jewel" he knew nothing.[9]

Perhaps he had it; perhaps not. Vincentio de Fonseca, one of the carrack's officers, thought it more likely that one of the English captains had the diamond. Fonseca told the commissioners that Captain Cross had stones and pearls to the value of 50,000 crusados, and that Captains Langston and Cock had been "of the first that entered aboard the carrack," having had report of the "great store of stones" in her cargo. Fonseca himself estimated the stones to be worth 400,000 crusados; "but," the commissioners ruefully wrote to Lord Burghley, "to whose hands any part thereof is come doth not yet appear."[10]

Much, probably most, of the plundered treasure had already made its way underground; but before long it began to surface. The first suspect to be interrogated was one William Bradbank of Gravesend, who was found early in October to be in possession of 1,300 diamond sparks, 150 rubies, sixteen ounces of ambergris, jewels, gold in chains, and some four ounces of pearls. Bradbank was questioned by Cecil's agents, and though he was of no help in locating the great diamond, he did name others: Hugh Merick, the captain of the *Prudence*, one of Cumberland's ships, who denied having any commerce with Bradbank; and a goldsmith named Shory, who admitted being in Bradbank's house and seeing the jewels but said that he was unsuccessful in dealing for them, Bradbank apparently preferring to do business with other goldsmiths in London.[11]

Fortunately for our purposes, Shory furnished Cecil with a list of those other goldsmiths in London, all of whom were, according to Shory, trafficking in the carrack's goods. Some of them, he said, had even gone down to Dartmouth to do their negotiating, despite Burghley's strict prohibition; for there was plague in London, and all such travel had been expressly forbidden on those grounds as well as for the more immediate reason. Those whom Shory implicated were "one Scott in Fenchurch Street, a merchant," "one Conway in Lombard Street at the sign of the Bull's Head," "one Robert Brooke in Lombard Street," "one Barker in Tower Street over against Barking Church," and more to the point of our subject, "Hannibal Gammon in Cheapside, a goldsmith, a great doer in those matters" and "young Howe, a goldsmith, that by report hath bought so much below at the price that he fears calling in question and hath shut up his shop and is gone." [12]

So our digression to explore one of the greatest sea adventures of Elizabethan times has brought us back to the door of the Saracen's Head in Cheap. Shory's accusations would prove to be well grounded; for Gammon and Howe, two of Langley's tenants in the Saracen's Head, were indeed dealers in the stolen goods from the carrack, Howe apparently to an imprudent degree. But it was not the almost routine recovery of the small diamond sparks, rubies, and pearls that most closely engaged Sir Robert Cecil. He still had every intention of finding the main prize, the diamond reputed to be worth half a million ducats. Howe and Gammon were no doubt interrogated; but no record survives, nor is there any evidence that they were detained.

Many months went by before the diamond came to light. The plague continued virulent, and the City's attention was elsewhere; but in the late spring of 1594 Cecil arrested a London goldsmith named Bartholomew Gilbert, who was said to have an uncut diamond of twenty-six and one-half carats in his house. Cecil must have had faith in his informant; for though the diamond was not found, Gilbert was kept imprisoned in the Wood Street Counter for half a year, until he confessed. Yes, he had purchased the diamond, "which cost me £500 and more to my utter undoing." It was a simple story: some months earlier his friend John Maddox had introduced him to a mariner who said he had a diamond he wanted to sell. Gilbert was of course interested, so Maddox and the mariner agreed to meet him the next day at a tavern called the Lion at Limehouse, a dock area downriver from London. Maddox and the mariner arrived as promised, and showed Gilbert the diamond. Maddox, acting as the mariner's agent, asked £700 for the stone. Gilbert saw at once that the price was very low, and agreed to the purchase with the proviso that the stone be appraised by a colleague. Maddox assented.[13]

The next meeting of the three men was at the appraiser's, "at John Terry's house in Cheapside." Once again we are at the Saracen's Head. Terry, like Gilbert, immediately recognized the value of the stone, but cannily suggested that the price was high. Gilbert then offered £500, and after some haggling the parties agreed upon a price of £550 in money plus certain vessels of gold. Once this agreement was reached Gilbert affirmed to Maddox his intention to buy, and set about to raise the money. His own resources were limited. John Terry was interested in participating in the purchase, but could not raise so large a sum. Robert Howe, Terry's neighbor, was invited to join the group, but the combined resources of the three goldsmiths were not equal to the task. Outside help was needed. Gilbert and Howe went to Robert Brooke, a goldsmith in Lombard Street (one of those named by Shory), and explained their need. Brooke, on seeing the stone, agreed to lend them £1,000 for three months; but he, too, was unable to raise such a sum, and turned for help to the ubiquitous Giles Simpson, who was able to accommodate him.[14]

Brooke received the money from Simpson and advanced it to Gilbert, with Howe as cosigner; they in turn asked Brooke to inquire about a possible purchaser for the stone, "to see the most that it would make." Gilbert took the thousand pounds and paid £550 to Maddox and the mariner, leaving himself and Howe with a momentary profit of £450. Brooke in his turn made inquiries about selling the diamond; "I did show the stone unto divers jewellers, and some did bid me £1200 and some did bid me £1300." The stone had obvious value, and Brooke soon resolved to purchase it himself: "having learned what it would make, I did fully buy it of the said Gilbert and Robert Howe for the sum of one hundred pounds more," that is, he offered to forgive them the debt of £1,000 and to give them an additional £100. But Brooke did not buy the stone as a keepsake. He was negotiating for a purchaser of his own, and in the meantime he gave the stone to his associate William Hamore, a scrivener, for safekeeping. The security of this arrangement was shattered with the arrest of Gilbert. Brooke was implicated, and made his own deposition. William Hamore, under examination, admitted receiving the diamond from Brooke and said that he had given it to his wife Alice to hide. Alice Hamore, when questioned, said that she remembered seeing the diamond and hearing that Mr. Brooke was going to buy it, but that she didn't know where it was.[15]

The news of Brooke's difficulties over the diamond caused his prospective purchasers to turn cool; Cecil was willing to wait. He had located the handful of men who would lead him to the diamond, and though Gilbert's imprisonment had not produced the stone it had produced some useful information. No one was likely to buy the stone at such a troubled time, and if Cecil was patient someone would likely make a mistake. Brooke, seeing the impasse in which he was caught, reneged on his offer to purchase, forcing Howe (for Gilbert was in prison) to take back the stone. Howe compounded with Terry, and reclaimed it from Brooke. Thereafter it disappeared from view for a time, perhaps hidden somewhere in the Saracen's Head.[16]

VII

The Swan

A pretty plot, well chosen to build upon!
HENRY VI, PART TWO

Francis Langley's life during this period seems to have been relatively untroubled, or no more troubled than usual, in contrast to the increasingly hazardous activities of his friends and tenants. From the evidence of the various lawsuits in which he was involved, it seems clear that he remained in London throughout the worst of the plague from mid-1592 to mid-1594. His was not the sort of livelihood that could easily be transported elsewhere: his post as alnager required his presence in the City, though traffic in woolens was greatly reduced because of the plague; and his broking activities required ready access to his contacts in Cheapside. He was constrained to stay and make the most of it. Philip Henslowe, Langley's near neighbor in Clink liberty, was similarly constrained; Henslowe collected rents from his tenements, lent out money on bonds or at pawn, and managed a nearby playhouse, the Rose. We learn from Henslowe's letters to his son-in-law Edward Alleyn in 1593, when Alleyn was touring with Lord Strange's players, that Henslowe found life in London fairly grim during the plague. "We are all at this time in good health in our house," he wrote, "but round about us it hath been almost in every house

about us, and whole households died . . . Robert
Browne's wife in Shoreditch and all her children and
household be dead and her doors shut up." Later he
ventured a grim guess: "I think doth die within the
City and without, of all sicknesses, to the number of
seventeen or eighteen hundred in one week."[1]

Henslowe's pawnbroking business actually increased during the plague, a grim reminder of the
straitened circumstances of his neighbors. His diary is
filled with pawn accounts from this period; Philip,
perhaps fearing to go abroad, employed his nephew
Francis Henslowe to make the necessary contacts and
bring in the pawned goods. They were mostly items of
clothing, probably from persons who would no longer
need them, and it is unlikely that many of them were
reclaimed, or that Henslowe grew rich in the enterprise. But he had no alternative. He asked Alleyn to
"commend me heartily to all the rest of your fellows in
general, for I grow poor for lack of them." And so it
must have seemed to the casual observer; for the Rose
playhouse, on which Henslowe had expended nearly a
hundred pounds for repairs and alterations at the beginning of 1592, had been standing empty and disused
for many months. In June 1594, when the Admiral's
company finally reopened at the Rose, Henslowe could
reflect that of the six hundred or so playing days available to him in the two years previous, he had been able
to offer plays on less than seventy. It was a chancy
business. The players could at least take to the road
and eke out a living in the provinces. But the playhouse owner was trapped. One can speculate that even
in June 1594, with all the excitement of a new season
about to begin, a certain rueful attitude would persist
about the hardships of 1592 and 1593. When would the
plague strike again, closing the playhouses for perhaps
another year? It would require a man of special temperament to contemplate, in 1594, the building of a
new playhouse.

By the autumn of that year, however, Francis Langley clearly had just such a plan in mind. By early November the news had even reached the Lord Mayor, John Spencer, who wrote a letter to Burghley asking that Langley be stopped. Langley's plans must have been fairly well advanced by November to have provoked such an official reaction. My guess is that Langley was struck forcefully by the popularity of the Rose when it reopened in June 1594. Langley had moved to Paris Garden perhaps too late to see such crowds as might have formed at the Rose in 1591; but in June 1594, looking across the grounds of the manor from the windows of the manor house, he must have had food for thought. He would have seen great numbers of Londoners who chose to cross the Thames by boat rather than by the bridge to get to the Bankside, and he would have seen them landing at Paris Garden stairs at the northeast corner of the manor near Pudding Mill, one of the most popular landing places on the south bank. The Falcon Inn was there, hard by the mill and just over the boundary in Clink liberty (not the Falcon over which George Chute, Richard Humble, and Francis Langley had had their dispute, for that was in the borough). After a bit of refreshment at the inn a short walk eastward would bring them to the Rose. Their numbers must have been impressive, and perhaps set Langley to thinking, even by the late summer of 1594, that a playhouse built even nearer to these landing places would intercept much of that traffic. All the manor grounds adjacent to the river were of course copyhold lands; but Langley's own demesne holdings came fairly close to the river in places, and in one place he could get quite near to the landing stairs and to the Falcon. Unfortunately, this particular site was also close against the millpond, with all the attendant hazards of that location, and a scant hundred yards from the manor house itself.[2]

These were not insurmountable problems, though their solution would require some planning. Langley must have been thinking about ways of reclaiming the

land near the millpond in any event, for he had apparently begun to contemplate a program of building
there. Though the plague in 1593 had been no respecter of boundaries, it must have seemed demonstrably safer to the populace in that year to be living on
the Bankside rather than in the heart of the City; perhaps Langley's plans to build dwellings on the manor
grounds began to take shape in this period, as a result
of the pressures of a citizenry bent on escape. Certainly Langley's neighbor James Austen had seized the
opportunity. In 1593 Austen purchased William Hobson's copyhold lands next to the millpond on the south,
on which eight messuages stood. Austen immediately
began to build; he had thirteen householders on his
property by 1594, sixteen by 1595, and twenty by early
1596. Langley no doubt viewed this expansion with interest, for it demonstrated clearly that there was a demand for living quarters in the area. Only a small roadway separated Austen's Rents from the millpond and
the demesne lands of the manor, and Langley's first instinct may have been to put tenements of his own in
that spot. He did not do so, however, choosing instead
to begin his construction several hundred yards away
at the western end of the manor. His thinking about
the land by the millpond presumably changed with the
opening of the Rose and the daily arrival of playgoers
at Paris Garden stairs; for that was just the spot on
which a playhouse ought to stand.[3]

Early evidence of Langley's determination to develop the manorial grounds may well be found in the
bold step that he took in February 1594 when he mortgaged all his Cheapside properties, including the Saracen's Head and the Horse Head, as collateral for a loan.
These holdings had provided his chief stable sources of
income, to the best of my knowledge—his nephew
Richard Langley had been paying him eighty pounds
annual rent on the Horse Head alone—and one would
think that Langley's own experience as a money broker
would argue against his putting up such valuable prop-

erties as security for a bond. But he went ahead, and on such security he was able to raise £1,650 from that unfailing source of capital, Giles Simpson. Langley mortgaged to Simpson all those messuages in Cheapside in the tenure of "John Terry, goldsmith, Robert Howe, goldsmith, Richard Langley, haberdasher, Hannibal Gammon, goldsmith, John Cornwall, goldsmith and Jane Clark, widow, citizens of London."[4]

One can only speculate why Langley needed £1,650 at the beginning of 1594. I have found no record of any debts or obligations of that magnitude, or of any sizable legal judgments against him in that period. I hope it will be safe to deduce that the sum was directly related to a decision to invest money in the manor. Between February, when he borrowed the money, and November, when the Lord Mayor wrote in alarm about the impending new playhouse, there are no specific records about the erection of a playhouse at the manor. But I presume that the Lord Mayor's letter was based on more than hearsay, for he would probably not have wished to trouble the Lord Treasurer with unfounded rumors. Perhaps the building of the foundations had begun by that time. If so, then we may conjecture that the playhouse was completed by the spring or summer of 1595. We do not know as much as we ought to know about the conventions of building in Elizabethan London, and in particular we have no very precise information about the length of time needed to erect a playhouse. The Rose, which was described in January 1587 as having had its foundations laid, seems to have been in operation before October of that year; the Globe, which was apparently open to the public by the summer of 1599, was built from the timbers of another playhouse which had been pulled down at about Christmas 1598; the second Globe, whose construction perhaps began in January or February 1614 with the renegotiating of the ground lease, was in operation that summer. All of these rough estimates argue for a construction time on the order of six months. If Langley had indeed begun in November 1594, the following spring or summer would seem to be a reasonable time for his playhouse to have been ready.[5]

Neither are we particularly informed on the matter of construction costs. A set of lawsuits found by C. W. Wallace suggests that the total cost of building the Theater was in the neighborhood of £700. Henslowe's indenture of partnership with John Cholmley in 1587 was based on a schedule of payments totalling £816, possibly the total cost of the Rose. One of the Globe sharers suggested in 1635 that the cost of erecting the second Globe had been some £1,400, though Wallace thought this was an inflated figure. If we may be allowed the liberty of assuming that these figures are substantially accurate, then one might hazard a guess that Langley could have erected a playhouse in 1594–95 for perhaps £900 to £1,000. The testimony of Johannes de Witt informs us that of the four playhouses in London in about 1596, "the largest and the most magnificent" was the one built by Langley in Paris Garden. The additional opulence suggested by de Witt's description may have raised the total cost of the playhouse, but to what extent we cannot know. All of this is simply to argue that the substantial loan of £1,650 that Langley received from Giles Simpson in February 1594 would have been adequate for the erection of a playhouse and for sundry other purposes as well.[6]

If Langley was inspirited by the sight of James Austen building new tenements on his copyhold land in 1593, it did not take him long to begin to do the same. I conjecture that the loan in February 1594 was intended to finance Langley's own new tenements, and that Langley momentarily passed over the property by the millpond, with its drainage problems, in order to begin building elsewhere on the manor grounds. The St. Saviour's token book for 1593 does not reflect any building activity on Langley's part, but in the book for 1594 the collectors have noted the presence of six new families adjacent to the Upper Ground near the western end of the manor, in a grouping that the collectors described as "Langley's new buildings to tithe." The newcomers were John Palmer, Christopher Moseley, John Bassett, Robert Fortune, William Rosby, and Richard Smythe. Among them these six families accounted for eleven tokens, all but Palmer apparently having wives. There were probably several children under sixteen, but the token books do not reflect this. In making their annotations for the tithing the collectors recorded that each of these families paid "40^s a year" in rent. The collectors also noted two unoccupied buildings on the grounds, which they marked as "new." The token book for the following year, 1595, shows "Langley's new rents" with nine families in residence: all the above except for Rosby, and in addition Richard Stone, a widow Parson, John Dankes and George Reynolds (sharing one messuage), and, interestingly, Francis Henslowe. In addition to these nine tenants, Langley was apparently ready for four more families, for the collectors have noted that "Mr Pope has four new-built houses new built in Mr Langley's ground." These thirteen buildings, nine of them occupied, must represent the extent of Langley's investment as of Easter 1595, or just prior, at the time when I have presumed that the playhouse was under construction.[7]

But if Langley was using his funds to build tenements in 1594, then the decision to build a playhouse —which I have presumed to date sometime after June 1594—would require a diversion of these funds. We might well expect that the building of tenements would stop while the playhouse went up. And indeed the token books support this assumption. There were thirteen tenements ready by Easter 1595, and two years later there were still only thirteen. But growth began again after that; the token books list nineteen families in 1598 and twenty-six in 1599, with the further annotation of "three new builded untenanted."

The playhouse, therefore, represented perhaps a two-year setback in Langley's other building plans; presumably he found this acceptable.

My reading, then, of the available evidence leads me to conclude that Langley had decided by the end of 1593 or the beginning of 1594 to build dwellings on his land; that he was confident enough of their financial success that he was willing to risk his Cheapside properties on the venture; that some time after he commenced building tenements he decided to build a playhouse as well; that he stopped the building of tenements in order to accomplish his new purpose; that the playhouse was under construction by November 1594; that it was completed sometime in the summer of 1595; and that it may have cost Langley £1,000.

It is also clear, I believe, that the playhouse was intended to supplement, and not to replace, Langley's tenements, for as soon as he had recouped some capital he not only returned to the erection of buildings in his "new rents," but began building another set of tenements beside the playhouse. The token collectors were soon constrained to distinguish between "Mr Langley's new rents" and "Mr Langley's new rents near the playhouse." At some point in its existence the playhouse came to be known as the Swan. The letter which Johannes de Witt sent to his friend Arend van Buchell contains probably the earliest reference to this name; scholars conventionally date de Witt's visit to London in the summer of 1596. The playhouse is mentioned by name in the lawsuit between Langley and the Earl of Pembroke's players early in 1598. I find no other references to the name before this date. Nor can I suggest a reason for the name. The names of the early London playhouses can usually be explained: the Theater is self evident; the playhouse at Newington Butts either had no name, or was named the Playhouse (on the analogy of the Theater), or had a name that is lost to us; the Curtain took the name of the property on which it was built, as did the Rose. The Swan was the first play-house with what might be termed an idiosyncratic name. The commonest assumption is that it was named for the swans on the river; but so were many other structures in London, including a prominent Bankside whorehouse mentioned by Stow. The matter is of no moment; it is quite likely that Jane Langley or one of her children suggested the name.[8]

The playhouse was conceived and built at a time of great economic uncertainty for the professional drama. The early summer of 1594, as E. K. Chambers has observed, was a significant moment in the history of the English stage. "The plague was now really over," he wrote, "and a reorganization of the companies became possible." Indeed, not only possible but necessary; for the comparatively haphazard arrangements under which stage players had associated themselves into companies in 1591 and 1592 had weakened and collapsed under the protracted pressures of enforced touring from mid-1592 until mid-1594. Some companies apparently could not afford to return to London; Worcester's, for example, or Sussex's, or Derby's, or even the formerly prestigious Queen's company, all of which were either heard from no more after 1594, or noticed only as troupes playing in the provinces. Pembroke's company apparently could not survive even in the country and went bankrupt in 1593. When it became evident in the early summer of 1594 that the plague was really over, only two playing organizations were in evidence in London: a company under the protection of Charles Howard, Baron Howard of Effingham, the Lord High Admiral, and another newly under the protection of Henry Carey, Baron Hunsdon, the Lord Chamberlain. These two companies played together for ten days at Newington Butts in June of that year, under the management of Philip Henslowe. The arrangement was apparently unsatisfactory to all concerned, and one must assume that it was not by choice. No doubt the Privy Council had required the players to keep a certain distance from the City. Within a fortnight, however, the two companies found means of moving nearer in and separating in the process, the Admiral's men moving to Henslowe's own playhouse, the Rose, and the Chamberlain's men moving presumably to the Theater or the Curtain in Shoreditch.[9]

Of the Chamberlain's men we have scant records from this year, but we know a fair amount about the Admiral's men. From the time the latter company began to play at the Rose, in the middle of June 1594, until the midsummer suspension of playing in June 1595, Philip Henslowe recorded some 275 performances in his account book. The only interruption in playing during that period was in late winter, beginning at the second Sunday in Lent and continuing through Easter, for a loss of about five weeks of receipts. Other than that, the Admiral's men maintained their six-day-a-week schedule throughout the year almost without pause. Henslowe's daily earnings from this highly satisfactory season ranged from a low of 4^s to a high of £3 13^s, and by June 1595, the time of the expected inhibition of playing in anticipation of the plague, his share of the takings had amounted to some £450. His earnings averaged 32^s to 33^s per day throughout the season and were particularly high at the beginning, when Londoners flocked to the newly reopened playhouses; Henslowe made on the average nearly £2 per performance between June 15 and July 30, 1594. One might have been able to make a rough estimate of this figure simply by watching the crowds each day. A man engaged in building tenements for rent might notice with interest that one day's earnings for Henslowe at a good performance easily equalled the yearly income from a newly built tenement. A great many tenements would be needed to bring in £450 in one year.[10]

It did not take Francis Langley long to commence his own construction. The Swan playhouse may have been completed in the summer of 1595 just in time for the building to be interdicted by the suspension of playing in June. If so, it may have caused Langley some momentary nervousness; but the threat of plague must have been remote that summer, for playing resumed on August 25, at least for the Admiral's men, and if Langley had managed to lease the Swan to a group of players during the summer they, too, might have begun their season at that time. One would like to find in Henslowe's accounts some reflection of the possible new competition from the Swan, but the figures are tantalizingly vague. In the 1595–96 season Henslowe recorded 232 performances as against 275 in the previous season; but this is only because the new season did not begin until August. However, his total income in this season was £340 as against £450 the year previous, and this drop reflects more than simply an attenuated playing period. The average daily earnings in the 1595–96 season were between 29^s and 30^s as against a daily average some 3^s higher the year before. The first six weeks of the season were, as was the case in the previous season, a time of increased business, but the daily average of Henslowe's earnings in this second season went up to just under 34^s, some 4^s per day lower than the previous year's figure. Henslowe's Lenten break was a week longer this season, commencing on the first instead of the second Sunday in Lent; but this longer break has no effect on my daily statistics, as they are based on performance days. One looks in anticipation at all these diminished figures, hoping to find some clues about the Swan; but the yield is inchoate, for the clues are simply too tenuous.

So, unfortunately, are all the other known facts about the Swan in the season of 1595–96. There is no solid evidence, indeed, to affirm that Langley had any tenants at all in the Swan during that season. We do not even have any substantial evidence about possible or prospective tenants, for there is no clear record of a third company of players active in London in that year. Nor is there any evidence that Langley's playhouse was licensed. This last need not give us pause, however, for the fact is that no licenses as such have survived for any of the playhouses in this period; we know only by hearsay and indirect reference that they were a necessary preliminary to operation, and nothing is proved by our inability to find one for Langley. But this total absence of hard facts reduces one, by default, to contriving a series of hypothetical answers to the very real questions that are raised. Such an absence of direct information is an invitation for guesswork to proceed, with all its attendant hazards; for the unwary reader, the wild surmise and the cautious suggestion may stand on equal footing in such circumstances.

One might surmise, for example, that the Swan was not even built in 1595 but was completed in the summer of 1596. This is a year later than is usually proposed, but the absence of evidence from the 1595–96 season might thus be readily explained, and no firm facts are at hand to disprove such an assertion. I find it too facile a suggestion, however, for if the construction of the playhouse was not under way by November 1594, the Lord Mayor's letter of that month becomes an anomaly. And if construction was under way I can see no reason why Langley should have spent more than the minimal time necessary to get the building up. My own belief is that the Swan was ready for occupancy by the summer of 1595, and that the absence of any further information about its occupants at that time must be explained otherwise.

Let me proceed directly, then, to the question of tenants. Though we do not know of a third company of players in London in 1595-96, there are grounds for entertaining the possibility of one. The reorganization of players into companies in the summer of 1594 left a number of loose ends unaccounted for. A great many men who had made their living from the theatre before 1592 had lost their livelihoods during the great plague, and there is no reason to presume that they had all quietly taken up other trades. In F. T. Rickert's phrase, London in the summer of 1594 "must have been seething with unemployed actors." Those who were fortunate enough were taken up into the two functioning companies, the Admiral's and the Chamberlain's. But there were other men, not so fortunate, who still hoped for work. Such men would do, presumably, what they had done in the past; they would try to organize themselves into troupes, try to find a patron, try to find a playhouse, try to find playscripts and properties, try to find financial assistance.[11]

On the first of June, 1595, at just about the time when I conjecture the Swan to have been completed, Philip Henslowe noted in his account book the loan of nine pounds to his nephew Francis: "lent unto Francis Henslowe the first of June 1595 in ready money to lay down for his half share with the company which he doth play withal, to be paid unto me when he doth receive his money which he lent to my Lord Burt, or when my assigns doth demand it." This loan was witnessed by "Wm Smyght player," "George Attewell player" and "Robert Nycowlles player."[12]

As might be expected, there is no additional documentation about this undertaking. The three witnessing "players" belonged to neither the Admiral's nor the Chamberlain's troupes. "Smyght" and "Nycowlles" are otherwise unknown to theatrical history, and Attewell has been further noticed only as a payee for Strange's men in March 1591 for Court performances during the previous Christmas season. Of Francis Henslowe's own histrionic aspirations there is prior evidence. A year earlier, Philip Henslowe had lent fifteen pounds to his nephew "to lay down for his share to the Queen's players when they broke and went into the country to play . . . to be paid unto me at his return out of the country." Of the witnesses to this earlier loan, at least one—John Towne—and perhaps all three were members of the Queen's company at the time. It is reasonable that Philip Henslowe would require Francis's proposed fellows to serve as

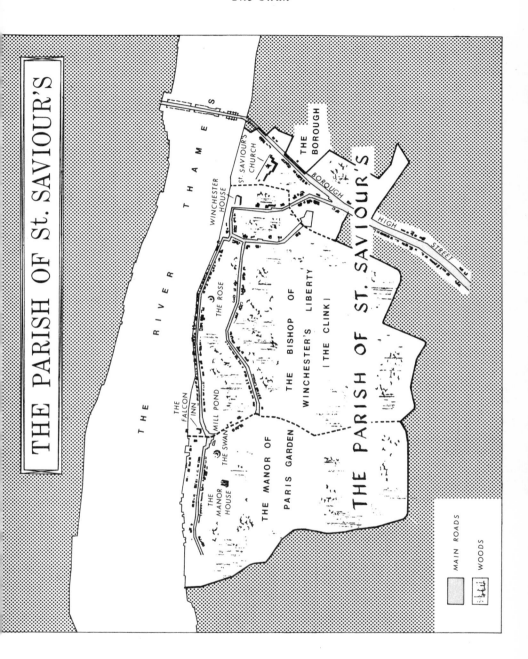

THE PARISH OF St. SAVIOUR'S

THE RIVER THAMES

WINCHESTER HOUSE

St. SAVIOUR'S CHURCH

THE BOROUGH

BOROUGH

HIGH STREET

THE ROSE

THE BISHOP OF WINCHESTER'S LIBERTY (THE CLINK)

THE PARISH OF ST. SAVIOUR'S

THE FALCON INN

MILL POND

THE SWAN

THE MANOR HOUSE

THE MANOR OF PARIS GARDEN

MAIN ROADS

WOODS

witnesses, and the logical inference from this assumption, as Sir Walter Greg observed, is that Smith, Nichols, and Attewell were fellow members of "the company which he doth play withal" in June 1595, "whatever that may have been," as Greg wryly concluded.[13]

Henslowe's two memoranda differ in that there is no mention in the later entry of any proposed travels in the country, or any suggestion that Francis might be absent when the time came to repay the loan. One might conclude from this that the second entry refers to a company being formed to play in or about London. This assumption is reinforced by Francis Henslowe's move, in the summer or autumn of 1595, into one of Francis Langley's new tenements at the further end of Paris Garden manor. I find it unlikely that he would take new lodgings as a preparative for departing, and in fact the token collectors for St. Saviour's church found him regularly present each year and able to buy communion tokens. The token book for 1595–96 shows "Mr Francis Henslowe" as newly arrived in Langley's rents; two tokens were assessed, presumably for himself and his wife, but in fact three were bought—"one pd for Alice Drant," the marginal annotation reads. Alice Drant, or Grant, was no doubt engaged in settling next door, for the following year's token book shows "mystris Grant" listed just before Francis Henslowe. In 1597–98 Francis Henslowe was again assessed for two tokens, but in 1598–99 the name "Francis Henslowe" has been marked through, and he and his wife thereafter disappear from the listings in this area. His tenancy in Langley's rents, then, coincides interestingly with the generally accepted period of activity assigned to the Swan, from 1595 to 1598.[14]

It would be helpful if one could show Attewell, Smith, and Nicholls also moving into the area in 1595 and out in 1598, but such a tidy collocation of data is not to be found. Chambers, in his paragraph on George Attewell, notes that a "Mr. Otwell lived in St. Saviour's Close in 1599." There is of course no indication that this is the George Attewell whom we seek, but on closer inspection a Mr. Otowell or Otewell can be found in St. Saviour's Close in 1595, 1596, and 1597. He is missing in 1598, but back again in 1599 and 1600. The first part of this pattern is strikingly like that of Francis Henslowe. The coincidence is weakened, however, by our inability to trace him in 1593 and 1594, the Boroughside token books for those years not having survived. Smith and Nichols are even more elusive. They did not live near the playhouse during this period, and their names are so common that no importance can be attached to their appearance elsewhere.[15]

Attewell's name is otherwise preserved for us as the eponym of a jig, entered in the Stationers' Register on October 14, 1595, as "A pretty new Jig between Francis the gentleman, Richard the farmer, and their wives," but commonly spoken of as "Attewell's Jig," George Attewell's name being printed at the end of it. The piece is a suitable exemplar of the formal stage jig as brought to popularity by Richard Tarlton, the famous clown of the Queen's company, who died in 1588. The next man to win lasting fame as an exponent of the form was Will Kemp, the leading comedian of the Lord Chamberlain's players. Between the death of the former and the rise of the latter, the art was presumably kept alive by such performers as George Attewell. There is no evidence that Attewell actually wrote the jig to which his name is attached; he is more likely to have made it famous through performance. Even this, however, would argue that he was a player not unknown, or at least less unknown than William Smith or Robert Nichols, the other witnesses to Francis Henslowe's loan. Attewell may indeed have been the nucleus of the company that Francis Henslowe joined in July 1595. The sale of the jig to a publisher in October of the same year may have been an attempt to gain publicity, or to raise money.

Admittedly, all of this is tentative, and I have no

119

dazzling piece of evidence to offer as a conclusion to the argument. I can only suggest, on the basis of the few instances I have been able to bring together, that there is a distinct possibility that a third company was formed in the summer of 1595, including among its number four players whose names are known; that the company may have contracted to play at the Swan, either on its own initiative or at Francis Langley's urging; and that some of the players either lived near the Swan already or else moved nearer to it at that time. I do not know who their patron may have been, who the other players were, or what plays they might have owned, though I have no doubt that such information is lying somewhere waiting to be found. My conclusion, then, based on such scanty evidence as I have adduced, is that the Swan was licensed and occupied in the autumn of 1595, possibly by the group of players formed around George Attewell. Their competition, a short stroll eastward on the Bankside, was Edward Alleyn and the Admiral's men. If Henslowe's accounts for 1595–96 show little decrease from the previous year, it may simply be that Attewell and his men were not sufficient competition to threaten the popularity of the Admiral's players.[16]

In fact, very little seems to have detracted from the popularity of Alleyn's company. A Fugger newsletter reports severe gales in London during the last week of December 1595 and the early days of January 1596; a ship called the *Samaritan* was apparently lost with all hands in the Thames on one of those days. Hardly fit weather for attendance at one of the public playhouses; yet the Admiral's men gave nine performances at the Rose between December 26 and January 5, presumably right through the worst of this blustery weather, and Henslowe's share of the profits from those performances alone was £17 17^s, or a daily average of just under £2. It is hard to imagine the players at the Swan, whoever they might have been, doing as well.[17]

VIII

Cadiz

How much unlook'd for is this expedition!
KING JOHN

One of the plays performed by Alleyn's group during that stormy fortnight was—as Henslowe recorded it—"harey the v." This play belonged to the Admiral's men; it was not the play written in 1599 by Shakespeare for the Chamberlain's men, and probably not the *Famous Victories of Henry V* played more than a decade earlier by Tarlton and the Queen's men, though it may have been derived from the latter. Between the end of November 1595, when it was first presented, and the end of February 1596, when Henslowe began his Lenten break, Alleyn's version of *Henry V* was performed at the Rose eight times and earned a commendable profit. Its theme, like that of the other Henry V plays, no doubt involved the celebration of English victories abroad. Such an emphasis would have been timely, for during that winter the thought of famous victories abroad occupied men's minds at the Court as well as in the playhouse. Plans had been forming since that autumn, in fact, for an attack against the forces of the King of Spain, and the Earl of Essex figured prominently in those plans. Shakespeare's recasting of the Henry V story in 1599 is thought by some to be linked to the disastrous Irish campaigns of the Earl of Essex in that year; it is an interesting coincidence that Alleyn's earlier version should come before the public in 1595–96 just in time to herald Essex's greatest victory, the spectacular sack of Cadiz.

Not since the Lisbon fiasco of 1589, which marked the decline of Sir Francis Drake's career, had there been a major expedition against Spain. By the winter of 1595–96, sentiment argued that it was time for another try. Plans were formulated throughout the winter, and by the middle of March 1596 the draft of a royal commission had been drawn up by the Queen, Cecil and Burghley. Lord Admiral Howard and the Earl of Essex were to be joint commanders. The target was to be a major coastal city. But there was to be no rash adventuring. The failure of the Lisbon expedition in 1589 was generally laid to Drake's casual disregard of the instructions and limitations laid down in his commission. Drake had, after all, made his reputation by a series of bold strokes taken in the face of royal commands to the contrary; the Queen knew as much, and on the Lisbon expedition she had sent along Anthony Ashley, one of the clerks of the Privy Council, to keep an eye on Drake, but to no avail.

The Earl of Essex had himself been a member of the Portugal expedition. He was a young man, as bold and rash as Drake but without his skill and experience, and his impulse to disregard instructions was as strong. But the Lisbon experience had left almost everyone wiser, and the commission drawn up for Essex in 1596 specified and circumscribed his actions in a number of particulars. Essex was particularly anxious to engage in the campaign, for he believed implicitly in his own skill as a commander and hoped that military successes would strengthen his power at Court and give him added leverage against the entrenched Cecils. The tension between the Essex and Cecil factions had increased over the winter, and separating the two men must have seemed a good idea to all concerned. But Essex's determination to be a hero often made him rash, and Cecil, as he drafted the commission, may have wondered if it wouldn't be better in the long run to keep Essex at home. An imprudent and impulsive action on Essex's part might plunge the whole country into danger.

One solution was to restrict the number of loyal followers who might accompany him, thereby lessening the incitement to acts of bravado. One by one they were ordered to remain at home: Southampton, Derby, Compton, Sheffield, Mountjoy, and other of his followers, leaving him in the end with only Sussex, Rich, Herbert, and Burgh. Another solution was to send along Anthony Ashley again. Ashley's services at Lisbon were apparently felt to have been valuable, though only Ashley himself could have known what they cost in exhaustion of spirit. He was instructed to accompany the Earl of Essex, and he knew perfectly well what was meant by that order. His brother-in-law, Francis Langley, may have been privy to his thoughts at this time. One would like to have a record of such conversation as may have passed between them, perhaps while watching the preparation of ships in the Thames. They would have been an interesting pair. Ashley, in his middle forties, close to the center of power for many years and yet, strangely, the more naive and innocent of the two. Langley, by now in his late forties, shrewder and more calculating than his wife's brother, inwardly wondering perhaps at Ashley's inability to grasp certain basic principles of human nature, or musing on the course of action he himself might be planning to take if their roles had by some chance been reversed. Idle speculation, of course; Langley was not, and never would be, empowered by a commission from the Queen or her Council; his talents were not destined for Her Majesty's service.

By the end of April 1596 Ashley was engaged in his own preparations for the intended expedition. But we learn, from a letter that he wrote on April 28, that he was also engaged upon some other business for Cecil, about which he was curiously vague. "I assure you," he wrote Cecil, "I do not slack the important matter committed to my charge, and shall find opportunity to satisfy her Majesty's expectation therein." And then, in language reminiscent of an earlier undertaking of Cecil's, Ashley pointed out that "albeit I might have gotten above a thousand pounds clear by this booty unseen, yet are you witness that I preferred my duty to her Majesty before all private." Ashley's own money was apparently involved in this unspecified undertaking, for he earnestly requested Cecil "to move her Majesty for the present dispatch of my bill remaining with you, that I may in part be able to defray the great charges I am at in my preparation to the intended expedition."[1]

Not since the disappearance of the great diamond in the depths of the Saracen's Head have we been troubled by references to a thousand pounds' worth of booty. The present letter gives no more than a tantalizing hint; but it is enough to put us on our guard. More than a year had passed since Cecil's interrogations of Gilbert, Howe, Brooke, and the others, but there is no reason to presume that he had given up hope of recovering the stone. The quest was a personal one for Cecil; one finds records of its progress among his own papers, but not in any public documents, for he did not trouble the rest of the Privy Council with his efforts. Anthony Ashley, for example, even though he was one of the Council's clerks, seems not to have known about the earlier interrogations, or even to have known that Cecil had pinpointed specific individuals.

But Ashley, by some strange devices of his own, had indeed managed to become involved in the business of the diamond. It may have been secretive at first; but Ashley was in too exposed a position to keep such a matter secret for long. My own guess is that in some fashion Cecil had got hold of a piece of information implicating Ashley in the affair and had confronted him with it. As I conceive the confrontation, Ashley then explained that he was indeed involved, but that he was trying to recover the diamond for the Queen, and was certainly not dealing underhandedly for his own gain. Cecil replied that if that was the case then Ashley had better get on with it, for suspicions had been aroused. But none of this fanciful speculation is vital, for the facts will make their own case. By the time of this letter, at the end of April, Ashley was ready to let Cecil know that he had located the elusive diamond on his own, and had put down some money on it. The letter says as much, though in veiled terms, and implies even more. But Ashley's suggestion to Cecil that only patriotism kept him from illegal profiteering was disingenuous; as an assurance of his sincerity it rang hollow, and if Cecil already had suspicions about Ashley they might have been deepened at this point. However, neither of them could afford the luxury of uninterrupted attention to the business of the diamond, for other matters kept intruding into the affairs of both men.

Early in April, from their stronghold in the Netherlands, the Spanish had launched an attack southward upon the port of Calais. The attack was successful by mid-April. The French defenders fled, and the English were left with the discomforting reality of an armed Spanish garrison facing them across the Channel. The ships of the Essex expedition had been hastily shifted from Plymouth to Dover when news of the siege first arrived in London, but the Queen was reluctant to commission Essex to make a counterattack, and while he waited and fretted impatiently at Dover, pacing the deck of his flagship, the citadel of Calais was overrun. Essex was hot to intercede, but Elizabeth and Burghley viewed the event more coolly, and they ordered him to return to Plymouth and to continue preparations for his expedition to the Spanish coast. He was told to wait at Plymouth for Anthony Ashley, who would bring him further instructions and would attend upon him during the voyage. Essex took his fleet to Plymouth, but by mid-May nothing further had happened. Ralegh's contingent of ships had not yet arrived, Ashley had not yet arrived, money to pay the men had not yet arrived. Essex wrote in some pique to Cecil on May 12, asking for a speedy resolution to all these hanging matters.

Ashley, indeed, had not even left London. As a man publicly identified with the Cecil faction at Court, he was understandably ill at ease about being assigned to the Earl of Essex. The Queen and Burghley, with Cecil's assistance, had so framed Essex's commission for the intended voyage that little room for maneuver was allowed him; their intention was simply to keep the impetuous young man within bounds. Essex might therefore be properly suspicious of any of Cecil's men placed in his retinue, and might require similarly detailed commissions from them. But Ashley had no such commission. Cecil had told Ashley in private what to do and what to look for, and had read some instructions to him, but had declined to furnish him with a written copy; some of the instructions were for covert activity on Cecil's behalf, and Ashley later remembered that Cecil "charged me I should not be known thereof to any, for the causes then delivered." [2]

As a result, Ashley's quite reasonable concern was that he would be treated by Essex simply as one of Cecil's spies. Nervous at the prospect, he took the tactless step of writing to Lord Burghley requesting a set of written instructions. When Cecil learned of this he was enraged; for reasons which are not wholly clear, it was his intention that Ashley should not have a written warrant. Ashley trembled under Cecil's ire, protesting that he had meant no disloyalty and was certain he had "given no just cause of least offense." On May 15 he wrote to Cecil, his puzzlement professedly the greater at Cecil's anger. "What offense, I pray you, can be conceived by you against me in making suit to my honorable good lord your father for his letter commendatory to the Generals, upon those grounds contained in my letter, namely, that I knew not certainly what to do in discharge of my duty by any letter or other direction given me in writing from her Majesty or their lordships."[3]

Ashley held that he would be quite unable to satisfy any inquiry about the authority under which he acted or about the extent of his commission. But with a letter, "then (as I take it) should I know certainly the limits of my duty and charge." Ashley felt he had been publicly embarrassed by the altercation. "It is some touch to have stayed thus long purposely for the instructions, and now to depart empty handed, the Generals being so formerly advertised of the cause of my stay; and the cause of my stay in town all night grew (as you know) upon the matter of the diamond and not of mine own desire . . . For had not this been, (for aught I know) I might have departed fortnight sithence . . . For the diamond, so heavily laid on me sithence my coming home, I have sent for the party, but cannot yet get him by reason of his absence at Lambeth."

We are of course teased by this reference to an unknown party absent at Lambeth, and Ashley's need to stay "in town all night" because of the diamond. The import is not yet clear. Cecil, for his part, seemed bent on humbling Ashley at this juncture. It may have been policy; the embarrassment, coupled with the refusal to furnish a written commission, may have been part of an effort to convince Essex that Ashley was merely a functionary with no special status, thereby lessening Essex's suspicions about his presence. Or it may have been a general dissatisfaction with Ashley himself, resulting in a decision to treat him frostily and put him on tenterhooks for a time. Whatever Cecil's reason, Ashley construed it in the worst light, seeing his years of dedicated service discounted and set at naught in the face of his present impropriety. Something was needed to restore his credit with Cecil, and swiftly. But it was already May 15, and he was to leave for Plymouth on the following day. Whatever he did, it would have to be sudden and dramatic. Ashley had no choice but to play his trump card; in one sudden outburst he told Cecil everything he knew about the diamond.

> One Terry, a goldsmith dwelling at the sign of the Black Boy in Cheap, is the party that first contracted with Mr Francis Langley and myself for the diamond, and took assurance by obligation for the sum of two thousand six hundred pounds in the name of one James Woolveridge, a Fleming, of purpose to conceal the true owner, who (as I am informed) is one Howe, a goldsmith that dwelleth in Terry's house at sojourn. Myself, with Francis Langley and Hannibal Gammon, a goldsmith, were jointly bound to this Woolveridge for the payment of this money. The stone is at this present in cutting at the said Gammon's house at the sign of the Horseshoe in Cheap, in a study in the second story of his house, by a Dutch cutter, and will be best recovered by his means. This cutter may be apprehended in the morning as he cometh from his house to work, and so be accompanied by some fit person to the place where it remaineth . . . But if her Majesty will be pleased for a time to forbear, I will undertake to deliver it her with mine own hand upon any penalty or displeasure, whereas by other means there may be some danger; but will write you somewhat more hereof in the morning before my departure if I prevail.[4]

So the secret was out at last. Everyone, it seems, was implicated in the diamond affair: Langley, Gammon, and Ashley, as well as Howe and Terry. The value of the stone had risen to £2,600, turning a tidy profit for Howe, along with some white hairs; Ashley and his associates were engaged to purchase it at that price, and Gammon was actually preparing to have it cut. Ashley's position in all this was of course that he was acting solely on the Queen's behalf, and had allied himself with Gammon and Langley surreptitiously, they not being aware of his underlying patriotism. "You will not easily imagine how beneficial the good opinion and acquaintance of these coistrels sometimes proveth," he

boasted nervously to Cecil. Cecil may have believed
this pose of innocence, but it seems unlikely. Apparently he had discussed Ashley's shortcomings with
William Brooke, Lord Cobham, who was not only a
member of the Privy Council but also Cecil's father-in-
law; for on the very day that Ashley finally determined
to write to Cecil about his dealings with Langley and
Gammon, Cobham wrote a stern and straightforward
letter to Ashley, threatening him in no uncertain terms
with the dire consequences of his duplicity. As a result, Ashley's final night in London—the night of May
15—was spent even more sleeplessly than the previous
one. Cecil had completely unnerved him. "The sudden
alteration of your conceit of me hath not a little distempered me, and could wish it had not happened; not
being one whit satisfied till I may understand that you
are. This night I protest to God I neither slept nor
came in bed, partly through the conceit of your letters,
and partly for the care I had to accomplish your expectation concerning the diamond, wherein I have not
slacked any moment of time."[5]

And indeed he had not. His sleeplessness had even
enabled him to locate his brother-in-law. "At last," he
went on, "have spoken this morning by three o'clock
with Langley, showed him my Lord Cobham's letter,
whereat I assure you, he was so far gone out of himself
that for a time I knew not what to make of him, fish or
flesh, wise or foolish, protesting solemnly that he
would rather choose to rot in prison than bewray or deliver the thing; and esteemed himself happy in that
the day precedent, upon some vain chimera or fantas-
tic conceit of his own, he had removed it from the
usual place. Nevertheless at the last the passion as-
suaged, and so by little and little became foolish kind,
and somewhat timorous, and in the end faithfully
promised that he would not fail forthwith to repair
unto your Honor (as so advised by me), and make offer
of the thing unto you to be disposed of either privately
to gain, or otherwise for good opinion, as should be

thought most behoofull in your wisdom for his good . . . But in any case that he should not repair to the Lord Cobham, by reason I utterly misliked the phrase of the letter, doubting thereby some danger intended to us both. Much ado there was, before this was, and I long to understand whether he hath been with you or not."

Ashley was unable to await the event, unfortunately, for he had to be on his way to Plymouth. He must have left London almost immediately after his interview with Langley, for the letter just cited was inscribed "from Hartford Bridge near Hartley Row the 16th of May 1596." Ashley's closing words were a reminder to Cecil that "Your Honor seeth that yourself might by mine industry have made your choice in share with me of the gain of two or three thousand pounds . . . I hope you will not forget immediately upon the receipt of the diamond to cause my three hundred and fifteen pounds to be repaid to this my servant, otherwise I shall make but a shrewd match of it."

And then Ashley was away. He arrived in Plymouth, presented himself to the Generals, and was taken to his quarters aboard the *Due Repulse*, a ship whose name could hardly have cheered him. From his cabin he wrote Cecil again on May 24. "It appeareth by your letter of the 16th of this month sent me hither in post with the packet, that you had not received my last letters written from Hartford Bridge; and therefore, not doubting but ere this her Majesty through you be satisfied touching the diamond (having received it), I hold it needless to trouble you any farther therein, with this hope nevertheless, that albeit I have with hazard of disgrace foregone my gain, I may not also lose or long time expect the repayment of my three hundred and fifteen pounds." One can almost appreciate Cecil's weariness with Ashley. In a postscript he expressed the hope that Cecil would "write me how she [the Queen] accepteth the jewel."[6]

On the last of May Ashley wrote again. "This afternoon we set sail," he announced resignedly. Cecil's continued silence on the matter of the diamond was surely galling to him, and by now Ashley must have begun to suspect the worst; that Langley had not kept his promise of a fortnight earlier to hand over the stone. If this was so—if Cecil still did not have the diamond—then Ashley's graceless efforts to regain his master's good will had produced just the opposite effect. To salvage what little he might of his reputation, Ashley took pains to make clear his own sincerity in the matter, and to hope that Cecil "would be pleased to save my credit by all good means possible with the parties that are touched in the diamond."[7]

Ashley's fears were of course well grounded. Cecil did not have the diamond. Francis Langley may have been distraught at three in the morning on May 16, or at least have feigned distraction to his brother-in-law, but he was certainly himself again in the daylight. The purchase that he, Gammon, and Ashley had negotiated with Robert Howe had not yet been consummated, though the money had been put forward; Langley promptly terminated the agreement, returned the stone to Howe from its hiding place, and pocketed not only his own share of the refund but Ashley's as well. No doubt Langley felt justified; for in a delicate matter, which had presumed mutual trust, he had been betrayed by his wife's brother, someone he should have been able to rely on. He would know better in the future. As for his brother-in-law, when he returned to England he might fend for himself in the matter. His welfare was no longer Langley's concern.

Ashley did not of course know any of this yet, but the uncertainty was a torment, and his conduct on the Cadiz expedition reflected his inner turmoil. He knew that if his position with Cecil was jeopardized, it would behoove him to conduct himself well before the Earl of Essex. Accordingly, he tried to promote a friendship with Essex's household steward, a wild Welshman named Gelly Meyrick. But Meyrick was no

fool; he saw Ashley's intent, and responded to his over-
tures with calculated and hypocritical enthusiasm.
Meyrick had his own master's concerns to attend to,
and his own advancement to protect; if Anthony Ashley wanted to play into his hands, so much the worse
for Ashley. An opportunity might arise to disgrace the
man further, and if Meyrick could manage this, Essex
would be pleased.

The opportunity was not slow in coming. The English fleet entered the harbor of Cadiz on June 22, and
after several hours of fierce fighting the port and castle
fell. Part of the commission to Essex and Howard had
forbidden the English forces to loot or plunder, and
after the victory a few half-hearted attempts were
made to enforce this prohibition, but to no avail. Everyone stole what he could. Common soldiers stole
trinkets; those in higher office had higher aspirations.
Ashley and Meyrick found a Dutch ship in the harbor
with a cargo of oil, and at Meyrick's urging Ashley appropriated it and demanded cash from the captain.
Later, in the Corregidor's own quarters in the castle,
Ashley claimed the Corregidor's own golden chain of
office, to Meyrick's delight. Sir George Carew wrote to
Cecil from Cadiz a few days after the victory to report
that the whole city had been pillaged. He did not wish
to implicate the generals, he went on, but many persons of his own rank had filled their coffers. And indeed, the number of persons of his own rank had
swelled considerably, for Essex, flushed with his military triumph, and Howard, not wishing to appear less
magnanimous, had jointly created sixty-four new
knights at Cadiz, more than doubling the number of
persons who held that dignity. Among those so elevated were Sir Gelly Meyrick and Sir Anthony Ashley.
Carew may have had these very men in mind when he
wrote Cecil, for Meyrick's activities with Ashley could
not have gone unnoticed. Meyrick's intention was that
they should be noticed.[8]

Once the city of Cadiz was secured, Essex turned to

grander plans. He proposed, for example, that the English forces should raid and recapture Calais on their way home. He was balked in this by Howard and Ralegh; but they capitulated to his demands that he be allowed to capture the smaller Portuguese forts at Faro and Lagos, neither of which ventures proved useful, and both of which ran counter to his commission. Toward the end of July Essex dispatched a ship to Plymouth to give the Queen and the Council advance warning of his return and a full account of his victories. The messengers on the ship were Sir Gelly Meyrick and Sir Anthony Ashley. Ashley's relations with Meyrick were cooling by this time, for Ashley had begun to sense that Meyrick was plotting his downfall. Meyrick would surely report Ashley's plunder to the Council; though he would implicate himself in the process, he need not fear his own punishment, for it would be at Essex's hands; but Ashley's penalty would be dealt out by Cecil. Ashley had to forestall this. The ship landed at Plymouth on July 28, and the men took lodging there for the night before proceeding to London. Meyrick found, some hours later, that Ashley had taken horse surreptitiously and ridden off ahead of him.[9]

Ashley arrived in London a few days later, made his presence known to Cecil, and was summoned to Greenwich to make his full report to the Privy Council at its next regular sitting on August 7. But Cecil was not oblivious of the charges laid against Ashley. Immediately on hearing of his arrival in London, Cecil had sent his man Richard Drake to spy on him. Drake stationed himself in a shoemaker's shop adjacent to Ashley's house in Holborn, and kept close watch. On August 4 he reported to Cecil that some seven or eight trunks were rumored to be newly arrived in Ashley's house, having been quietly brought in at two in the morning. They were immediately seized and searched. "I am ashamed to particularize what I have lost by this late inordinate search of my coffers (besides the touch of credit)," Ashley later wrote to Burghley. Cecil had some further news from Sir Ferdinando Gorges at Plymouth; Lord Howard's own pinnace, the *Lion's Whelp*, laden with Ashley's goods from Cadiz, had put in at Plymouth but had turned round on seeing the commissioners and departed without unloading.[10]

Ashley's report to the Privy Council was full and circumstantial. In part he told Cecil and Burghley what they wanted to hear—that the terms of the commission had been exceeded, that Essex had attempted unauthorized military ventures, that Cadiz had been plundered—and the result was a strongly worded letter from the Council to the Lords Generals. "Her Majesty hath entered into divers doubts what she might expect from you . . . since this information given to her . . . by Mr Ashley." Ashley had thus cast his lot with Cecil, seeing no future in currying the favor of the Earl of Essex in the light of Sir Gelly Meyrick's unfriendly treatment of him. Ashley attempted by candor to win Cecil's confidence; in his relation of the pillaging of the city he did not exculpate himself. The Council accordingly questioned Essex's assurances "to stay such disorderly spoils" when they had heard "by common report and in some part by Mr Ashley's confessions" that "great spoils hath been made and robberies of the riches there."[11]

But Sir Gelly Meyrick recognized his obligation to protect his master's name and reputation, and in the face of Ashley's damaging testimony it behooved Sir Gelly to attack him at once. Ashley was promptly accused of confiscating a variety of treasures, from a shipload of oil to a golden chain. Ashley was taken aback by the force of the accusations. On August 10, and again on August 12, he wrote Meyrick, imploring him to "proceed gentlemanlike with me" and to deal "friendly and faithfully with me." Cecil of course understood Meyrick's game, but nevertheless was not disposed to overlook the peccadilloes of his own servant. Within a fortnight he had made it clear to Ashley that his performance had been unsatisfactory; that since his first failure in the diamond enterprise he had been a constant discredit to Cecil, and that Cecil's displeasure would soon become manifest. When Ashley realized that disgrace and imprisonment were to be his lot he was completely overcome. He absented himself in confusion from Greenwich, and retired to his house in London. He wrote Cecil that he had been "constrained through extreme and sudden indisposition of mind and body to depart the Court"; he lamented that "Sir Gelly Meyrick hath prevailed herein against me to his own benefit," and professed himself "extremely distempered . . . to the overthrow both of body and mind." In particular, Ashley expressed bewilderment at the cause of Cecil's coldness: "[I] cannot enough marvel whence this extreme alteration should come, for from so slender a cause as the diamond (knew you once the truth) it could never grow."[12]

Ashley was promptly imprisoned in the Fleet, whence he wrote to Cecil lamenting "my grief in this increase of disgrace and shame," and exclaiming "Woe worth the time that ever I meddled with the diamond, that I went this journey, or did return untimely before the Generals." To Ashley it appeared perfectly clear that the diamond, and Langley, were the chief causes of his present disgrace. "And touching that unfortunate diamond (the ground of all this mischief) I would to God you would be pleased (notwithstanding my bad brother-in-law's assertions) to command him to show my sundry letters heretofore written to him in that matter, and then judge of me accordingly. No man yet (excepting her Majesty) hath interest therein but myself with Langley."[13]

Early in September Ashley was charged by the Corregidor himself with the theft of the golden chain, and he confessed to having sold it to a goldsmith in Cheap for £530. Cecil also noted that Ashley had reputedly made between £500 and £700 in ransoming prisoners, and Sir Gelly Meyrick managed to remember that Ashley had said while in Cadiz that he would make the expedition, and his commission therein, worth a good manor. By the end of September Ashley was broken, and Cecil had made his point. An agreement was reached between them, which apparently required Ashley's commitment to pursue the diamond matter further, and early in October he was released from the Fleet. On October 7 he wrote Cecil from his house in Holborn, vowing the good performance "of your promise made unto her Majesty in my behalf upon my deliverance."[14]

The symmetry is sadly depressing. When we picked up the thread of Ashley's story in April 1596 we found him promising good performance in an important matter committed to his charge; six months later, having been to Plymouth, to Cadiz, and to prison, and having shown consistently poor judgment, we find him reiterating the same pledge. He must have sensed that his wheel had come full circle and that he was seeking once again, like a beginner, for ways to ingratiate himself. His career was in jeopardy: the summer of 1596 had been an eventful one for Sir Anthony Ashley, but not a profitable one.

It seems to have been an eventful summer for Francis Langley too, though of course the documentation is sadly deficient by comparison. If Langley wrote any letters, they have not survived or have not been found; so we cannot have his own words for anything that transpired in this period. It would be useful, for example, to have his own version of the diamond incident. As it is, we can do no more than surmise. With Bartholomew Gilbert's arrest in the spring of 1594, Robert Brooke had reneged on his offer to purchase the stone, and Howe and Terry had bought it back from him. Their prospective purchasers had melted away under the threat of Cecil's determined pursuit, and if Howe and Terry were to realize any sort of profit from their risk they would have to find more covert confederates with whom to negotiate. The "great doer" in all such matters, according to the goldsmith Shory, was their colleague Hannibal Gammon, and it is reasonable that they might have turned to him with a proposal.

He would of course be interested. Gammon would have spoken with Langley about financing the arrangement, and Langley with Ashley about protecting it. The three no doubt would have been quite willing to purchase the diamond from Howe and Terry if they could see therein a means of profit to themselves; this meant that the assurance of their own sale of the stone to others had to be reasonably certain before they would bind themselves to buy it. This would explain the delay in the consummation of the purchase and would also explain why, in the interim, the prospective purchasers had possession of the stone and the sellers had the purchase money. During these negotiations Cecil's curiosity about Ashley's conduct might first have become aroused. Ashley, indeed—if we read his letters aright—seems to have attempted to interest Cecil himself in the purchase of the stone: "Your Honor seeth that yourself might by mine industry have made your choice in share with me of the gain of two or three thousand pounds." That this tactic did Ashley irreparable damage seems certain; he ought to have known Cecil better than that, after so many years of association.[15]

Ashley's last-ditch confrontation with Langley, on May 15 at three in the morning, marked the end of the negotiations from Langley's point of view. The protection that Ashley might have afforded was gone, shattered by Cecil and Cobham, and worse yet, Langley had now been identified and pointed out to Cecil as a main participant in the scheme. For some reason Ashley refrained from implicating Gammon beyond the mention of his name; but Cecil now knew about Francis Langley, and he was not a man to let such information slip. My guess is that very soon after his receipt of Ashley's letter describing the nocturnal visit, Cecil sent his agent Richard Topcliffe to inquire after

Langley; for in the week immediately following the final meeting with Ashley, Langley found it expedient to be away from home. By May 21 he was in Croydon, Surrey, where he remained until at least the first of June.

It is also possible that one or more of the Surrey Justices were instructed to look for Langley. As bad luck would have it, Justice William Gardiner happened upon him in Croydon on May 21, and the encounter was apparently noisy. Gardiner reported later that Langley had railed slanderously against him and called him a liar. The result was of course a lawsuit, brought by Gardiner against Langley in the Court of Queen's Bench. Another result may have been that Cecil was notified of Langley's whereabouts. But if Langley was apprehended and brought in for questioning, no record of it has survived among Cecil's own papers. In any event, Langley was in a reasonably secure position; he did not have the stone, such information as he did have could only serve to implicate Ashley further, and Cecil already knew whatever Langley might offer to tell him. For Cecil, Langley was a man who had made too many wrong moves. Imprisonment was not in order; but sooner or later an occasion for punishment would present itself. Langley could be broken in the same way that Ashley had been broken. Cecil would merely bide his time.[16]

IX

Langley and Shakespeare

Which is the justice, which is the thief?
KING LEAR

So May passed into June, and June into July, and an expectant populace awaited news of the great expedition. On July 19 Lord Cobham wrote to Robert Cecil from Dover, "I have heard such diversity of occurrences of our fleet since I came to these parts as I durst not write them." Cobham also reported the more disquieting news of a spreading plague in Boulogne, Abbeville, and Dieppe. On July 20 William Stallenge wrote Cecil from Plymouth, that there was "no farther . . . news from the fleet"; he also reported the arrival of some trading ships from France. The fear of plague crossing the channel into England moved the Privy Council to immediate action. At its very next meeting, on July 22 at Greenwich, it took measures against infection. All playing was suspended in and about the City of London, effective immediately. Henslowe learned of the inhibition on the following day, and promptly closed down the Rose. Langley must have done the same. Thereafter there was no playing in London until late in October.[1]

Nor was this the only blow suffered by the players in the summer of 1596. On the very day of the Privy Council's order, the Lord Chamberlain—Henry Carey,

139

Lord Hunsdon—died of a lingering illness. His death was not unexpected, but its effect on theatrical activity was twofold; it left one of the two major companies in London without a patron, and deprived the profession as a whole of his moderating presence on the Privy Council. The first of these problems was soon remedied, for Hunsdon's son George Carey, on assuming his father's titles, took also the responsibility for continuing the company of players—Burbage, Kemp, Shakespeare, and the rest—previously maintained by his father. But George Carey did not succeed his father in the office of Lord Chamberlain. The Queen chose instead to do honor to a loyal baron who had grown old in her service. Her new Lord Chamberlain, chosen a fortnight after Hunsdon's death, was Sir Robert Cecil's father-in-law Lord Cobham, the man who had written the threatening letter to Ashley in May.[2]

Cobham's appointment was viewed by many as a statement of policy. In the City it was interpreted as the harbinger of a clamping-down on players and playing, and the aldermen were not long in following suit. Thomas Nashe wrote that "the players . . . are [now] piteously persecuted by the Lord Mayor and the aldermen, and however in their old Lord's [Hunsdon's] time they thought their state settled, it is now so uncertain they cannot build upon it." Not that Cobham was an enemy of the theater, as many have inferred from this well-worn passage; he was simply not interested. He was not, like Hunsdon, the patron of a respected acting company with interests to safeguard, and he refused to follow his predecessor's practice of serving as a buffer between the City and the players. The Lord Mayor might do whatever he wanted, as far as Cobham was concerned; let the players work it out among themselves.[3]

E. K. Chambers thought that 1596 might have been the year in which the City was successful in prohibiting playing in inns, and this suggestion seems subsequently to have hardened into a fact, though scarcely anyone can explain the petrifaction. If Chambers's conjecture is accurate, the period of Cobham's tenure as Lord Chamberlain may have been the indicated time for such a bold move; Chambers may indeed have had this in mind when he suggested that in 1596 the aldermen "appear to have at last obtained the assent of the Privy Council to the complete exclusion of plays from the area of their jurisdiction." But even if Chambers's hunch is correct, it still indicates only that the City was successful in obtaining the necessary legislation; its success in enforcing the legislation, in actually stopping the presentation of plays within the City, was embarrassingly slight, as subsequent records show all too clearly. Whether or not such an ordinance was actually passed in 1596 is therefore an academic question; its answer, if forthcoming, will merely be part of the chronicling of legislative enactment, not of the history of actual social or theatrical change.[4]

Still another event usually ascribed to the summer of 1596 is the visit to London of the Dutch tourist Johannes de Witt. There is no clear evidence to date de Witt's stay in London with any accuracy; but during that time he wrote down, in academic Latin, some of his "Observationes Londinenses," and made some sketches; on his return he showed the work to Arend van Buchell, his friend since their student days at Leyden in 1583. Van Buchell copied some of de Witt's notes into his own commonplace book, including the passage in which he described the four playhouses in the City, two in Shoreditch and two on the Bankside, the largest and fairest of the four being the Swan ("cuius intersignium est cygnus"). Van Buchell also copied de Witt's drawing of the interior of the Swan, showing a play in progress. These few facts establish the limits for de Witt's visit. He must have been in London before the end of 1598 in order to see the Theater still standing, and after August 1595 in order to see a play at the Swan. If we are to accept, as E. K. Chambers does, that de Witt was in London in 1596, then his drawing of a play at the Swan requires that we place him there either before July 22, when playing was suspended, or else after October 27, when it resumed.[5]

De Witt's own notes have vanished, but van Buchell's commonplace book was discovered in the library of the University of Utrecht in 1888, and his copy of the drawing of the Swan has since become a shibboleth among historians of the stage. Its value as primary evidence has been debated at length, and I will not pause here to rehearse the various arguments it has engendered about the structure of the Elizabethan playhouse. One scholar, however, has allowed his mind to wander far enough from this field of battle to suggest that we can identify the play shown to be in progress—an intriguing prospect. And though his argument that the drawing portrays Olivia and Malvolio in *Twelfth Night* fails to convince, it does add to the growing consensus that the company occupying the Swan when playing resumed in the autumn of 1596 was Shakespeare's company. If de Witt was in London after October 27, the possibility becomes quite real that he may have seen a Shakespearean play at the Swan; one inclines, however, despite this temptation, to favor a summertime visit for de Witt, if only on the grounds of ease in traveling, a consideration surely as weighty then as now.[6]

The arguments in favor of Lord Hunsdon's players being at the Swan in the autumn of 1596 were strongly advanced in 1931 with the publication of *Shakespeare versus Shallow*, in which Leslie Hotson argued, on the basis of some legal documents he had found, that Shakespeare and Francis Langley were in association in November of that year if not earlier. Evidence placing Shakespeare in Surrey in this period of his life had already been assembled by E. K. Chambers, and has since been expanded upon by N. E. Evans. Evans's summary of the argument is succinct: "The chain of evidence [is] usually interpreted as follows. Until

142

1596, or at latest until February 1597, William Shakespeare lived somewhere within the parish of St. Helen's, Bishopsgate. Thereafter he cannot be found in that parish, and, after some delay, he is traced by the tax officers to a Liberty of the Bishop of Winchester in Surrey which can only be the Clink, Southwark." Such conclusions command assent when supported by the documentation that Evans analyzes. And yet there is a minority report, which seldom finds its way into print these days though it is not unknown. If Shakespeare lived at any time in the Clink liberty he would have been, like Philip Henslowe and other Clink residents, a member of St. Saviour's parish for that time; and yet his name does not appear in a single one of the annual lists made by the token collectors for that parish. If Shakespeare did live in the Clink, as all the other evidence seems to suggest, then he was singularly invisible every year at token time.[7]

The evidence for the presence of Shakespeare's company in the Swan, however, is not dependent on our verifying the location of Shakespeare's dwelling place. Hotson's arguments, as they directly involve Francis Langley, are more to the point of our inquiry. We have already observed that the Privy Council on July 22, 1596, dispatched letters to the Justices of the Peace of Middlesex and Surrey requiring them to suspend all playing for fear of the plague. We have no way of knowing which of the Surrey Justices was chosen to communicate with Langley in this regard, but in Hotson's view a vengeful man like Justice William Gardiner would have sought out such an opportunity. Gardiner, it will be recalled, had engaged in a name-calling altercation with Langley in Croydon two months earlier, by the end of which Langley had managed to insult him rather too much. Gardiner did not lack for means of revenge. He went to law, of course; but the opportunity to close down Langley's playhouse as well would have been a source of additional satisfaction. Gardiner may have done it in person, or he may have sent his creature William Wayte; another altercation must subsequently have ensued between Langley and one or both of these men, for among Hotson's new documents we find a writ of attachment sworn out against both of them by Francis Langley.

A writ of attachment was, in essence, a directive to the sheriff of a given county to apprehend a specified person or persons, resident in his county or sheriff-wick, on the formal grounds that he or they constituted a serious threat to the life and safety of the person entering the complaint. Once so apprehended, the person complained of was required to enter into sufficient bonds before the court, with the requisite cosigners, to ensure his keeping the peace in particular towards the person complaining as well as generally to the community at large. If he should break the peace within the specified period, usually a year, the bonds would be forfeit and the default sum promptly payable. Such writs were not meant to be issued on whim; the person requesting the writ had to swear before a magistrate of the Court of Queen's Bench that he stood in fear of his life or of bodily harm at the hands of the person complained of, and that concern for his own safety, not malice or revenge, motivated his request. Once the plainant had so sworn, the magistrate then directed the appropriate sheriff to seek and attach the person against whom the complaint was made. Needless to say, many such writs were sworn out of malice, despite the official precautions, and the documents Hotson found may be no exceptions.

Hotson discovered a writ issued in October 1596, whose essence is as follows: "scire scilicet Franciscus Langley petit securitates pacis versus Willelmum Gardener & Willelmum Wayte ob metum mortis &c" (be it known that Francis Langley craves sureties of the peace against William Gardener and William Wayte for fear of death, and so forth). The writ was directed to the sheriff of Surrey, and was to be returned on November 3. There is, however, no evidence that either of the men against whom the writ was issued was attached or constrained to post a bond. What Hotson found instead was a second writ of attachment, issued a fortnight or so after the one just cited and possibly in retaliation against it. Its contents were, however, vastly more exciting: "scire scilicet Willelmus Wayte petit securitates pacis versus Willelmum Shakspere Franciscum Langley Dorotheam Soer uxorem Johannis Soer & Annam Lee ob metum mortis &c."[8]

As in the earlier case, there is no evidence that attachments were made or bonds drawn in consequence of this latter writ. As the writ was directed only to the sheriff of Surrey, one must conclude that all four persons named therein were, or were thought to be, residents of that county. If Shakespeare neither lived nor worked in Surrey, such an assumption about him would be hard to explain; but if he were seen on the Bankside daily, and in occasional association with Francis Langley, such an assumption on William Wayte's part would at least become explicable whether or not it was justified. Further pursuit of this line of reasoning requires, of course, that we accept (as Hotson did unquestioningly) that Wayte's William Shakespeare is the player and not some other of the same name. On the whole, I am inclined to think it was the player, though, like Hotson, I have no supporting evidence to bring forward in that regard.

Hotson was unsuccessful in identifying Dorothy Soer or Anne Lee, the other two parties named in Wayte's writ; they may also be mislocated in Surrey (Hotson searched for them only in Surrey records), or they may be mere contrivances of Wayte's. Wayte's writ of attachment is in fact a curious document, containing as it does four quite ill-matched names, only one of which can be demonstrated from other evidence to have any connection with him. That he might have been genuinely afraid of Langley is quite possible; but I have my doubts about the "fear of death" likely to be engendered by two women, or by a player generally characterized by his friends as "gentle." Shakespeare may have found his way into the writ not because he represented any real danger, but rather because he was associated with Langley. The same may be true of the women; if this should be the case, then Wayte's purpose in swearing out the writ must be understood as essentially vengeful or provocative, and therefore perhaps done at the instance of Justice Gardiner, who would have felt it demeaning to swear out such a writ in his own name.[9]

The hostility between Langley and Gardiner is an interesting phenomenon; we have seen that it provoked a writ on Langley's initiative against Gardiner and Wayte, and another writ in response from Wayte, or perhaps from Gardiner by means of Wayte, against Langley and assorted others. Hotson traced this hostility to the slanderous encounter in Croydon, where Langley called Gardiner a false perjured knave; but such an outburst on Langley's part surely argues a history of nursed grievances rather than a spontaneous flux of invective against a stranger. True, Langley had only a few days earlier learned of Ashley's duplicity in the matter of the diamond, and of Cecil's unfriendly interest in him, and he may have been on edge during his sojourn in Croydon. But there is evidence that the two men had confronted one another even before that time, evidence that Hotson would have found had he pressed his search for Langley further through the records of Queen's Bench.

Some two years before the time of these writs one William Moyerghe brought suit against Francis Langley in that court, claiming that in October 1593 Langley had assaulted him in Southwark "and made an affray and wounded and maltreated him so that he despaired of his life." Moyerghe sought redress at the law through the agency of his attorney John Fell, and upon his plea the sheriff of Surrey was ordered to impanel a jury and hold an inquisition to determine the true extent of the damages. The inquisition was held in

Southwark on February 18, 1595, and appropriate damages were adjudged due to Moyerghe. The outcome must have pleased the sheriff, for he brought the judgment into court himself and insisted on serving personally as Moyerghe's attorney for the remainder of the case, dispossessing John Fell of the office. He represented Moyerghe's interest well and had the pleasure of hearing the court order Langley's arrest, receiving that commission himself in his capacity as sheriff. The sheriff's desire to oppose himself personally to Langley in this suit seems curious until we discover that he was William Gardiner.[10]

I have found no evidence that Gardiner actually arrested Langley on that occasion, but I have no doubt that he did, making his authority felt and increasing their mutual enmity in the process. The subsequent slander in Croydon, the resultant lawsuits, and the associated writs of attachment all cohere to show us two unscrupulous men at odds with one another, one of them having the advantage of civil authority. Gardiner's harassment of Langley might conceivably have extended to his business associates; perhaps it occurred to Gardiner that if the players occupying the Swan were sufficiently troubled they might consider vacating, thereby depriving Langley of income. If it was indeed his plan to vex Hunsdon's players, it may be significant that he chose to begin with Will Shakespeare.

This last is of course predicated on the assumption that the occupants of the Swan in the autumn of 1596 were Hunsdon's players. Among the reasons customarily offered to support the argument that Shakespeare and his fellows were on the Bankside that season, the most common seems to be that the imminent expiration of their ground lease for the Theater had motivated the company to test the theatrical climate on the other side of the Thames, with an eye to determining the feasibility of relocating there when the time came to make a permanent move. This is perfectly reasonable insofar as it clarifies why they might have been—though of course it is not evidence that they were—in the Swan. Since in this, as in so many other matters, we have no hard proof, we may as well try another hypothesis or two. Earlier I attempted to analyze the figures in Henslowe's diary in an effort to determine whether the presence of a company of actors in the Swan in 1595–96 might be ascertained; and my results were inconclusive. We might look at these figures again for the autumn of 1596; for if Hunsdon's men were playing in the Swan—playing *A Midsummer Night's Dream*, perhaps, or *Romeo and Juliet*, or *The Merchant of Venice*, or *Richard II*—they might conceivably have made a greater dent in Henslowe's income than did the unknowns of the year previous.

Henslowe's accounts for the 1596–97 season present us with a new difficulty, however, for in mid-season—near the end of January—Henslowe shifted to a new system of bookkeeping involving five columns of figures, and no one has since been able to explain this system to universal satisfaction. We will need to restrict our analysis, then, to the fifty-seven entries between October 27, 1596, and January 22, 1597, for which the figures are clear and unambiguous. This will do perfectly well, as it happens, for it is only during this period that Hunsdon's men were likely to have been in the Swan and competing for patrons; we know that another group, Pembroke's men, occupied the playhouse beginning in February. And when we look at the figures for those fifty-seven performances of the Admiral's men, it becomes evident that something had happened. Henslowe's total income for the period was just over seventy pounds, or an average income of less than twenty-five shillings per performance. This compares badly with his record over the two previous years. For the first few weeks of the season, a time of year when Henslowe had been accustomed to making nearly two pounds per performance, he earned barely 21^s on the average.

Another indicator may perhaps be found in what I like to call Henslowe's three-pound plays, that is, performances at which his own share of the earnings reached £3 or more. In the 1594–95 season, before the Swan was built, Henslowe enjoyed thirty-three such days. In the following year there were only twenty-one. But in the first half of the 1596–97 season there were only three, and two of those were in the week of Christmas. The holiday fortnight was in fact the only part of the 1596-97 season during which Henslowe's income assumed its old brilliance. In the previous year, during storms and blustery weather, he had earned almost £18 during that period; his earnings now for the same span fell short of this earlier figure by only one pound, even though it was again a time of bad weather. "From London," a Fugger newsletter tells us, "comes news that the rain lasts day and night, and the country is waterlogged. The roads are in such a state that it is impossible to travel by carriage or on horseback." Nothing, however, seems to have stopped the populace of London from visiting the playhouses between Christmas and Twelfth Night.[11]

There is, however, a curious explanation even for the phenomenon of Henslowe's increased holiday revenue. The London citizenry was not alone in enjoying theatrical entertainment at Christmastime; the Queen and her Court had acquired the same tastes. Responsibility for arranging dramatic entertainment at Court in holiday time, as well as for overseeing the licensing and censoring of plays in general, fell to the Lord Chamberlain through his deputy, the Master of the Revels. During the 1590s the latter function, and perhaps the former as well, were probably carried out in their entirety by the Master of the Revels, Edmund Tilney, whose continuity in office must have made for a smoother transition between Hunsdon's and Cobham's tenures as Lord Chamberlain than would otherwise have been the case.

It remains to observe, however, that the entertainments at Court for the Christmas season of 1596–97, the only season of Christmas entertainments arranged during Cobham's tenure as Lord Chamberlain, were unique in that one company and one company only— Lord Hunsdon's—gave all six of the performances. The company belonging to Lord Cobham's colleague the Lord Admiral, which had played at Court every holiday season from the reconstitution of the companies in 1595 until the end of Elizabeth's reign, was not represented at all during this one season. This is a curiosity, and I do not have an explanation for it. There was no antipathy between Cobham and Lord Admiral Howard that I know of; though they were not personally close, they were united in 1596 by their affection for Robert Cecil and their dislike of Essex. It has been customary to look to the internal arrangements of the Admiral's company, as reflected in Henslowe's diary, to find some evidence of disorder that would prevent them from appearing at Court that season; I merely suggest that the explanation may as easily lie elsewhere, perhaps in some undiscovered predilection of Cobham's.

Whatever the cause, the Court calendar for the 1596–97 holiday season had the effect of keeping Hunsdon's players very busy, perhaps too busy to attend to their offerings in the public playhouse with as much care as they would have liked. Concurrently, it left the Admiral's men with nothing to devote their energies to but public performances. The loss of vigorous competition during that fortnight seems to have done wonders for the Admiral's receipts. In the year previous, with Shakespeare's company presumably at the Theater, safely distant and not strongly tempting to the Bankside crowds, no such drastic effects on Henslowe's accounts were observed. It may well be that his comparatively poor showing in the autumn of 1596 was due to the unwelcome proximity of such glamorous competitors, a scant few hundred yards away in the Swan. If so, it was a harbinger of things to come.

X

Pembroke's Men

*What lenten entertainment the players
shall receive from you.*
HAMLET

The popular acclaim that ushered in 1597 for the
Admiral's players was shortlived. Henslowe's third
three-pound play of the holiday season was a revival on
January 7 of the *Spanish Tragedy*. Thereafter his receipts worsened again, averaging only 22^s per performance, until January 24. After that date we lose
track of his exact takings, for at that point he commenced his new system of accounting. Compared to
the old way in which he kept his records, the new
method was quite elaborate. His original system involved simply entering the amount of his receipts
against the name of the play—as in "Rd at Joronymo
xix^s," the entry for January 22 and the last to be written in this fashion. The new method involved five separate columns of figures, the significance of which is
now lost to us. The entry for January 24 reads "Rd at
that wilbe shalbe 00 17 00 . 19 - 07." Various pro-
posals have been put forward in an effort to explain
why Henslowe might have needed a more complex system of bookkeeping at this juncture, all of them pre-
supposing some alteration in the financial relationship
that had existed until that time between him and the
Admiral's players.

Bookkeeping aside, it does seem probable that the company was experiencing some sort of difficulty during January and February. In February an indeterminate number of players, two at the least, took their leave of Alleyn and Henslowe and went to Paris Garden, where they joined with others and took a lease from Francis Langley to play for a year in the Swan. We were not aware of this latter development until 1911, when C. W. Wallace reported his discovery of a lawsuit from the Court of Requests that made clear—in fact, made known—the relationship between Langley and this new group of players. The former tenants of the Swan had already left, perhaps in January, perhaps even before Christmas; the new players later recalled, in pressing their lawsuit, that at the time of their shift to the Swan the playhouse "was then lately afore used to have plays in it"; but they neglected to identify the former occupants.[1]

It would be helpful to know why the earlier group of players had left, especially if they were Hunsdon's men; but we have no information on this score. It would be useful, too, to be able to demonstrate a rise in Henslowe's revenues after the departure of the rival company, but his new system of accounting works against us here, depriving any of our conclusions of the necessary certainty. There have been, of course, various theories proposed for making sense of the new bookkeeping; if we use these theories to guide us as we do our arithmetic, we can arrive at a shaky figure of about 25^s per performance for the remainder of the season. This is pretty consistent with the receipts recorded in the earlier part of the season under the old system. To the extent that it is a reliable figure, of course, it suggests merely that Henslowe was having a bad year all round, and it vitiates any claims to the autumn having been particularly bad because of the company occupying the Swan. We are on pretty thin ice here; with some relief, perhaps, we may return to matters for which there is substantiating evidence.[2]

152

From the lawsuit that Wallace discovered we learn that "about February" a group of players—"Robert Shaa, Richard Jones, Gabriel Spencer, William Bird alias Borne, and Thomas Downton . . . together with others their accomplices and associates," all of them having "of long time used and professed the art of stage playing, being lawfully allowed and authorized thereunto," presented themselves to Francis Langley as "servants to the Right Honorable the Earl of Pembroke." The identification, and the description, are both perplexing. Only a year or two earlier, Jones and Downton had both been Admiral's men, and nothing whatever is known of the other three before 1597, despite their claims of long service in the profession. Further, the last notice we have of a company of Pembroke's players dates from September 1593, at the height of the plague; Henslowe wrote at that time to Edward Alleyn, then on tour, that "my Lord of Pembroke's [players] are all at home and have been this five or six weeks, for they cannot save their charges with travel, as I hear, and were fain to pawn their apparel for their charge." Such evidence of bankruptcy bespeaks a company in the last stages of existence, and modern scholarship has concluded from this entry that the Pembroke's group of which Henslowe wrote did indeed cease functioning in 1593. The corollary of this position is necessarily that the group that called itself Pembroke's players in 1597 was a new company. This may well be true, though we must be on our guard against the implicit assumption that a new company requires a full complement of new personnel. We do not know whether such players as Shaa, Spencer, and Bird belonged to the older Pembroke's, but they may have, and I am inclined to accept their description of themselves as experienced in their craft.[3]

Let us accept, then, that these men were just what they claimed to be, "long time" professional players; "during which time" they also claimed to have been "familiar and acquainted with one Francis Langley,

153

citizen and goldsmith of London." The nature of their familiarity was not expanded upon, but the observation is nevertheless useful; for they might simply have stated, in the conventional formula, that they had entered into an agreement with one Francis Langley, goldsmith, without offering the prefatory observation that they had previously known him. If we place a strict construction upon this gratuitous remark, we might attempt to understand by it that Shaa, Spencer, and Bird were members of the group that had played in the Swan in the 1595–96 season, perhaps the same group to which George Attewell and Francis Henslowe had belonged, and that they were "familiar and acquainted" with Langley by way of a professional relationship. It is also possible, in turn, that Attewell and Francis Henslowe might be among the "accomplices and associates" spoken of in the present document. Indeed, the Earl of Pembroke may have been the patron in both cases. All of this is only conjecture, of course, but if it should happen to be the case, then the "new" company in the Swan in February 1597 might simply be an old company returned, with a few new members.

The plainants explained that "about February" they "fell into conference and communication with the said Langley for and about the hiring and taking a playhouse of the said Langley situate in the old Paris Garden . . . commonly called and known by the name of the sign of the Swan." They found Langley receptive; in fact, they were impressed by "his forwardness that your said subjects should take the same." Langley's own recollection was that "Shaa and the rest" were rather "earnest suitors unto the defendant to have the defendant's house for to play in." Both these observations are likely to be true, for the two parties needed one another. The plainants went so far as to suggest "that the said house of the defendant might have long continued without gains if they, the said complainants, had not upon request of the defendant exercised their playing therein."

The financial arrangements between them with respect to the leasing of the playhouse were presumably the conventional ones. The takings for general admission at the entry door or doors would go to the players; the additional takings at the galleries would be divided, half to go to the players and half to Langley. For any extraordinary expense on Langley's part, such as the purchasing of costumes, the players would reimburse him out of their half of the gallery takings; "the defendant should be allowed for the true value thereof out of the complainants' moiety of the gains for the several standings in the galleries of the said house which belonged to them."

But in addition to these conventional arrangements, Langley required of Pembroke's players a new form of contractual agreement. He required, as the plainants were shocked to discover, "that your said subjects would become bound to him, the said Langley, in some great penalty with condition that they should not absent themselves nor play elsewhere but in the said playhouse called the Swan." There was of course nothing new in the use of bonds as guarantees for the fulfillment of contractual obligations. They were a necessary adjunct to the borrowing of money, as we have seen. Merchants used them as protection against defaulted agreements, and the state used them as a means of securing the peace. Langley himself had to sign a bond with the City Chamberlain in 1586 for his good performance as alnager. But no one, apparently, had ever thought before to require bonds of players as a condition for the letting of a playhouse.

Pembroke's men had no choice, however; they needed a house to play in. They all (presumably there were eight of them) gave Langley "obligations in one hundred pounds apiece," each man thereby affirming that he would "play in the said playhouse . . . called the Swan without absenting himself at any time from the company when they should so play there" for one year, or until the "twentieth day of February now next

ensuing." Provision was made for replacement: if a
man had unavoidably to leave the group, he might "in
his place and stead bring in or procure a sufficient person" to take over his duties "until the said twentieth
day of February." If these conditions were satisfied,
the bond was to be void; otherwise, it would stand in
full force, and Langley would move to collect the penalty sum.

It was no doubt only a matter of time before someone
thought to require bonds of players. Once begun, the
practice may have become common. Later in the same
year we find Philip Henslowe requiring bonds of certain of Pembroke's men when they sought once again to
play at the Rose. Henslowe may have gotten the idea
from Langley, as Bernard Beckerman suggests. At
first, indeed, he may have used the bonds punitively
against the Pembroke returnees, to ensure the contin-
uance of men not otherwise noted for their length of
service in one place; but later he began requiring them
of other players as well. It is possible that Langley, too,
required bonds of the Pembroke players in February
1597 for punitive reasons; if they were the same
players who had been in the Swan in 1595–96, and if
they had left him unexpectedly after that first year—
so that he had to cast about for tenants in the autumn
—then the bonds might have been Langley's way of securing their uninterrupted presence once they decided
to return. Langley, after all, needed stable tenants in
the Swan if he was to hold his own against Henslowe
and the Rose; a series of transients simply would not
do.[4]

As the expiration date on the bonds was February
20, 1598, we may assume that Pembroke's men began
playing at the Swan shortly after February 20, 1597.
February 20 fell on a Sunday in 1597; Ash Wednesday
had been on February 9, and Lent was therefore already some ten days under way. The Admiral's men
had stopped playing on February 12, but apparently
not in observance of Lent, for they began again on

March 3 and played thereafter erratically but steadily into the summer, pausing only for the last few days of Holy Week. We may perhaps assume that Pembroke's men also continued to play through this period.

The irregular schedule of performances of the Admiral's men for the three weeks or so after March 3, coupled with their failure to play at all for the three weeks prior to that date, led Wallace to assume that the loss of personnel to the Pembroke group had "caused a temporary interruption of the performances of the Admiral's company at the Rose, until the places of the withdrawing players could be supplied." To support this perfectly reasonable inference, Wallace chose to presume that Jones, Downton, Shaa, Spencer, and Bird had all been Admiral's men before leaving for the Swan. We know nothing about the latter three before the dates mentioned in this lawsuit, and therefore Wallace may well be right, though clear prior connection with Henslowe exists only for Jones and Downton. The withdrawal of so many men (Wallace supposes even more, naming Humphrey and Antony Jeffes as fellow travelers to Paris Garden) would surely have a crippling effect on any company's ability to maintain regular performances; if Wallace is right, then one must marvel at Alleyn's ability to keep going at all in the face of seven departures.[5]

But if the Admiral's men were so delayed in getting back to normal operations, what difficulties must the Pembroke's group have faced in getting their own season under way? I have assumed as an article of faith that no group of experienced players would associate themselves into a company and engage themselves financially to rent a playhouse if they had no playbooks, or insufficient playbooks, to enable them to commence rehearsal and performance with minimal delay. If the Pembroke group were all former Admiral's players, they would of course carry many plays with them in their heads, which they might easily reconstruct for their own use. But it would seem to be sheer folly for

157

Pembroke's men to attempt to compete with the Admiral's players at the Rose by offering the Admiral's own repertory warmed over again at the Swan. There are many legal and moral reasons, aside from the sheer impracticality of such a move, which make this proposed solution impossible of serious consideration.

Two possibilities remain: that the new Pembroke's group owned no playbooks, or insufficient playbooks, and proceeded to purchase a repertory of new plays as rapidly as possible; or that the nucleus of Pembroke's players was a pre-existent group—already distinct from the Admiral's men—with some old playbooks of its own, already licensed, and ready for rehearsal. I find the latter possibility the more reasonable, biased as I am in favor of assuming that professional players would be sensible and cautious in such matters rather than impetuous and pound-foolish. But my favored solution requires a continuing group of players from elsewhere, and a consequent reduction in the number of deserters from the Admiral's company proposed by Wallace. I would prefer to suggest that the bulk of the new Pembroke group came from an older group, perhaps an older Pembroke group, with only Jones and Downton certainly from the Admiral's players. Their readiness to begin playing, which I take to be a necessity, is thus accounted for; but Wallace's handy explanation of Henslowe's troubles is thereby made less convincing, for if only two players departed from the Admiral's group, as I suggest, then Alleyn's three weeks of closure and three weeks of unpreparedness seem too drastic a result. Perhaps, despite Wallace's confident conclusion that the departures explain everything, the Admiral's troupe was having more problems in February 1597 than those caused by two defectors. There may indeed be more to Henslowe's shift of bookkeeping procedures than we have yet been able to learn.[6]

Wallace claimed that the Pembroke group "began acting at the Swan Feb. 21, 1597," which may or may not be true; but they must have begun playing fairly soon after the signing of the bonds, for the plainants in their lawsuit insisted that Langley, between the commencement of playing and the end of July following, "hath gained at least a hundred pounds and more" as his share of the takings. Henslowe's receipts from the same period (as calculated from the new bookkeeping system, it must be remembered) came to perhaps £130 or £140, an increase over Langley's reputed earnings which is only to be expected, given the talent and resources of each group. But Pembroke's players would have had to play a fairly full season in order for Langley to realize even the £100 that they claimed for him; the corollary of a short season is a high average income per performance, an unlikely eventuality unless all of our assumptions about Alleyn's popularity are in error.[7]

On the fifth of March, midway between Ash Wednesday and Easter Sunday, just as the Lord Admiral's players were beginning to play again, the Lord Chamberlain, Lord Cobham, died. His death occasioned no civic observance, playing was not suspended, and the Privy Council continued its daily deliberations without any memorial hiatus. Cobham had served in the office of Lord Chamberlain for seven months, neither distinguishing nor discrediting himself. But he was elderly, and not well. After the death of his daughter, near the end of January, he had stopped coming to Privy Council meetings; then he himself sickened and died. These two deaths, within six weeks of one another, deprived Sir Robert Cecil first of a wife and then of a father-in-law. The former loss precluded Cecil's own attendance at Council through February, though he did not miss a single day in respect of the latter. This is not to be misconstrued: it speaks more of Cecil's sharpened sense of duty after an extended absence than of any lack of grief. He and Cobham had been of like minds in many ways. But with Cobham's death a number of offices fell vacant, and there would have been an importunate clamor for them that would not permit the luxury of a discreet interval of mourning. Among those posts was that of Lord Chamberlain, and for that particular vacancy the Queen turned to her cousin George Carey, Lord Hunsdon, appointing him on March 17 to the post once held by his father.[8]

Thomas Nashe had lamented, after the death in July 1596 of George Carey's father, the old Lord Hunsdon, that "in their old Lord's time" the players in London had "thought their state settled," but that under Cobham's control it had become "so uncertain they cannot build upon it." Whether the restoration of a Hunsdon to the office of Lord Chamberlain brought any immediate and tangible succor to the players is not certain, and indeed not likely; but it probably engendered a sense of expectancy, a feeling of optimism about the more secure and perhaps even more prosperous times that might now lie ahead. Good feeling, in fact, seems to have been the order of the day: it was generally understood that during the last month of Cobham's final illness even Robert Cecil and the Earl of Essex had become reconciled, largely through the good offices of Sir Walter Ralegh, and that a new period of tranquillity had subsequently commenced at the Court. Such a development, if true, could only conduce to a general feeling of satisfaction in the whole City, which the players, as mirrors of their time, might well reflect.

And in truth there had been some sort of an accord between Robert Cecil and the Earl of Essex, though only superficially of Ralegh's doing. The truce was impelled by a variety of considerations on both sides. During Lady Cecil's final illness Essex had confined himself to his house because of an alleged illness of his own, which may have been no more than fatigue mingled with pique, and he remained away from Court during the period of Robert Cecil's bereavement. But the two men began to communicate with one another at that time, perhaps using the occasion of Lady Cecil's death as a pretext for opening communications under the guise of commiseration. But neither of these exotic leopards had changed his spots. Cobham's death brought Essex promptly back to Court, for the Wardenship of the Cinque Ports had thereby fallen vacant; Essex immediately chose to make a trial of his influence, and a test of Cecil's amity, by backing Sir Robert Sidney for the post. Cecil was not impressed by the nomination, and neither was the Queen. Various other persons were suing for the Wardenship, including Henry Brooke, Cobham's son, but Essex disliked the young man even more than he had disliked the father, and Brooke reciprocated the scorn. The Queen was not slow to put Essex in his place, however, by bestowing the office on Brooke, the new Lord Cobham: Essex had moved Sidney's candidacy on March 7; on March 9 the Queen told Essex that the post was to be Cobham's. When Essex left the Court in anger the Queen mollified him by appointing him Master of the Ordnance, a post he had coveted. Cecil concurred in this latter appointment, for reasons of his own.[9]

Some dispute then arose over the matter of a new Lord Chamberlain, but Essex seems to have acquiesced in the Queen's choice of her cousin George Carey, Lord Hunsdon. The post of Vice-Chamberlain, which had been vacant since the death of Sir Thomas Heneage on October 17, 1595, became the next issue, with Essex once again backing Sir Robert Sidney and boldly declaring himself an enemy to any other man who might seek the office. In this case the Queen responded by doing nothing, and the office continued vacant until 1601. *Plus ça change,* Robert Cecil might have mused as he contemplated the new amity between himself and Essex. The concord had broken down at its first test, but in outward form it continued unabated. Essex and Cecil became warm correspondents, each of them finding an advantage in perpetuating the image of solidarity, though the struggle for power continued. The new Lord Chamberlain could not avoid involvement, but he managed to remain above factionalism. His sympathies, however, were not with the Earl of Essex.

One immediately visible result of Hunsdon's appointment to his new office was that his players could now once again call themselves the Lord Chamberlain's players. The two major companies in London were now both under the patronage of Privy Councillors—men who were brothers-in-law, in fact—and both groups of players were thus persuaded that they should have a fair and sympathetic representation in the Council if they should ever have the misfortune to become a topic of conversation there. As a corollary to this assurance, the Admiral's and Chamberlain's players may have felt more heavily the need for decorum in their daily conduct and in their performances. If there was a general exhilaration in the air it must have been tempered by sobriety. Cobham was too recent a memory, and though St. George may have arrived at last, all the dragons were still at large. The Lord Mayor and aldermen were not about to become quiescent, nor would the moralists cease their efforts. Indeed, with Cobham gone, additional vigor would be called for from these vigilants.

Unexpected opposition might come from other quarters as well; it has been argued, for example, that the Cobham family forced certain adjustments in the text of *The Merry Wives of Windsor*. This play, with its trenchant topical satire, may indeed represent the threshold of acceptable impertinence in 1597, beyond which the Chamberlain's players chose not to venture. But other groups of actors, not so fortunately placed in their patrons nor so conscious of the need for restraint, might from time to time cross this threshold and engage in portrayals a bit too scurrilous for conservative judgment to ignore. The image of the Queen's Council as bathed in a new euphoria was a dangerous one, and such players courted disaster by their assumption of laxity, for their patrons had no voice in the inner circles of government, and the increasing sense that there were simply too many groups of actors in London would assuredly find its easiest outlet in the suppression of all troupes except those sponsored by the Lord

Admiral or the Lord Chamberlain. The players in the Swan comprised such a troupe; one might almost expect that they would misread the signs and sooner or later find themselves in trouble.[10]

But in the spring of 1597, as in the spring of 1596, the Privy Council was occupied with matters of greater import to the realm than the danger of scurrility on the public stage. Preparations were once more in hand for an expedition against Spain. The assault on Cadiz in the previous summer had moved King Philip to anger, and in the late autumn of 1596 he had dispatched a fleet to Ireland to make contact with the rebellious Earl of Tyrone and to foment discord. A December storm scattered this fleet and sank forty ships, reducing the expedition to impotence. But during the winter the Privy Council received intelligence that troops and supplies were being assembled at the port of Ferrol, near Corunna, and a new attack in the summer was deemed likely.

To forestall such an undertaking, a fleet of English ships was ordered assembled at Plymouth, and by the time of Cobham's death the preliminary preparations were well in hand for the expedition. Essex of course became involved in the planning on his return to Court in March; he was the popular hero of Cadiz, "Great England's glory and the world's wide wonder, / Whose dreadful name, late through all Spain did thunder, / And Hercules' two pillars standing near, / Did make to quake and fear," as Edmund Spenser chose to describe him late in 1596. There was no doubt in anyone's mind that Essex would participate in the new venture. His recent appointment as Master of the Ordnance gave him further responsibilities, and on May 22 he was delighted to learn that he was to be in sole command of the expedition—for the first time in his career—with Lord Thomas Howard de Walden as vice admiral and Sir Walter Ralegh as rear admiral. Letters were sent to the Lords Lieutenant of the several counties and to the Commissioners for the Musters for the levying of troops; the City of London was ordered to furnish five hundred soldiers from "the City and other parts near unto it," and later to furnish as well "six sufficient drummers" for the captains of the three London companies.[11]

Armor and horses were to be furnished by persons of means, according to a schedule worked out by Parliament in 1557. Francis Langley was thus required to furnish "one pair of almain rivets, or one coat of plate, or one pair of brigandines, two long bows, two sheafs of arrows, two skulls or steel caps, and one black bill or halberd." No record survives of his compliance with this order. One may presume that such equipment was not part of the regular household furnishings of the Lord of the Manor of Paris Garden, and that Langley's compliance would have required the purchasing of such items. In May and June 1597 Langley borrowed money on four separate occasions from Robert Shaa, one of Pembroke's players, perhaps in connection with these purchases. The loans were properly secured by bonds drawn up at St. Mary le Bow, for £20 on May 1, £10 more on May 21, £10 more on June 1, and a final £30 on June 21. According to Shaa, Langley paid back £54 of this amount, but refused to pay back the remaining £16. Shaa eventually sued Langley for debt in the Court of Common Pleas.[12]

By June 15 Essex's orders and commission had been signed, and the assembled fleet was ready to set sail. But bad weather, and a persistent strong wind from the west, made it impossible for the ships to get beyond Plymouth harbor, though they tried without success on June 25 and again on succeeding days. Each subsequent attempt to put to sea was met with failure or disaster, as violent storms and tempests beat back every English effort. The frustrations were interminable. For seven demoralizing weeks the fleet was unable to depart, and did not make its way finally into the open sea until August 14. Needless to say, the Privy Council was concerned that its advantage was slipping away, and the month of July was spent in strengthening the army in Ireland and securing additional revenues for the increasing cost of maintaining the fleet, as victuals were being consumed and wages falling due despite the immobility of the expedition.

The raising of revenue was, as usual, fraught with complications. Early in July the Lord Mayor responded to the Council's request by complaining that many Londoners, though they "have dwelling houses and remain in the said houses the most part of the year," nevertheless "do refuse to contribute to those public charges which are imposed on the citizens for the setting forth of soldiers and other public services," using as their argument "that they have habitations or are assessed in the Subsidy in other counties of the realm." The result of such conduct, the Lord Mayor explained, was that "the burden doth light more heavily on the rest of the citizens." [13]

The Council responded by setting guidelines to reinforce the Lord Mayor's authority, and then reprimanded him for his slackness in mustering, claiming that he had taken up "in all this time" only fourscore persons, "most part of them being base people and without apparel, and that you conceive our meaning to be that you should be at no charge to apparel them." The Council informed the Lord Mayor that while military armor would be provided from other sources, the City ought to consider it "a very unmeet thing to send men over to serve in the wars in such naked sort . . . seeing they are to be sent over into a foreign country, both in regard of the men and the honor of the realm." The Lord Mayor was directed to "furnish a greater number." [14]

The Lord Mayor—Henry Billingsley, haberdasher—seems not to have exerted himself unduly, for by the middle of July he had impressed only twenty more men. The Council wrote him again on July 18, angered that he had mustered "a certain number only of 100 men," and further angered at the Lord Mayor's tactic of publicly announcing the muster. This move, perhaps intended to inspirit the young men of the City, had served only "to drive them out of the City into the counties adjoining." The requisite number of men was still to be furnished, "which number we doubt not but may easily be found within the liberties." The Council cautioned that further reprimands would be in store "for your default herein." [15]

XI

The Isle of Dogs

Their faults are open; arrest them
to the answer of the law.
HENRY V

So July came to an end, with little amity between the
Lord Mayor and aldermen in the City and the Lords of
the Council at Westminster. Historians of the theatre,
however, are accustomed to thinking of the end of July
1597 as one of those times when the City and the
Council acted with rare unanimity in an effort to
suppress stage plays. In support of this notion, the theatre historian will argue that at the end of July the
players in the Swan, by staging a scurrilous play called
the *Isle of Dogs*, brought down upon themselves the
wrath of both City and Council, and that a Council
order for the cessation of playing and the pulling down
of playhouses was the direct and immediate result of
this affront. As a reading of the published evidence,
this proposal is not without its merits, but a more careful look at a wider range of evidence—my intention in
the following pages—will suggest other readings. We
might begin with the musters, and note that the City
and the Court were both preoccupied in July 1597
with matters of some moment, though the City was
less involved than the Court and therefore able to dis-
engage itself far earlier. The City, indeed, hastened to
dispatch its work by the end of July so that all but the

most routine sort of activity could be suspended during the month of August. There had been little or no threat of plague during the summer, and most of the aldermen must have felt they had earned a vacation. Her Majesty's forces, under Essex, were still battling high winds off Plymouth; but in London, life settled slowly into the doldrums. The Town Clerk hastened to draft his final batch of official correspondence so that he, too, might enjoy a respite. He was apparently successful, for the *Remembrancia* contains no letters sent out by the City during the month of August. The docket was apparently cleared by the letters sent out in July.

One of the last letters to be so dispatched was sent on July 28; it was signed by the Lord Mayor and addressed to the Privy Council. The letter was on a matter of routine business, the annual reiteration of the City's plea that plays and playhouses be suppressed. As all the public playhouses lay outside the jurisdiction of Guildhall, it was only proper that such an appeal be addressed to the Council. The letter, like its predecessors in former years, asked that the Council empower the Justices of the Peace of Middlesex and Surrey to close down all such playing places. The Lord Mayor, Henry Billingsley, approved the letter, and it was no doubt forwarded in due course to the Privy Council, which was then sitting not at Westminster but several miles distant at Greenwich. If the letter was posted from Guildhall in the morning, it might have reached the Council that afternoon; otherwise it would have arrived the next day. Either way, it is unlikely to have arrived in time to form part of the agenda of the Council's own meeting on the 28th. There is no reason to presume any undue haste in the delivery of the letter, as it contained no urgent matter. But the letter has been part of a continuing controversy among historians of the English stage, and has in recent years assumed an importance utterly out of keeping with its contents.

The letter was straightforward. "We have signified

to your Honors many times heretofore the great inconvenience which we find to grow by the common exercise of stage plays," it began. The traditional arguments were then rehearsed: plays contain "nothing but profane fables, lascivious matters, cozening devices, and scurrilous behaviours;" they give opportunity "to the refuse sort of evil-disposed and ungodly people, that are within and about this City, to assemble themselves and to make their matches for all their lewd and ungodly practices;" in particular, certain wayward apprentices upon examination "have confessed unto us that the said stage plays were the very places of their rendezvous" with subversives who would incite them to "designs and mutinous attempts." For these and other reasons, all of them general and none particularly topical or immediate, the City found itself constrained once again (so the letter concludes) to ask the Lords of the Council to prohibit stage plays in the public playhouses.[1]

Such an appeal from the City was not unusual. In 1594 John Spencer, then Lord Mayor, had asked Burghley for help in "the stay and suppressing" of plays in the same letter in which he complained of Langley's intended new playhouse. In 1595, on the thirteenth of September, the Lord Mayor, Stephen Slaney, sent a letter to the Lords of the Council, noting in the traditional formula that "we have been bold heretofore to signify to your Honors" the traditional complaints, and asking them "to direct your letters to the Justices of Peace of Surrey and Middlesex for the present stay and final suppressing of the said plays, as well at the Theater and Bankside as in all other places about the City." The letter of July 28, 1597, in the same vein, asked them "to direct your letters as well to ourselves as to the Justices of Peace of Surrey and Middlesex for the present stay and final suppressing of the said stage plays, as well at the Theater, Curtain, and Bankside, as in all other places in and about the City."

169

The similarity of phrasing in the last two extracts, and in the two opening statements, is not mere coincidence; in fact, the extent to which the entire letter of July 28, 1597, is merely a redrafting of the letter of September 13, 1595, will be evident to anyone wishing to compare them. I presume that a similar letter was sent in 1596 as well, though it has not apparently survived. In the passage just cited, the only notable difference lies in the City's desire in 1597 to have itself included in the list of addressees; where in 1595 the Lord Mayor was concerned about playing in "places about the City," in 1597 he was concerned about playing in "places in and about the City." But playing within the City had always fallen under the purview of the Lord Mayor and Court of Aldermen; a request for authorization from the Privy Council to enable the Lord Mayor to take action within his own jurisdiction —which he had every right to do even without their authorization—argues that the Lord Mayor's authority had not proven entirely effective by itself in the previous year in suppressing playing within the City. It does not suggest, I am persuaded, that the Lord Mayor wished to encroach upon the jurisdictions of the Justices of Middlesex or Surrey by taking upon himself any responsibility for the public playhouses beyond his own jurisdiction. This position has been recently argued, but I find it untenable.

Nor do the circumstances surrounding the dispatch of the letter from the Court of Aldermen to the Privy Council provide support for such a position. Rather they make clear, I believe, that what the Lord Mayor and aldermen wanted for themselves—apart from having directives sent to the Justices—was a formal statement from the Council that would authorize them to take such action, within the City, as they might at some future date deem necessary. That they had no immediate application in mind is evident from their working schedule; though the aldermen had maintained their twice-weekly (Tuesdays and Thursdays) meetings throughout June and July, and had scheduled additional meetings in those months as the need arose, there was no business transacted at the meeting of July 28 except the swearing-in of Roger Clarke as the new alderman for Bridge ward (the vacancy in the Court having been caused by the death of Sir Rowland Hayward), and the posting of the aforementioned letter. The letter had been neither discussed nor debated in any of the meetings held in June or July. Its dispatch on the 28th was probably just an ordinary part of the ritual of the Town Clerk's office. Thereafter the Court of Aldermen did not meet again until the thirtieth of August. There can hardly have been anything urgent in the letter, given the long suspension of aldermanic activity that it heralded.

The Privy Council, meanwhile, was holding its own meeting on July 28. The troublesome matter of the fleet, battered once again in its efforts to get out to the open sea, had been its central topic of discussion all week. But even these deliberations had been interrupted by the arrival of an ambassador from Poland, a most undiplomatic visitor whose effrontery toward the Queen compelled the Council's immediate attention. At his first audience this ambassador had startled the assembled lords in the Presence Chamber by his presumption in boldly addressing a long speech to the Queen in—inappropriately—Latin. The Queen, to the delight of all present, responded vigorously and angrily to his ostentation with an extempore Latin speech of her own, which occasioned considerable comment in the surviving records. Sir Robert Cecil thought it one of the best extempore Latin speeches he had ever heard. Essex, still aboard the *Bonaventure* struggling to get out of Plymouth, found time to write Cecil in praise of the Queen's triumph over "that braving Polart."[2]

The ambassador had of course misjudged, and he was immediately out of favor as a result of his impudence; the Council informed all parties having inter-

course with him that they "forbear all offices of ceremony toward him, as of visitation, sending presents or
whatsoever else of like gratification." There may, however, have been some ceremonial function scheduled
for the afternoon of the 28th, for the Privy Council,
like the Court of Aldermen, recorded very little business at its own meeting on that date. One William Col-
son, who had arrived from Bristol, was ordered to attend on the Council until released; and the Council's
clerks were instructed to send a letter to the Justices of
Middlesex, and another to the Justices of Surrey, ordering that stage plays be prohibited and that playhouses be dismantled—"plucked down," as the Lords
phrased it. No letter was to be sent to the Lord Mayor.

The Privy Council minutes for this meeting are
characteristically terse; there is no suggestion that the
order to suspend playing is the result of any communication from the Lord Mayor. It was, in fact, customary
for the Privy Council to suspend playing in and about
the City during the hot summer months, for a variety
of reasons. In the previous year, 1596, they had issued
a similar order on July 22. It is an odd coincidence that
in 1597 the order from the Privy Council and the letter
from the Lord Mayor should bear the same date; such a
coincidence does not, however, prove any causal relationship, for letters from the Lord Mayor and orders
from the Privy Council were the conventional expecta-
tions of summer; in some years one came first, in other
years the other. To presume that the Council would respond swiftly, with a carefully worked-out order, at a
time when it was otherwise occupied, to a request that
it had just received, is to ask too much of the evidence.
We must note in passing that the one new request in
the Lord Mayor's letter—that the City itself be the recipient of an order—is nowhere acceded to in the minutes of the Council. To me, the evidence points clearly
to an independent initiative from each party, occurring coincidentally on the same date.[3]

Indeed, the Privy Council minute of July 28, like the

172

letter from the Lord Mayor, stressed only the traditional arguments in support of an inhibition, nowhere alluding to any immediate cause or concern. The Lords merely noted "that there are very great disorders committed in the common playhouses, both by lewd matters that are handled on the stages and by resort and confluence of bad people." Some two or three months earlier the Privy Council had learned of the intention of the citizens of Hadley, Suffolk, "to make certain stage plays" in celebration of Whitsuntide, "and thither to draw a concourse of people out of the country thereabouts, pretending herein the benefit of the Town; which purpose we do utterly mislike, doubting what inconveniences may follow thereon, especially at this time of scarcity when disordered people of the common sort will be apt to misdemean themselves." The town was prohibited from having the plays and was ordered to "cause the stage prepared for them to be plucked down." One cannot help noting the similarity of argument, and even of phrasing, between this order and the other. In both cases the Privy Council felt the danger to be great "especially at this time" and that it would presumably lessen with the onset of autumn; the order of July 28 specified only that "there be no more plays used in any public place within three miles of the City until Allhallowtide next."

The Admiral's men were playing at the Rose at the time of the inhibition, and Henslowe's record of their receipts stops after July 28; this fact has been adduced as evidence that playing did indeed terminate on that date. But Henslowe's receipts for July 1597 show the Admiral's men playing erratically; performances were recorded with fair regularity until the nineteenth of the month, and then a hiatus with no receipts recorded until the twenty-seventh; after the twenty-eighth no receipts were recorded until October 11, when the Admiral's men and some of Pembroke's men from the Swan began playing together at the Rose. Henslowe's failure to record receipts after July 28 may, therefore, be of dubious value as an indicator of his instant compliance with orders that had only that day been posted to their recipients, the Justices. In the ten days previous, Henslowe had recorded only three playing days, and it may well be that no performances were planned for the twenty-ninth or thirtieth (a Friday and Saturday) in any event. On July 31, a Sunday, there would of course be no performance, and by August 1 presumably the inhibition would have been generally proclaimed and in effect.

This point may perhaps be substantiated by considering the corresponding events in the previous summer. The Privy Council order for suspension of playing in 1596 was issued on July 22. If we look at Henslowe's account book for that period, we find that the final entry before the cessation of playing was a performance of "The Tinker of Totnes," recorded as on the eighteenth. But this is one of those sections in the diary where, as W. W. Greg has pointed out, Henslowe got his dates mixed up. The dates that Henslowe wrote after July 7 and July 8 in his accounts are July 4 and July 5 instead of July 9 and July 10—Henslowe may have misread his 8 as a 3, or his 9 as a 4—and from that point on, according to Greg (and here he must be right), Henslowe's dates are five days out. If we make the adjustment called for, we find that "The Tinker of Totnes" was played not on July 18 but on July 23, the day after the Privy Council order. The confusion about the dates makes this instance less persuasive than it might otherwise be; but as neither Henslowe's original date nor Greg's emendation correspond to the date of the Council's order, the point may perhaps stand.[4]

So playing need not have stopped on the date of the Privy Council order in 1597. But let us, for the sake of argument, assume that it did; that the letters to the Surrey and Middlesex Justices, which were drafted on July 28, were promptly copied over and dispatched; that the Justices received them immediately; and that the Justices for Surrey were able to notify both Henslowe and Langley by that very afternoon or evening. Henslowe, being the more conscientious of the two, would be likely to communicate such an order directly to his son-in-law Ned Alleyn, who lived very near, and thence to his fellows. A performance scheduled for the next day might well have been canceled in this manner, and due public notice of cancellation provided; for we know that the Admiral's men did not play on the twenty-ninth. Langley, by contrast, had less contact with Pembroke's players than Henslowe had with Alleyn and the Admiral's men; they were neither his neighbors nor his friends. He may have tried to reach them and failed; he may simply have been negligent and put it off; or he may himself have been unreachable on that date. (The order instructed the Justices to "send for the owners" of the playhouses in question, not to notify the lessees.) Justice William Gardiner may well have been the man designated to notify Langley, and as there was no love lost between these two men it may be that the Justice was at no great pains to locate the recipient. We have, in other words, no clear evidence for declaring that playing stopped at the Swan on the twenty-eighth, or even on the twenty-ninth.

But some of Pembroke's men—Richard Jones and Thomas Downton, to name two—had formerly been Alleyn's fellows at the Rose, and they still lived near the Bankside along with their new colleagues Robert Shaa, William Borne, and some others. If these men were still on sociable terms with the Admiral's players whom they had deserted in the previous winter, they might have gotten word of the inhibition in that manner despite a possible failure on Langley's part to communicate with them. On the whole, I think it probable that playing did stop before the hour of performance on July 29, by one means or another, though I repeat that there is no evidence to rule out a performance at the Swan on that day. One may be conjectural here, but not dogmatic.

I stress this point because the traditional explanation for the closing of the playhouses in July 1597 has remained unchallenged for so long that it has, like most uncontested theories, become an article of faith among writers on the stage history of the period. As a result, few modern accounts suggest that there is any difficulty in explaining the event. One would be hard pressed to find any recent work on the subject that did not tell us, as E. K. Chambers did in 1923, that the "inhibition of plays near London on 28 July 1597 [was] caused by the production of *The Isle of Dogs*" by Pembroke's players at the Swan. This argument was not new with Chambers; but he accepted it without question, and there has been little effort in the intervening years to retreat from it, even though we know nothing about the play in question or the circumstances of its production. We often sound, however, as though we know something. A recent and reputable reference book tells us unblinkingly that the *Isle of Dogs* "contained such explosive political satire that its performance at the Swan by Pembroke's Men on July 28, 1597 resulted in the closing of all the London theatres." An even more recent study assures us that the *Isle of Dogs* brought about the closing order "by criticizing the government," and by "its rowdy reception in the auditorium," which "embarrassed both the Queen and her Council." One hesitates to swim upstream against such a full tide of received opinion, but I believe it might be time for all of us to take a fresh look at the evidence.[5]

We may dismiss at the outset three pieces of evidence that are spurious. John Payne Collier, more than a hundred years ago, was so anxious to demonstrate a connection between the *Isle of Dogs* and the suspension of playing that in his edition of Henslowe's *Diary*, published in 1845, he boldly offered as genuine three passages bearing on the topic which all subsequent editors of the diary have rejected as nineteenth-century forgeries. The first two of these passages read as follows:

Lent the 14 May 1597 to Juby, upon a note from Nashe, twenty shillings more for the Isle of Dogs which he is writing for the company.

Pd this 23 of August 1597, to Harry Porter, to carry to T. Nashe, now at this time in the Fleet, for writing of the Isle of Dogs, ten shillings, to be paid again to me when he can.

Collier had presumed, of course, that the *Isle of Dogs* was played by the Admiral's men at the Rose, a common enough assumption in his day; an assumption not overturned, in fact, until 1911, when C. W. Wallace published his newly discovered lawsuit between Langley and five of Pembroke's players. Prior to that time everyone, even Wallace himself, had accepted Collier's "evidence," not only the foregoing entries but this one as well:

Pd unto Mr Blunsones, the Master of the Revels' man, this 27 of August 1597, ten shillings, for news of the restraint being recalled by the lords of the Queen's Council.

To ensure that this entry would be properly interpreted, Collier attached to it an explanatory note: "The restraint upon the company, in consequence of the offensive performance of Nash's *Isle of Dogs*, had by this date been recalled, and Henslowe paid Blunson ten shillings for bringing the welcome news." Surely a touching moment in Henslowe's life, as conceived by Collier; but quite unrelated to the truth.[6]

This is not to suggest that there is no authentic mention of the *Isle of Dogs* in Henslowe's diary; there is one, but only one. The play did indeed exist, though it is now quite lost. On the tenth of August, less than a fortnight after the inhibition was proclaimed, Henslowe accepted a bond from William Borne, one of Pembroke's players from the Swan, "to play with my Lord Admiral's men at my house aforesaid, and not in any other house public about London, for the space of three years, beginning immediately after this restraint is recalled by the Lords of the Council, which restraint is by the means of playing the Isle of Dogs." Four days earlier, on August 6, Henslowe had similarly bound Thomas Downton and Richard Jones, two other of Pembroke's players. The terms are similar, but there is no mention of a play called "the Isle of Dogs" in the entries concerning Downton and Jones. I interpret these two sets of entries to mean that at some point between August 6 and August 10 Henslowe perceived a connection between the inhibition and the performance of the *Isle of Dogs* at the Swan. For his perception to make sense, one must assume that the *Isle of Dogs* was performed a reasonable time before the word of the inhibition reached the Bankside.[7]

It need not tax our ingenuity to determine what event, between August 6 and 10, brought forth Henslowe's observation. It must surely have been Richard Topcliffe's characteristically flamboyant arrest of Gabriel Spencer, Robert Shaa, and Ben Jonson for having participated in the production. Topcliffe was never one to minimize his own importance to the security of the realm, and it may have pleasured him to encourage the view that his present business and the inhibition were of a piece, perhaps even that both were the result of his own conscientious activities. It is curious that he did not also arrest Borne, Jones and Downton; they were surely as accessible as the three men who were taken. Nor is there any evidence that Topcliffe intended to arrest the entire company. His purposes may have been adequately served by a few token arrests, to make clear that something was amiss and to strike terror into collaborative hearts. Topcliffe was in his sixties, a veteran hunter of heretics and traitors, a master of the arts of torture; his very name was a byword in Elizabethan London. He knew the value of a theatrical gesture; the arrest of Spencer, Shaa, and Jonson would be sufficient.

It was certainly sufficient for Thomas Nashe, who was utterly convinced by the demonstration. Nashe had been one of the writers of the play, and he learned, perhaps concurrently with the news of the arrests, that his room had been searched and some papers taken. He fled at once, secluding himself in Yarmouth and turning his mind to other matters. In *Nash's Lenten Stuff*, written in praise of red herrings, and printed in 1599, he nevertheless found time to muse on the "strange turning of the Isle of Dogs, from a comedy to a tragedy two summers past," and called the play an "unfortunate imperfect embryon" of his idle hours: "An imperfect embryon I may well call it, for I, having begun but the induction and first act of it, the other four acts without my consent, or the least guess of my drift or scope, by the players were supplied, which bred both their trouble and mine too."[8]

Nashe surely felt that whatever might be seditious in the play was none of his doing, and he must have been right. He was no neophyte writer, and he understood the need for decorum and the limits of scurrility. He had known Marlowe, and understood what had happened to him. Ben Jonson, who had also written a part of the play, no doubt maintained the same position, and was probably right as well, if our understanding of his other works may serve as testimony in his behalf. Nor is it reasonable to presume that the players were so unaware of the constraints upon their profession that they would undertake to present such a play. We know enough about Edmund Tilney's conduct as Master of the Revels to be certain that he would not license a play full of "very seditious and slanderous matter"—which is precisely the charge laid to this play—and yet no one at that time or later suggested that the play had been performed without a license, nor does Tilney ever seem to have become involved in the subsequent investigation. We cannot finally judge in the matter, unfortunately, without being able to read the play. We can only note that at this stage two positions were taken: one by those associated with the play, who claimed that it was misunderstood; and the other by those associated with the government, who claimed that it was seditious.

The first official notice of the *Isle of Dogs* is dated

August 15. The Privy Council, acting "upon information given us" about "a lewd play that was played in one of the playhouses on the Bankside, containing very seditious and slanderous matter," claimed on that date to have "caused some of the players to be apprehended and committed to prison, whereof one of them was not only an actor, but a maker of part of the said play." This is unacceptably vague, of course, but it probably represents the extent of the Council's information at that point. The Council wished to pursue the matter further—Howard and Hunsdon in particular, I suspect, for Howard's men played regularly on the Bankside and Hunsdon's numbered a playwright among them. The company in question might be one of their own. Richard Topcliffe was directed to examine "those of the players that are committed, whose names are known to you," with an eye to determining "what is become of the rest of their fellows," who were sharers in the "lewd and mutinous behavior" allegedly presented or countenanced in the performance.[9]

The wording of this entry suggests to me that the Council did not know as much as it wished about the matter; that it did not know who the players were whom Topcliffe had arrested, nor in which playhouse they had done their deed; and that Topcliffe, having made the arrests on his own initiative, was to be given the support of the Council in his actions but also directed to produce some substantiating evidence. A genuinely seditious play was of serious concern to everyone. Its perpetrators might well be made public examples for the common weal; but proof was needed first. All of this was on August 15, however, and Topcliffe had made his arrests, as I conjecture, between the sixth and the tenth. We need to account for the intervening dates.

To the best of my knowledge, no one has attempted to trace the steps by which the news of the play traveled from the playhouse in Paris Garden to the Privy Council, sitting at the time at Greenwich. But the path is reasonably clear. The Council received its first detailed information about the play from its Secretary, Sir Robert Cecil; Cecil had been told by his agent Topcliffe; Topcliffe had in turn been informed by a shadowy creature of his own, a man whose name has not been preserved for us, but whom Topcliffe described as being in "exceeding grief" because of heavy debts "for the which he hath been arrested." The man had come to Topcliffe perhaps on August 7 or 8 with information about a "seditious play called The Isle of Dogs," which was "in his opinion" venomous and mischievous. Topcliffe heard all this with interest, and, as I interpret the evidence, promptly went out and arrested a few of the players. He then wrote to Cecil at Greenwich, probably on August 8 or 9, telling him of the informer and of the arrests. Cecil responded, indicating that he was "well pleased with him," and requiring an interview with the informer. Topcliffe wrote the man on the evening of the ninth, conveying this news, and was visited by him promptly the next morning. Topcliffe then hastily penned a letter to Cecil for the informer to deliver: "this gentleman the bearer hereof, to whom I did write yesternight, did this morning come speedily unto me." [10]

There is no evidence to suggest that Topcliffe was himself familiar with the play in question, or that he had been at any pains to seek corroboration of the man's report. In his letter to Cecil, written "in great haste, at my lodging, this tenth of August 1597," Topcliffe displays his accustomed delight at the prospect of apprehending enemies of the realm. The motives of the informant appear to be somewhat different, perhaps not so complex. Topcliffe speaks of the man's poverty, voicing the hope that the news might be worth "some extraordinary favor." He speaks of the man's "wife, and four children, his wife being big-bellied," and allows that if Cecil will not reward the man, "must I lay myself to pawn for him." Cecil will find the man "careful to perform any service you will prescribe him," and suggests that his report on the *Isle of Dogs* "was good proof of his loyalty." All of this may lead us to suspect that the informer's motives were less lofty than a disinterested concern for the well-being of the commonwealth.

Cecil's own pleasure in hearing the news was of a different order. Perhaps the *Isle of Dogs* was a scurrilous play; perhaps not. We have no evidence. But it certainly suited Cecil's purposes to accept, for the nonce, that it was, and we must explore this further. For the plain fact is that we know nothing about the text of the *Isle of Dogs*, or the circumstances of its performance, except what certain government functionaries have chosen to report of it. My own view is that their judgments of the play were self serving, from Topcliffe's informant on up. Their reports cannot pass for impartial witness. I think we are also constrained to observe that the bulk of the evidence points to the period between August 6 and August 10 for the Privy Council's first notice of the play—first from Topcliffe's report of his arrests, and later from Cecil's own interview with the informer—and that we really have no evidence at all for assuming that the restraining order of July 28 was issued because of the Council's concern over this play. We have, in fact, no evidence that the Council was even aware of the play when it framed the restraining order.

Positions such as these, if accepted, will of course introduce their own problems. If the *Isle of Dogs* was performed on or before July 28, that is, before the inhibition, then we need to explain the informer's delay of more than a week before calling upon Topcliffe. If the story of the seditious play was fabricated or embellished for his own advancement, then the man's delay might be explicable; I can think of no other reasonable ground. Topcliffe may have been away from London for those few days, of course, though he nowhere excuses his lateness in reporting the seditious event on that account. The probability is that the delay was the informant's; it was not in Topcliffe's nature to linger if he could act boldly, and he is quite unlikely to have kept information of this sort to himself for several days before acting. His credibility before Cecil, as well as his own temperament, postulated speed in such matters. But if the informer came promptly, and if Topcliffe acted promptly, then the play would have had to be performed after the twenty-eighth; such a construction of the event makes nonsense of Henslowe's perceived correlation between the inhibition and the performance. On the whole, the informant's inexplicable delay seems the most probable of these uncertainties.

Henslowe was, of course, close to the event, and he believed, or professed after August 6 to believe, that the *Isle of Dogs* had brought about the inhibition. But I think, with all due respect, that he was under a misapprehension. It is likely that the play was performed before the twenty-eighth, if we are to make sense of Henslowe's observation; but we merely indulge in wishful reshaping of events if we try to make the *Isle of Dogs* the motivating factor in the Council's order, or in the Lord Mayor's letter. There is not a glimmering of evidence in either of these documents that such an event was present in the minds of the framers. In neither document is a specific play mentioned; in neither document is there any mention of sedition or slander, the charges later laid to the play; in neither document is the Swan playhouse mentioned by name or even alluded to except under the general term of "playhouses on the Bankside." One would expect more precise wording in documents supposedly written in direct response to a known seditious play at a known playhouse. The Privy Council was precise enough on August 15, in its memorandum to Topcliffe and his associates, though even there one senses that their information was scanty.

And, in fact, the charge of sedition seems not to have held up. As the Privy Council had ordered the three prisoners interrogated, we must presume that in due course they were. The details have not survived. One hopes, however, that the procedure was supervised by someone other than Topcliffe, the man whom the Jesuit John Gerard called "the cruelest tyrant of all England, Topcliffe, a man most infamous and hateful to all the realm for his bloody and butcherly mind." Topcliffe had always maintained that the rack was insufficiently persuasive, and during his long career as a recusant-hunter he had devised a number of ingenious instruments intended to better assist prisoners in the proper answering of his questions. We may presume that the depositions made by the three players, however they may have been gotten, were conventionally forwarded to the Council for evaluation; no harm seems to have been found in them, for the Council directed the Keeper of the Marshalsea prison on October 3, 1597 to release the three "stage players," Gabriel Spencer, Robert Shaa, and Benjamin Jonson. Nor is there evidence that any other of Pembroke's players were arrested or interrogated.[11]

It is not clear to what extent Francis Langley was considered a party to these doings, or responsible for them. There is no record of his apprehension or interrogation, even as there was none in the previous year at the height of his involvement in the diamond affair. It is hard to imagine that he escaped questioning on either occasion, but in the absence of documentation there is little to say. Cecil had surely not forgotten him, and among the public benefits intended to accrue as a result of the Council's calculated display of official outrage at the *Isle of Dogs* Cecil might have numbered not only the sobering effect upon players and playwrights in general but also the more immediate effect upon this impertinent manorial lord. And it is clear that the popular image of the Council's reaction to the *Isle of Dogs* was a powerful one. Thomas Nashe, secluded in Yarmouth, grew increasingly bewildered by the news, not daring to return to London for some years. No doubt he could have returned that very autumn, for he was probably in no greater actual danger than Jonson, another "maker of part of the said play," who was released quietly and without penalty at the summer's end. Nashe may even have heard about the release of the other players; if so, he nevertheless preferred to stay away.[12]

Langley, too, may have been bewildered by it all. No doubt there were consequences for him of which we are unaware; the only immediate effect for which there is any evidence is that Langley was unable to get a license for his playhouse in the autumn. This was a relatively mild form of punishment if it represented Cecil's measured retaliation for past wrongs. The Privy Council order had in fact required that all the playhouses "within three miles of London" that were "erected and built only for such purposes" were to be "plucked down"; the owners of the playhouses were "forthwith to pluck down quite the stages, galleries and rooms that are made for people to stand in, and so to deface the same as they may not be employed again to such use." The Justices were required to inform the Council if any owner did not "speedily perform" these orders. These are strong terms, and it is clear from subsequent evidence that Langley for one did not comply. No one, in fact, seems to have taken this order seriously.

Glynne Wickham has called us all to task, and rightly so, for pretending for too long that there was no problem here. Surely if a pretext were needed for bringing the full pressure of the law to bear upon Langley, the twin offences of housing a seditious play and flouting a Privy Council order would have furnished that pretext. The opportunity seems to have been declined. Nor were any of the other playhouse owners apparently called to account for their manifest disregard of the order. The terms had been clear and unambiguous; the letters had been signed by eight Councillors, among them the Lord Admiral, the Lord Chamberlain, and Mr. Secretary Cecil. We may wonder what

consideration would move the first two of these to endorse such an order, and what would constrain the
third to countenance its disobedience. But these are
the facts of the case, at least as they appear to us now.
Two or three months earlier the sheriff of Suffolk had
been directed in similarly straightforward terms to
prohibit the citizens of Hadley from staging Whitsun
plays, and "to cause the stage prepared for them to be
plucked down." We do not know whether he carried
out the order as directed. The Council must have been
equally serious in its statements to the Justices of
Middlesex and Surrey. Wickham sees the order of July
28 as a cleverly deceptive counter in an elaborate stratagem by which the Council hoped to entrap the City;
my own feeling is that the situation was much more
straightforward than that, and that no such complex
explanation needs to be attempted. I think that on July
28 the Council meant exactly what it said, that the
playhouses were to be pulled down; and that, at some
later date, it changed its collective mind, for reasons
that are lost to us.[13]

The Privy Council order had also stipulated that
"there be no more plays used in any public place
within three miles of the City until Allhallowtide
next"; but the Council seems to have changed its mind
about this matter as well, for Henslowe allowed performances to resume at the Rose on October 11, just a
week after the release of Shaa, Spencer and Jonson,
and some twenty days before the prohibition was formally due to be lifted. No penalty seems to have followed on this decision. The group that resumed playing at the Rose on October 11 was made up not only of
the old Admiral's regulars but also of several new
members who had formerly been with Langley at the
Swan. Shaa, Jones, Bird, Downton, and Spencer, the
erstwhile Pembroke's men, had all transferred themselves to Henslowe during the suspension of playing,
and had even (all but Spencer) signed another set of
bonds with Henslowe that they would play only at the

Rose for the next three years, in direct contravention of their earlier bonds to Langley.

They seem also to have brought with them a collection of playbooks, for among Henslowe's earliest offerings after his resumption of playing were three plays, *Hardicanute, Bourbon,* and *Friar Spendleton,* not formerly in the Admiral's repertory. Greg felt that the first two were "old play[s] of Pembroke's men" and that the third was "new and probably common" to both groups. Greg further suggested that *Branholt, Alice Pierce, Black Joan,* and *Stark Flattery,* plays subsequently offered by Henslowe, may also have come from the returning Pembroke players.[14]

From Langley's point of view, of course, only one construction could be placed on these events: his tenants had decamped, violating the conditions of their indentures, and those indentures were now forfeit. When the players refused Langley's demands for payment, he threatened to sue them at the common law for defaulting on their bonds. I have found no evidence that he actually commenced a suit in this fashion; but his threat was sufficient to move the players to file a counter suit in the Court of Requests, asking that Langley be enjoined from prosecuting them. All of these encounters took place within a month after the resumption of playing.

In their plea the five players complained that Langley "doth threaten to commence suit at the common law" against them contrary to "all right, equity and good conscience"; Langley's response was that he did not "threaten to commence suit at the common law" on any grounds "otherwise than is lawful for him to do." The problem, he went on, lay with the players themselves, for they had brought on their own difficulties by "withdrawing and absenting themselves from the defendant's house and continuing of their plays in other houses," more specifically "in the house of one Philip Henslowe, commonly called by the name of the Rose on the Bankside." They had been doing this,

Langley pointed out, ever "sithence their liberty to play," and "without any just cause offered unto them by the defendant."[15]

Nonsense, responded the players: "touching the departure and absence of these complainants from the house of the said defendant, the cause thereof was well known, as well to the said defendant [as] to others." The players had left the Swan because "a restraint was publicly made as well of the said complainant's as all other companies of players in and about her Majesty's City of London," and the various playhouse owners were "likewise prohibited to suffer any plays in the same several houses." The restraint, as the players recalled, extended "from about the feast day of Saint James the Apostle until about the feast of All Saints last past," that is, from about July 25 to about November 1. It is useful to note that neither party made mention of the *Isle of Dogs* during the course of these legal proceedings. It would have strengthened Langley's case to demonstrate that the players had brought about the inhibition by their own folly in presenting a seditious play, but he nowhere made such a claim. It was not in Langley's nature to overlook such opportunities if they might be profitably employed; my own sense is that the *Isle of Dogs* was not, even to Langley, a matter germane to the question of the closing of the playhouses. The thrust of Langley's argument, however, was not so much the suspension of playing as the disappearance of his lessees when playing resumed.

Once the inhibition had expired, and "after that these complainants had obtained license to play again," the players claimed that they had returned to Langley and attempted to resume their playing. Their company had been diminished in the interim by the departure of two or three men, thereby reducing the constituency of their troupe and technically violating their bonds. The players nevertheless (so they said) "resorted to the said defendant" and suggested that "if the said defendant would bear them out" in the sincerity of their intentions despite their diminished numbers, they would once again "play in the house of the said defendant according to the condition of their obligation as formerly they had done." We must regard this claim with a certain suspicion, for we know that four of the five complainants, and perhaps all of them, had already signed bonds with Philip Henslowe to play at the Rose for this same period. They may, indeed, have made this offer to Langley in the expectation of refusal, for by their own testimony Langley "answered that he would not bear the complainants out, but said he had let to them his house and bade them do what they would." [16]

The players, however, contrived to have the last word. They "replied and said that they durst not play in his house without license, and that it was to their undoing to continue in idleness; and that Philip Henslowe (in the said answer named) had obtained license for his house and would bear the complainants out." The argument was thus complete: the licensed players required a licensed playhouse, which Langley could not provide for them; therefore they "exercised their playing at the house of the said Philip Henslowe (as lawfully they might)." It is curious to note, however, that in their original bill of complaint the players neglected to mention this matter of the license; the legal process had reached the stage of replication and rejoinder before it occurred to them to bring up the point. We may wonder at this; for much has been made of the importance of licenses in recent scholarship. But Langley's failure to get one in the autumn of 1597 did not seem to be a consideration of paramount importance to the players, nor did it deter Langley. Langley told the Court that "sithence the feast of All Saints last past" the five complainants "might have played if it had pleased them in the defendant's house, as other of their fellows have done," and the players themselves affirmed that since their departure Langley "had his said house continually from time to time exercised with other players, to his great gains." That the practice of offering plays in an unlicensed playhouse not only continued unabated but could be proclaimed in a court of law without hesitation or fear of consequence must give us pause.

Langley spoke of "the great costs and charges he hath disbursed and laid out at and by [the players'] appointment and direction for the making ready of the playhouse, and furnishing himself with sundry sort of rich attire and apparel for them to play withal, whereof the defendant hath ever sithence had little use"; he claimed to have spent "the full sum of £300" for "making of all things ready." The players disallowed this charge, claiming "that for the making of the said house ready and fit for the complainants to play in, the said defendant was at no cost at all, for the said house was then lately afore used to have plays in it." Further, as his house was still occupied, he could hardly claim to have little use for the playing apparel. The complainants argued that they had in fact reimbursed Langley for these expenditures out of their own half of the gallery takings, and that the garments more properly belonged to them and not to Langley.[17]

The judges were not inclined to favor Langley's arguments. The case continued through Easter term, and their decree was entered on May 29, 1598: Langley was ordered to "surcease and stay and no further prosecute or proceed at the common law upon the said obligations" until the Court made its determination of the point at issue in this suit; further, "an injunction under her Majesty's Privy Seal upon pain of £500 shall be awarded forth of this Court and directed to the said defendant" to ensure his compliance with the decree. There is no record of any further proceeding in this matter, and we may assume that the case was quietly closed, Langley recognizing the futility of further litigation. The players had carried their point. They had assured the judges that "the said Langley" was "of a greedy desire and dishonest disposition," and the judges seem to have concurred. They were neither the first nor the last to have such feelings about Langley.

My attentions to Langley the playhouse owner in this section must not be allowed to suggest that in 1597 there had been any diminution in the activities of Langley the goldsmith, Langley the alnager, or indeed Langley the lord of the manor, at whom we have scarcely glanced. The goldsmith had in fact undergone a curious transmutation. His activities as a lender of money had been sharply curtailed, by necessity or perhaps even by design, and Langley, heedless of both sides of Polonius's maxim, had now become an active borrower. He may have persuaded himself that the threat of litigation would hold his creditors at bay; if so, he miscalculated badly. In April 1597 one George Benyan went to court against Langley for defaulting on a bond for £100, which Langley had signed in connection with a loan made to him by Benyan in 1592. The case was tried in June 1597 by a jury at the Guildhall, before Edmund Anderson, Chief Justice of the Court of Common Pleas, and the judgment was awarded to Benyan. Langley was ordered to pay the debt of £100, and also £3 15ˢ damages, which he did.

In the same month, April 1597, Edmund Shepperd sued Francis Langley for default on a bond in the amount of £100. A day in June was similarly given for this trial, and a jury summoned, but nothing further is recorded of the case. In the same April Langley borrowed £100 from William Pitchford, with Hannibal Gammon as cosigner, and later defaulted. Pitchford sued them both—"Hannibal Gammon, citizen and goldsmith of London" and "Francis Langley of Bankside, Surrey, yeoman, alias citizen and draper of London"—in October 1597 and won his suit. In May 1597 Langley also borrowed £100 from Thomas Hassould, with Gammon and Richard Langley as cosigners, and again defaulted; Hassould sued in 1600. In July 1597 Langley borrowed £100 from Elizabeth Sutton, with the same cosigners, and again defaulted, and was sued,

191

and lost. In October 1597 Langley sued John Lever for default on a bond, and was awarded the verdict, collecting £150 on the bond and one pound damages. In the same month he also served as a cosigner for a bond of Hannibal Gammon's on a loan from one Tidsley Monk, gotten through the agency of his friend Thomas Chapman, the scrivener of Soper Lane. Gammon defaulted, and Monk took them both to court and collected.[18]

Langley the alnager was equally busy. In addition to the weekly extortion that he practiced on simple clothmakers in Blackwell Hall, and in his newly erected "office" nearby, Langley and his colleagues had taken to patrolling the major City fairs as well. In 1597 the suspension of playing freed Langley to devote more of his time in August to the exploitation of Bartholomew Fair, the annual celebration of St. Bartholomew's Day in Smithfield. Ben Jonson has immortalized the festivity for us, complete with a vignette of a clothmaker named Northern, sodden with drink, who "changes cloth for ale in the Fair here," as Captain Whit observes of him. Bartholomew Fair was among other things a popular place for clothmakers to bring their wares, and therefore an apt place for Langley to engage in his own favored forms of larceny. Of the many clothmakers who came to the Fair in 1597, several had cause to remember Langley.

John Cole, a clothmaker of Balson, Suffolk, complained of Langley's activities "in Bartholomew Fair." Cole remembered "being there with a remnant of cloth, color french green, containing eleven yards or thereabouts," and that "Langley and Hugh his man came and violently took it from [him] and carried [it] to a place within the fair, where the [alnagers] pretend to keep an office for the fair time." Langley's confederate John Leake was there, "and there they detained the cloth till this deponent paid them 3ˢ for it, Leake scoffingly saying he would cut it in half and this deponent should have the one half, and he would have the other to make his men clothes."[19]

Zachary Whale, a clothmaker of Edwardston, Suffolk, remembered several encounters with Langley and his fellows, "and especially he remembreth that about Bartholomewtide 1597 there was taken from the inn called the White Horse, upon Mile End Green near London, five or six packs of cloth from Robert Clark, the carrier of Boxford, by the [alnagers] or some by their appointment, and carried to their office so called near Blackwell Hall, at which time this deponent and other clothiers going between Mile End and Aldgate were enforced for fear of the [alnagers] to flee back again to Mile End, and to take up their inn there at the said White Horse, not being their usual inn, whither the [alnagers] pursued them and would have taken their cloths also, but that before their coming they had locked them up in a chamber."

Salomon Richardson of Carsey, Suffolk, another clothmaker, remembered that on the day of Bartholomew Fair, "the 24th day of August anno 1597, the [alnagers] took away from one Colborne, his carrier, four cloths at one time which they would not deliver again till this deponent paid them forty shillings, and that about a year before the said 24th of August [presumably at the previous Fair] the said [alnagers] took four cloths more of this deponent's, whereupon one Mr Offley sent his man to their office, as they term it, who could not have them till he gave them 20^s."

John Upcheare, a clothmaker from Dedham, Sussex, remembered that Langley and his associates "came into Bartelmew Fair near London, and as soon as this deponent had laid down his cloth in the fair they came and took them from him and carried it to their office whereby this deponent lost his market, and was enforced to pay them 2^s 6^d before he could get it again." Joseph Brooke, a fellow townsman of John Upcheare's, remembered that Langley and his fellows "came into Bartelmew Fair, London, and took from this deponent one cloth and carried [it] to their office which they hold, and did only weigh it, and had 5^s of this deponent before he could have it again." Brooke also remembered that a few months earlier, "in April 1597," Langley and some others "came into Blackwell Hall and took away one cloth from this deponent and did but weigh it and made him pay 4^s before he could have it again."

Nicholas Strutt, clothmaker of Hadley, Suffolk, remembered that "in May anno 1597" he had "hired a carman of London to carry him 24 cloths to one Mr Alderman Clark's," but that Langley and other of the alnagers "came and violently enforced the said carman to carry the same cloths to their office, and this deponent was constrained to give them £20 for the redemption of the said cloths: also within two months after, the [alnagers] took, from Jerome Burman the carrier, eight cloths more of this deponent's, which he was to carry to the said Mr Alderman Clark's, but the [alnagers] compelled him by force to carry them with them, and this deponent paid them 30^s before he could have them again."

The alnagers' "office, so called," was clearly the place of much fraudulent dealing. John Hayward of Nayland, Suffolk, affirmed that "he knoweth the said place near Blackwell Hall which is called the searchers' office, whither the clothiers have used to repair for the redeeming of their cloths, and saith he hath heard the said office was erected by Leake and Langley, two of the [alnagers], and others, who there pretend to keep an office for the searching of cloth."

From these few depositions one can see that the ambitious alnager of the 1580s had not lost his touch, even after a dozen years of activity. Indeed, this method of securing an income now seemed to have a greater fascination for Langley than his earlier device of ensnaring the needy with punitive indentures; at least it moved him to greater exertions. Perhaps the confrontation with angry clothmakers served to enliven the daily tedium or provided an exhilaration beyond the power of bond-defaulters to engender. The insolence of office was no doubt a source of pleasure to Langley. He was, after all, the nephew of a former Lord Mayor, and was now the lord of a manor in his own right. The dignity of age was also settling upon him; he was now fifty, and could lay claim to a certain amount of deference on that score. Over the years he had developed a taste for the special satisfactions that lay in requiring the obeisances of others. He was himself not intimidated by aldermen, or sheriffs, or even Lords Mayor, for he had seen their lives from the inside during his early youth in his uncle's house. Now he might scoff openly at them. For those yet lower in authority, such as the local officials who lived near him on the Bankside, his scorn was even greater.

The churchwardens of St. Saviour's parish probably knew of Langley's activities in the City only by hearsay, but they had ample evidence near at hand to document his activities in the parish. The whole of the manor of Paris Garden lay within the parish limits, and the wardens could hardly fail to notice the new tenements and the new playhouse. Nor could they fail to be irritated by Langley's cavalier treatment of them. Though he purchased communion tokens every Lent, he refused to pay more than one pound for tithes, and the attempts of the wardens to negotiate with him proved fruitless. On the last day of June 1597 Langley was invited to a vestry meeting at which the wardens offered to settle for a flat sum: "At a vestry holden this present day, offer was made to Francis Langley of all his tithes, by consent of the whole house, for £4 a year." But Langley demurred, and "would not accept of" this figure, instead "offering but four marks a year," or about £2 13^s 4^d; "and so the same was left to be further considered of."[20]

The further deliberations took some months, but finally the vestry reached its determination in the matter. At a vestry meeting held on October 5, 1597 "it was ordered that Mr Langley shall pay £4 a year for all those tithes of the tenements and lands . . . for which he hath heretofore paid but 20^s, if he will accept thereof; which if he refuse, then the wardens to proceed by law against him."

The Christmas holidays came, marking the end of 1597, and the matter of the tithes had not been resolved. The festive season called forth no generosity in Langley's soul, but impelled him instead to an increased abuse of country clothmakers come to town for the holiday market. He continued to borrow money, and to lend it, and to appear in court as either plainant or defendant, though tending toward the latter. By all accounts he continued to have players in his playhouse, despite his failure to secure a license for such activity. For the historian of the theatre, 1597 is remembered as the year of the *Isle of Dogs* and the Privy Council order for the destruction of the London playhouses. For Langley himself, 1597 was filled with a variety of events. The one that may have seemed the most ominous to him, as the year drew to its close, was the arrest of Richard Renching, a money speculator like himself who also engaged in clipping coins. Coin clipping carried with it the harshest of penalties; if convicted, Renching's goods would be forfeit and his life at pawn. In 1591 Langley and Gammon had borrowed money from Renching, and had defaulted; Renching still held the bond. Upon his conviction the bond would become the property of the Crown, and Langley might look forward to the full machinery of government moving to collect the debt from him. He may have been musing on all this as the year closed. But there was good news too; the death of Justice William Gardiner in November no doubt buoyed Langley's spirits through most of Advent.[21]

XII

The Diamond

Sir, I must have that diamond from you.
THE COMEDY OF ERRORS

For Sir Anthony Ashley the end of 1597 brought its own kind of activity. Still engaged in restoring his credit with Cecil and in glozing over his complicity in the diamond affair, Ashley spent the month of December constructing a series of careful letters to Cecil purporting to reveal the full details of the venture. On December 6 he wrote Cecil that he had "more diligently informed me than before touching the diamond," having gotten some new information from the peccant goldsmiths themselves, "out of the bosom of those that pretend interest thereunto." Ashley claimed to have learned that the diamond "came to their possession about three years sithence by the means of a mariner" who "by all likelihood" had gotten it "out of the carrack." According to Ashley's version of the story the mariner, "meeting with these goldsmiths by chance at a play at the Theater in Shoreditch," spoke covertly of his purloined goods and aroused their interest. The situation is a classic, of course, and might well have come out of any of the Puritan tracts decrying the moral hazards of playgoing.[1]

For the better striking of an agreement, so Ashley's narrative continued, the mariner and the goldsmiths

197

left the playhouse and went "all together into Finsbury fields to take private view both of the diamond and of a ruby and a carbuncle." The goldsmiths resolved to buy the lot, but to give their transaction the color of legitimacy they insisted that the mariner "should expose his merchandise to vent in some open market"; more specifically, he should "bring it to their shop in Cheapside" where "they would not fail to deliver the price agreed on," which price, according to Ashley, "did not pass £500 for all three jewels by their own confession."

These details are not too wide of the mark. According to Bartholomew Gilbert's testimony, taken in the spring of 1594, he, along with Terry and Howe, had indeed purchased the diamond from a mariner, through the agency of his friend John Maddox. But the place of meeting, in Gilbert's deposition, was a tavern on the Thames at Limehouse, not a public playhouse. Ashley's detail of the playhouse, though probably fanciful, was appropriately circumstantial; it lent a certain immediacy to the narrative, and was perhaps Ashley's attempt to achieve verisimilitude by appealing to Cecil's distrust of public playhouses. Further, there was no mention in Gilbert's deposition of any ruby or carbuncle. But the price of £500 in Ashley's version is close to the £550 plus some plate that Gilbert claimed to have paid. Details of this sort, however, could hardly be of any interest to Cecil, who had been in possession of such information for years. Nor could Ashley have furthered his cause by the puerile iteration of his plea that Cecil "be mindful for my restitution to her Majesty's good opinion," or that Ashley "be repaid the £300 disbursed long sithence purposely to make the diamond her Majesty's." Ashley was even so bold as to point out that he had "entered into bond" for the rest of the money, upon payment of which the diamond "is by law mine and not the goldsmiths'."

On December 9 Ashley wrote another letter to Cecil, in which he claimed to be "now this morning thoroughly informed of the truth of the diamond," as a result of his having apprehended "such a one as had once a share in it himself," a man who was the "chief means that Howe and the rest that are now pretended proprietaries had interest in the diamond." Ashley's coyness in declining to name the man is in keeping with the general tone of these letters. The man is described as one "much grieved with [the] hard usage" he had suffered at the hands of Terry and Howe, and one who "would be contented (as it seemeth) to be revenged, as more particularly I can deliver unto your Honor when it please you to command mine attendance." The description could only fit Bartholomew Gilbert, as Cecil would have noted with a yawn, but Ashley was determined to spin out his tale. Each new letter gave him the opportunity to develop a few more details, and also a fresh chance for a plea: "I beseech your Honor make my service known . . . were I privately disposed, means and good occasion is offered to make myself a gainer . . . I could have clearly gotten well nigh £1000 . . . but in all duty I prefer her Majesty's good opinion and service before any private respect, not doubting but now at last her Majesty will be pleased to restore me to her good favour, and take course for my satisfaction of the £300."[2]

Ashley's persistence was indeed commendable. He closed by describing himself as "attending your Honor's direction herein," but soon concluded that no direction was forthcoming. He must have been piqued by Cecil's failure to respond, by his lack of curiosity about who the man was. On December 23 Ashley could restrain himself no longer. "I have by good chance taken hold of Bartholmew Gilbert," he announced, and promptly turned his confession into an occasion for further suspense. More information was promised for a later time; for the nonce, Gilbert "refuseth to answer particularly to the matter of the great diamond," claiming that he was bound to secrecy by the terms of "his bond wherein he standeth endangered to his partners Howe and Terry." By this juncture Ashley was probably telling the truth; he had indeed encountered Gilbert, and even arrested him after a fashion, for he noted that "I have him at this present in my house till your Honor's farther direction." Upon receipt of this direction—on receipt of any acknowledgment at all from Cecil, no doubt—Ashley predicted that Gilbert would be of service "not only in disclosing the truth of all proceedings concerning the great diamond yet unknown, but some other matters also (as he saith) little thought on."[3]

But Cecil was able to resist even so open-ended a temptation as this, leaving Ashley with no recourse but to keep writing, and perhaps to commence a bit of genuine investigation to sustain his lengthening narrative. From his actual apprehension of Gilbert, Ashley apparently did learn some new things. He learned that Howe and Terry, proceeding in the full confidence of their ownership of the diamond, and with an utter disregard of Ashley's own pretended claim thereto, had given the stone to a cutter—not the Dutchman in Gammon's shop this time, but another cutter—and that the stone was already cut and shaped. Howe and Terry had gone so far as to commence negotiations with the Queen herself, through the agency of her intermediary Sir John Fortescue, the Chancellor of the Exchequer and a member of the Privy Council. Howe and Terry had shown the partially finished stone to the Queen, shaped to hang as a pendant, and she had encouraged them to proceed, sweetening her words with an advance of £500, "delivered by Mr Chancellor," as Ashley ruefully noted.

The details of this further development were also already known to Cecil, but they were new, and astonishing, to Ashley. Ashley learned that Howe and Terry had no sooner commenced cutting the stone than they had grown apprehensive about a possible betrayal by Fortescue; accordingly, they directed the cutter to lop off a portion of the diamond that they might keep for themselves before completing the cutting. The cutter, unidentified but perhaps a Huguenot judging from Ashley's description of his speech, was annoyed at this command, for it seemed unprofessional to him. The man had grown in self-esteem upon receiving the Queen's encouragement in his work; he "is become a gallant with the pride of her Majesty's honorable largesse, and sweareth by Cotes Sacre Malt, he will be her Majesty's faithful servant." It was he who told Ashley about the breaking of the stone. "They broke it off before it was full cut off, fearing the stone might have been called for before the piece was clean cut off, and in so doing they impaired the pendant above one hundred pounds in the value and show." Howe and Terry, in turn, had "threatened and much abused" the cutter, "calling him knave, etc., for disclosing the secrecy of the piece that was cut off." The two men apparently also destroyed two other stones worth a thousand pounds by too hasty cutting, "all wasted into powder by their direction, not intending to hazard so long stay about a thing that might turn to her Majesty's only benefit and not to their own."[4]

Ashley was nonplussed by the unearthing of so much unsuspected activity, for it rendered nugatory all his earlier claims to discovery. There was now, it seemed, little left for him to do but to bring together the remaining threads of the story in the interest of completeness. Cecil missed the conclusion of the affair by reason of his absence from London, which circumstance furnished Ashley with the occasion for writing his final installment. The matter was now virtually settled, he wrote to Cecil; Robert Howe had, to the very last, "played his accustomed saucy parts, both by exhibiting petitions to the Queen and otherwise intimating to her Majesty that your Honor and Mr Chancellor did promise and undertake to give them £2100 besides all charges of cutting and the interest of the long forbearance of their moneys, all which amounting at least to some £2600 or £2700." This amount was "besides the great piece they indirectly caused to be cut away," which they were "not ashamed to claim (as well saved and gained) by their own art and industry" and "accompting it no manner of offense." If the Queen would pay the full price they were asking, they "would be contented to bestow on her Majesty the said stolen piece of free gift." This last gesture went too far: "her Majesty being herewith justly moved to indignation for this audacious part, especially in your Honor's absence, commanded them to the Marshalsea;" but "upon their humble submission, within short time released them and hath out of compassion (as I understand) yielded to give them some hundreds of pounds above the £1200 formerly yielded."[5]

And so, after many vicissitudes, it would seem that Howe and Terry had finally made their venture profitable. Their original plan had been to sell the stone in 1594; according to Robert Brooke, there had been a ready market for the stone in that year, but it had collapsed with the arrest of Gilbert by Cecil's men. Brooke had promptly reneged on his own offer to purchase it, and Howe and Terry were forced to take it back. Gilbert himself had lost all taste for the adventure after his year in prison, and he readily allowed himself to be bought out by the other two. Howe and Terry paid Gilbert £600 for his share of the stone, giving him £400 in hand and entering into bonds of £400 for the remaining £200. The final £200 was to have been paid to Gilbert on the first of March, 1598, by which time Terry and Howe had hoped to sell the stone.

But March came and went, and the Queen had not made up her mind. The promises of large sums reported in horror by Ashley were indeed merely promises, given in the finest monarchal style but quite insubstantial in reality. On the default of the bonds, Gilbert sued Terry and Howe in Queen's Bench; to forestall his suit, Terry and Howe entered a counter suit in the Court of Requests, in the conventional form of a petition to the Queen. They acknowledged that

they had "cut and perfected the said stone or diamond" and that it had been "sithence in most humble
sort presented unto your Highness for to view and
see." Howe and Terry had been hoping for some time
to learn "your gracious pleasure of your Highness' liking," but "as yet your Highness is not resolved whether
to allow it or to refuse it." Until the Queen made up
her mind, the plainants continued, they would be unable to make good on their bond to Gilbert, and so they
pleaded relief from Gilbert's suit on the grounds of
deference to the royal whim.[6]

The plea was successful; Gilbert was ordered to desist from his suit at the common law, and the Requests
suit continued through the spring and summer. Terry
and Howe had filed their plea on June 16, and the stay
was issued on June 17; Gilbert answered on June 26.
Then the summer vacation supervened, and the case
was not resumed until Michaelmas. Howe and Terry
filed their replication on October 14, and thereafter
the records of the proceeding cease. We may presume a
settlement out of court. Perhaps we may even presume
that the Queen finally paid for the jewel, though this is
more problematical. And so the diamond affair seems
finally to have come to an end, with the stone in the
Queen's possession, though perhaps not in the way
Cecil had intended, and with varying degrees of dissatisfaction as the lot of almost all the others who had
been touched in the business. It was a singularly undramatic ending to what had promised to be a suspense-
ful tale.

Nor did its resolution bring any satisfaction to Anthony Ashley. He longed to be reinstated as a Clerk to the
Privy Council, and had hoped that the completion of
the diamond affair might mark his reinstatement. The
new Lord Cobham had casually reassured Ashley one
day that his fortunes were bound to improve, and Ashley could not resist passing this news on to Cecil: "I
have had in your absence very honorable and gracious
thanks and promises from her Majesty by the media-

tion and intercession of my singular good Lord Cobham
. . . assuring me . . . that I shall not fail to obtain my
restitution, with some other good testimony of her
plenary remission, immediately upon your return,
without whose vote and applause (as Principal Secretary) in her princely wisdom it was not thought meet
to dispose of any thing concerning that place." But
Ashley was not restored to his former position in the
Council upon Cecil's return. His loss of favor, like his
correspondence, continued unabated for many years,
and Cecil was not moved to pity by the contemplation
of either phenomenon. Ashley was not destined to
prosper at his hands.[7]

XIII

The Community

What would you with me, honest neighbour?
MUCH ADO ABOUT NOTHING

A similarly undramatic ending seemed to be in store for the Swan. Indeed, its career as a public playhouse is generally thought to have been effectively suspended in the early part of 1598. Letters from the Privy Council to the Justices of Middlesex and Surrey and to the Master of the Revels on February 19, 1598, are assumed to be addressed to this problem. The letters began by noting that "license hath been granted unto two companies of stage players retained unto us, the Lord Admiral and Lord Chamberlain, to use and practice stage plays" so that the Queen's entertainment might be provided for "at times meet and accustomed, to which end they have been chiefly licensed and tolerated." This is a somewhat different state of affairs than that described by Shaa and his companions in their lawsuit against Langley, where the five plainants maintained that they, as Pembroke's men, were also duly licensed, "lawfully allowed and authorized," as they put it. The Privy Council version is no doubt the correct one, implying as it does that not only Langley's playhouse but also Pembroke's players, as a distinct group, were not relicensed in the autumn of 1597. We know already that the Pembroke group had split

205

over procedural questions with Langley that summer; some of the company had signed on with Henslowe, others had remained to play at the Swan. It is not clear which of these segments might properly claim to retain the license of the Pembroke group, though Henslowe seemed to feel that "my Lord of Pembroke's men" had formally come under his wing as a group in October 1597. Perhaps Shaa was the patentee; he certainly moved quickly into a position of importance under Henslowe, a fact that might argue his prominence in the earlier and larger troupe.[1]

But the remainder of the company, those men who elected or were constrained to continue at the Swan, would also have needed some sort of sponsorship. No doubt they insisted on their own identity as Pembroke's men, and may even have secured a duplicate license by exemplification. Some such process seems already to have taken place in connection with the activities of a group calling itself "Pembroke's men" which was touring the provinces at the very time that the Shaa troupe was in London. This provincial group may have returned to London in the autumn of 1597 just in time to combine with the remnants of the company left at the Swan. Whatever the explanation, the Privy Council was careful to point out in its letters that two and only two companies had been licensed. The letters were intended to alert the Justices to the rumor that "there is also a third company who of late (as we are informed) have by way of intrusion used likewise to play, having neither prepared any play for her Majesty nor are bound to you, the Master of the Revels, for performing such orders as have been prescribed and are enjoined to be observed by the other two companies before mentioned." The recipients of the letter were required to "take order that the aforesaid third company may be suppressed and none suffered hereafter to play but those two formerly named."[2]

Other than the Admiral's and Chamberlain's companies, the Pembroke group is the only identifiable company for which we have any evidence of activity in late 1597 and early 1598. That evidence, to be sure, is slight; it consists of Langley's assertion in November 1597 that the "fellows" of the departed players were continuing to play at the Swan, and also of some contemporary notices in the parish to be discussed in a moment. A grudging consensus has developed among theatre historians that the "third company" spoken of by the Council must have been Pembroke's, though the matter is by no means closed, and there are those who argue that a troupe in the Boar's Head was the real occasion of the letter. Again we might note that the Council's action in suppressing the "third company" is based on some sort of vague report: "there is also a third company . . . as we are informed." Topcliffe at work again, perhaps, though no evidence survives. Perhaps the Justices were able to furnish the Councillors with more precise information, so that appropriate steps could be taken to suppress unlicensed troupes in unlicensed houses. And then again, perhaps not. There is no clear evidence to support the general assumption that the Swan was closed down as a public playhouse in the early spring of 1598.

If playing had been stopped at the Swan, the churchwardens of St. Saviour's church would have been among the first to notice; but they seemed unaware of any such news. On April 20, at a meeting of the vestry, they ordered not only "that a view shall be made by the churchwardens how many new tenements Mr Langley hath builded since the order set down for his tithes," but also "that they shall speak to Mr Langley and Mr Henslowe and Jacob Meade for money for the poor, in regard of their plays." The order was repeated at a later vestry meeting on May 1: "Item, it is ordered that Mr Langley's new buildings shall be viewed according to an order the last vestry, and that he, Mr Henslowe and Jacob Meade shall be moved for money for the poor in regard of their playhouses." Apparently no one suggested to the vestrymen or wardens at either of these meetings that there were no plays or players at the Swan; nor is it likely that this dedicated group of men would be unaware of such a moral victory as the closing of a playhouse in their midst. The only reasonable construction to put on this evidence from the parish church, it seems to me, is to assume that playing was still in full career at both playhouses.[3]

By the early summer matters had evidently gotten worse. The vestry determined on July 19 "that a petition shall be made to the body of the [Privy] Council concerning the playhouses in this parish, wherein the enormities shall be showed that come thereby to the parish, and that in respect thereof they may be dismissed and put down from playing." The Globe was not destined to make its appearance in the parish until early in 1599, so the "playhouses" referred to by the churchwardens in this minute can only be the Rose and the Swan. Here, as elsewhere, we have the familiar pattern of conflicting evidence: an order from the Privy Council from the previous February which, if enforced, would have suppressed playing at the Swan some months earlier; and the periodic responses of the local parishioners to suggest that nothing of the sort had happened. Examples such as these teach us to be properly chary of equating the pronouncement of regulations with their effective enforcement.[4]

One must conclude that Langley was not yet finished as an entrepreneur at the Swan. Nor was he finished with the harassment of Shaa and his fellows. The players' suit against him was still pending in the Court of Requests when, at the end of March 1598, he had William Borne arrested for his default on the bond. Borne had by this date been incorporated into the company at the Rose, and his arrest represented an upsetting development in Henslowe's repertory. Productions can easily falter when actors are clapped into prison unexpectedly, and Borne was not the only new member of Henslowe's company to be financially en-

St. Saviour's church, formerly the priory of St. Mary Overy. The drawing shows the old cloisters and conventual buildings. The Bishop of Winchester's London residence is on the far left, beside the priory landing dock. In the background, the bridge leading to the City.

tangled with Langley. Henslowe no doubt anticipated the worst, a series of weekly arrests of various of his personnel, and must have seen the need to straighten matters out between himself and Langley with dispatch. He recorded in his diary on March 29 that he had lent five marks (6^s 8^d) to Borne "to discharge the arrest betwixt Langley and him," and later that day ten marks more, for a total of £10, "to discharge the arrest of Langley's." What confrontation, if any, then ensued between Henslowe and Langley we do not know.[5]

Within the month, however, Downton and Shaa retaliated by suing Langley in the Court of Common Pleas for default on his own bonds to them. Thereafter the relations between the players and Langley seemed to stabilize somewhat; by the following autumn Langley and Henslowe even seemed to be engaged in a business transaction of some sort, though the details are missing. Henslowe noted in his diary that on September 19, 1598, he had lent "the company" thirty-five pounds "about the agreement betwixt Langley and them." A fortnight later the agreement had come to fruition: "Lent unto Mr Jones, Robert Shaa, Thomas Downton, Wm Bird, the same time they paid Mr Langley his money for the agreement and fetched home the rich cloak from pawn . . . the sum of £3." The cloak must indeed have been rich; Henslowe noted separately that he had lent "the company" £19 "to buy a rich cloak of Mr Langley which they had at their agreement."[6]

But such apparent amity must not be misconstrued. If the players were successful in reaching an agreement with Langley, they were more fortunate than the churchwardens. The decision on April 20, 1598, to view Langley's new tenements in order to determine "how many new tenements Mr Langley hath builded since the order set down for his tithes," was not one calculated to conciliate Langley. The running battle over the appropriate amount of Langley's tithes had not been resolved, and the reiteration by the wardens in the summer of 1598 of their earlier figure had led merely to another response by Langley of his former counter-offer. Early in October, after a discussion in the vestry about whether to accept Langley's proffered payment, the wardens decided to hold out for the full amount: "Item, concerning the suit for the tithes of Parish Garden, it is ordered that advice shall be taken before receipt of the same, or any further proceedings therein."[7]

As a result of this order, the expedition to view the new tenements was apparently also put off. But by the following winter it had become evident that the increased building on the manor grounds had effected an increase in Langley's tithe obligation, and on February 21, 1599, the vestry resolved once again "that a view shall be taken of Mr Langley's new buildings for the rating of the tithes thereof accordingly." A view was therefore taken, a new figure proposed, and a new refusal received. A year later, on March 21, 1600, the vestry confronted the problem yet again. "Item, it is ordered that the churchwardens shall talk with Mr Langley and his tenants about their tithes and arrearages according to their discretions, to take order for the payment of the same if they can, if not to make report thereof and of their answers at the next vestry." This recalcitrant behavior on Langley's part merely confirmed the unfavorable impression Hugh Browker had formed of him when first they met, at the time of Langley's purchase of Paris Garden. Browker had been an active vestryman at St. Saviour's throughout the decade of the 1590s, and had served as parish auditor on many occasions. Langley's continued effrontery must have been a particular trial to him; but such trials were given to Godfearing men to test their patience, and Browker could be patient.[8]

On March 28, 1600, the vestry also determined that "the churchwardens shall talk with the players for tithes for their playhouses." The determination to meet with the players was no doubt intended to supplement, not to replace, the discussions with the playhouse owners on the same topic. By this year, however, the Globe was an active presence on the Bankside, so the plural use of the word "playhouses" may no longer serve as evidence for any activity at the Swan. Indeed, the other term is equally inconclusive; for in the case of the Globe, the occupants and the owners were both "the players," an ambiguity of which perhaps the churchwardens themselves were not yet fully aware.[9]

It must not be presumed that Langley was the only recalcitrant parishioner in these matters. On August 29, 1600, the vestry recorded that "there is some controversy between the parish and my Lord Montague, Mr Walter, Mr Langley and others for tithes." The personal dynamics operant in these altercations are unfortunately lost to us; but on this occasion we are afforded a glimpse of the stresses at work within the vestry. Richard Humble, vintner, who had purchased several properties from George and Thomas Cure in 1589, was at the meeting. He had been chosen a vestryman in 1592 and a churchwarden in 1594. He knew most, if not all, of the people under discussion. To everyone's surprise, "the said Mr Humble did openly, in the hearing of many, seem to defend their causes in words against the parish, and offered to lay a wager that the parish should never recover those tithes." Further, he said "that he would take part with them against the parish what he could in the hindering thereof." As if that were not enough, Humble also "did greatly abuse them, the said churchwardens, in regard of their said office, calling of them Knaves and Rascals, with other like most injurious speeches."[10]

The outburst must have astonished the vestry. Humble was a wealthy and respected elder of the parish, a warden of the church, and a man destined to be an alderman within a twelvemonth; age had perhaps made him testy, but the only specific prior disagreement on record was an altercation between him and some workmen making repairs on parish property. Nevertheless, the wardens were offended, and at a subsequent meeting on November 1, 1600, Humble, "for divers his misdemeanors and practices against the good of the parish, and denying to be censured by the orders of the house, is exempted the house [that is, ejected from the vestry] forever." As Humble's successor the vestry chose Hugh Browker's brother-in-law, Thomas Cure.[11]

Humble's defense of Langley is not readily understandable. True, they shared some common interests; they had first come together in 1589 to feast upon the inheritance of the younger Cure. As a result of that feast, however, they had found themselves on opposite sides of various lawsuits, and there could have been little love lost between them. As an investor, then, Humble would have known Langley the goldsmith. In later years, in his capacity as churchwarden, he had probably come to understand a different aspect of Langley's character, that of the playhouse owner and builder of tenements. In still another capacity Humble had encountered Langley the manorial lord; this last was the result of Humble's having been a jurator for the sewer commission for Surrey East since 1593, a sewer commissioner since 1597, and the foreman of the sewer commission jury for Surrey East since April 1599. Humble's rise in the sewer hierarchy may seem on the face of it to provide little opportunity for confrontation with Langley, but just the opposite is in fact true.[12]

As lord of the manor of Paris Garden, Langley was obligated to observe the customary duties of lordship, among which were the maintenance of the estate of the manor. The copyholders, enfranchised and in charge of their own affairs since 1580, were outside his authority as lord of the manor; but he did have certain responsibilities toward them of a custodial nature, though he was in fact little interested in their welfare. Indeed, when he succeeded Thomas Cure as lord of the manor in 1589 it must have seemed to the copyholders to be a change for the worse. Cure had apparently done nothing to improve the manor during his nine years of tenure as lord, but he had at least performed a few of the ordinary chores of maintenance. After 1589, however, there is evidence of general neglect in the common areas of the manor, which traditionally had been the lord's responsibility. Paris Garden wharf, on the Thames, was soon found in need of repair; Mill Bridge, on the main road through the Upper Ground, was shortly in a decayed state; the drainage ditches were blocked and in need of "scouring, casting and cleansing," the terms used by the sewer commissioners to describe the scraping out of underbrush growing in the ditches, the shoveling away of sludge and muddy deposits, and the removal of waste and rubbish.

The maintenance of these drainage ditches was of prime importance, for the very habitability of the area was at issue. The Surrey lands along the southern bank of the Thames consisted for the most part of flat, open country, large portions of which were below the river's daily high water mark. These areas had long since been protected against daily flooding from the Thames by a line of reinforced embankments built up along the river. These dikes kept the river water off the land at high tide, but they also prevented the drainage of ground water into the river at low tide. And, indeed, the ground behind the embankments often became soggy from other causes. Much of it was swampy to begin with, like Lambeth Marsh, which lay just to the west of Paris Garden; at times of heavy rain, these marshes and other low areas would normally be covered with water that might remain for weeks. Drainage of this recurring surface water was therefore an imperative, and was accomplished by a network of small ditches leading into a system of common drainage sewers. Water was carried through these ditches and sewers into a series of large sluices that emptied into the Thames at low tide and that were protected by barriers to prevent backflow at high tide. These sluices—Whitewall sluice, Heath's Wall sluice, Duffield sluice, Boar's Head sluice, Earl's sluice—along with the system of sewers and ditches that fed into them, were

vital to the welfare of the region, and their maintenance was a matter of continuing concern.

The early Commissions of Sewers were created to
remedy just such abuses as those that were becoming
evident in Paris Garden. The Surrey and Kent Commissions of Sewers, under whose purview the manor of
Paris Garden fell, had as their charge the preservation
of those lands in Surrey and Kent, generally opposite
to London, that lay within a few miles of the Thames
bank. Their jurisdiction extended upstream to the vicinity of Hampton Court, downstream to a point near
Greenwich. The commissioners were appointed by the
Queen. The elder Thomas Cure had been a commissioner; so had Rowland Hayward; so had James Bacon,
the uncle of Francis. The commissioners in turn appointed a number of jurators, whose duty it was to inspect the sewers and ditches, as well as the river wall,
in the area assigned to them, and to report any deteriorating conditions to the commissioners. It was also
the responsibility of the jurators to determine the
identity of the person responsible for the maintenance
or repair of the deteriorating portion, and to present
his name to the commissioners when they sat formally
as a court. The Surrey and Kent Commission sat as a
court at St. Margaret's Hall (formerly St. Margaret's
church) in Southwark; there the jurators made their
presentments, to be recorded in the official proceedings of the Commission.

By good fortune the early records of the Surrey and
Kent Commissions of Sewers, commencing in 1569,
have survived; and by reading through them one can
see how the various sewer commissioners, and their
presenting juries, set about identifying the landowners
and tenants of the various parcels of land lying along
these common sewers, and how the commission required them not only to pay periodic assessments for
the maintenance of the river embankments and the
major sluices, but also, under penalty of fine, to clean
and maintain those portions of the common sewer

which abutted their lands. One such sewer, on the Bankside, ran along Maiden Lane past the Rose play-house; accordingly, about six rods of its length became the responsibility of Philip Henslowe, and we find the commissioners repeatedly ordering Henslowe to clean and repair "the common sewer before his playhouse." After 1599 the names of Richard Burbage, John He-minges, and others appear periodically for neglecting the ditch by the Globe. Even the elusive Newington Butts playhouse makes a few appearances in the rec-ords, its owner, Peter Hunningborne, being presented for maintenance.[13]

Other kinds of entries are informative in other ways, giving us insights not only into the workings of the Commission but also into the behavior of the local in-habitants. Nicholas Dalton was presented "for that he hath not pulled up a tree that doth lie in the sewer ditch and doth stop the water going to the Earl's Sluice." Richard Dodson and Thomas Cuckowe were presented "to lay a lawful pisser at their ditch end there, that the water may have his course as in old time it hath had." Peter Williams was presented "for that he doth greatly annoy the common sewer with the cast-ing in of the filth that he maketh of his harp strings, which is also a great annoyance to the neighbors in-habiting there." The Masters of St. Thomas Hospital in Southwark were presented "to take down a privy that they have set upon a pisser which is to the great annoyance of the Queen's Majesty's people passing that way." The parishioners of Camberwell, having al-lowed a common bridge to decay, were presented "not only to make and maintain the same bridge, but also to pay a good fine in right to teach them to be more dili-gent another time."[14]

Nor were the jurators or commissioners deterred by considerations of rank: the terms of their commission were clear, and it is not unusual to find presentments of the following sort: "Item, we present my Lord of Winchester to amend and cleanse a rod of length under the bridge going into the park in the parish of St. Saviour's"; "Item, we present My Lord of Canterbury his grace to cleanse and scour his sewer leading to the Prince's Mead in Lambeth"; "Item, we present the Lord Montague"; "we present The Archbishop of York"; "we present our Sovereign Lady the Queen's Majesty." Such was the august company in which Francis Langley found himself on December 5, 1593, when he was first presented before the sewer court for negligence.[15]

In the autumn of 1593 the jurators had found the banks of the manorial millstream collapsing. This stream, in addition to furnishing power for Pudding Mill, was the main drainage sewer for the manor, and thus came properly under the purview of the jury. The function of the millstream as a sewer was complicated, however, by its use as a millstream; for the proper functioning of the mill required that the stream be open to the Thames, and filled to its maximum at every high tide of the river. The various ditches that emptied into the millstream were accordingly provided with their own sluice gates, but the millstream itself had none. The walls along the millstream were therefore of particular concern, for an unexpected breach anywhere along their length might inundate the whole area at the next high tide. When the danger was detected the jury moved promptly. "We present Francis Langley or Matthew Dawson the miller, to fill, cope and make higher 6 pole more or less of the wall from John Wrench's garden house to Robert Face's sluice by Our Lady Day next, upon pain of every pole then undone 16^d." [16]

Langley apparently shared the concern of the jury and made the necessary repairs; the clerk of the court has written "done" in the margin opposite this entry. Langley soon went even further. In 1597, presumably in an attempt to lessen the pressure on the millstream walls, he devised some sort of sluiceway to cut off the water from the Lambeth ditches, keeping it out of the millstream and away from Paris Garden. News of this device reached the commissioners, and they determined on July 29, 1597, just one day after the Privy Council order for the closing of the playhouses, that "a warrant shall be directed to the jury for the east part of Surrey to view a sluice which Francis Langley hath now made in his ground, whether the same be prejudicial or no to the lands and grounds of the Lord Archbishop of Canterbury, and at the next Court to certify their opinions concerning the same." The judgment of the jury must have been in Langley's favor, for no further notice of this matter occurs in the records of the Commission.[17]

At this same Court Langley was assessed his proportionate share of the costs of maintaining the major sluices and the river wall. The costs were shared on the basis of acreage: Langley was rated "for divers parcels of ground with the utter wall . . . in his own tenure, containing in all 60 acres: 20^s." The sixty acres on which he was assessed represent the extent of the demesne lands of Paris Garden manor. The ditches that ran through the copyhold lands of the manor were the responsibility of the copyholders themselves; but the maintenance of the millstream, the roadway bridge that crossed it at the Upper Ground, and the millpond—even the parts that lay within the copyhold portion of the manor—fell to the lord of the manor or to his tenant the miller. The millpond was notorious for overflowing; and even though Langley might go to elaborate lengths to keep water from Lambeth out of the millstream, he had not the slightest compunction about letting millstream or millpond water spill into other parts of the system. "Item, we present Francis Langley, or his farmer or occupier of the mill in the Upper Ground, to pile board and fill up the millpond bank with earth, and to make his bank higher, so as the water do not flow out of his mill pond cross the highway, to the annoyance of her Majesty's people, into the other common sewer leading to the Boar's Head sluice on the Bankside."[18]

In the winter of 1598–99 Langley was ordered to scour the western half of the millstream; a date was given for completion and a penalty set, but Langley failed to comply. On June 29, 1599, the commissioners noted that Langley had "forfeited £30 for not scouring of the sewer between the little bridge leading into St. George's field and the garden of John Wrench, which sewer the said Langley affirmeth he is now scouring, and hath promised to scour the same before the next Court." The commissioners duly noted the promise, and recorded that "at the humble entreaty of the said Langley [they had] given their consents . . . that the said Langley shall be acquitted of the said fine so as he do cleanse the said sewer before the same next Court day." The commissioners were moved to make this concession, they noted, "the rather for that the said Langley paid the charges of their dinner this present day."[19]

The next court came and went, and Langley failed to comply. On October 5, 1599, the savor of their meal long since forgotten, the commissioners noted that although Langley had been given a deadline "to cleanse and scour all that the common sewer leading from the corner next the little bridge in St. George's field all along the green wall down towards John Wrench's new garden gate, containing 120 poles," he had not done so, even though the cleaning "should have been done by Allhollandtide last, upon pain of every pole then undone, 5^s"; the same "was not done," and the penalty was therefore "£30," which amount was communicated to the Collector by the Court.[20]

Even as Langley was attempting to mollify the commissioners with his gustatory distractions, the copyholders were complaining about him on another head. They, together with some of Langley's own tenants, had sent a letter to the Commission requesting that the jurators inspect the mill bridge. The jury was sent out on September 6, 1599, and its finding was that the bridge was so badly decayed it needed to be made anew: "and we do find that Francis Langley ought to make the same, in respect he is owner of the manor of Parish Garden, which hath always repaired the same bridge." The jury made this report to the Court on December 17, 1599, and the Court ordered Langley to make a new bridge by the feast of St. John the Baptist [24 June] or pay £20. A marginal entry reads "not done."[21]

At the next Court the commissioners ordered "a warrant to be made to summon Francis Langley, gentleman, to appear here the next Court day to show cause why he doth not new make Parish Garden bridge according to the order made the last Court, and why he should not pay £20 which he hath incurred for not making the same bridge; and further to stand to the order of the same Court." There is no evidence that Langley ever appeared before the Court as a result of this summons, however, nor is there evidence that he paid the fine. To Hugh Browker, who was one of the commissioners at this time, such behavior would have come as no surprise. The decay of the manor would have seemed to him merely the outward and visible sign of the inward and spiritual condition of its lord.[22]

I have perhaps laid too much stress in the foregoing passage on Langley's neglect of the copyholders of the manor; he was not entirely unmindful of them. It is true that they had been running their own affairs ever since 1580, when they took a lease of their own copyholds under the trusteeship of Thomas Taylor and Richard Platt. By the terms of this lease the copyholders were enabled to hold their own court baron, oversee the transfer and inheritance of their own portions of the manorial land, and adjudicate minor disputes among themselves. Their rents and fees were payable to their own trustees instead of to the lord of the manor. But after the death of Thomas Taylor, one of the original trustees, Richard Platt had demised his whole interest in the lease to a syndicate of five overseers: Richard Wilbraham, esquire, Roger Jones, dyer, James Cullymer, haberdasher, Lawrence Caldwell, vintner, and James Gunnell, stationer. These men all described themselves as "of London," but Caldwell and Gunnell were also copyholders in the manor. The management of the copyhold estate by this board of overseers seems to have worked less well than the original trusteeship under Taylor and Platt, and some of the copyholders may have begun to feel that there might be advantage in attempting to strengthen the old manorial relationship between lord and tenant. At some point in 1598 it must have seemed to a majority of the copyholders that the services due to them from the lord of the manor might be better secured if the lord had a closer interest in the copyholders, and some preliminary conversations may have been held with Langley at that time.

With the death of Gunnell the remaining four members of the syndicate may themselves have become more receptive to the idea of selling the lease back to the lord of the manor. On January 10, 1598, an indenture was actually drawn up, by which Wilbraham, Jones, Cullymer, and Caldwell were to demise to Langley all their interest in the copyhold lease and the trusteeship. Such an indenture, if properly sealed and recorded, would have made Langley truly the lord of the manor, in fact as well as in name; but for some reason now lost to us the negotiations never reached completion. The indenture is carefully slashed through in several places, and the word "cancelled" written across the dorse. It has fortuitously been preserved among the other early papers of the manor, else we might never have learned how close Langley came, early in 1598, to its possession.[23]

Early in 1598 the trial of Richard Renching intruded upon Langley's affairs. In the previous December the Privy Council had directed Sir Richard Martin, the warden of the mint, to arrest Renching for "the clipping of her Majesty's coin"; Renching's house in Fetter Lane had been searched earlier, and "a great quantity of clippings and coin clipped" had been found.

Renching styled himself "gentleman," as Langley did on occasion, but he was a goldsmith by training. Like Langley, he had been a recalcitrant apprentice, and had departed from his master's service without leave, occasioning a confrontation with the wardens of his company. Like Langley, he eventually gained his freedom and soon after was engaged in moneylending. In 1589 he and Langley had combined to entrap Christopher Percy by lending money to him on hard terms, as the reader may recall. In the same year Renching also loaned money to Langley, taking his bond for £200 on a loan of £100. Langley characteristically defaulted, and Renching successfully sued him in Queen's Bench in October 1590. The judgment no doubt resulted in Langley's paying the debt, for on September 28, 1591, Renching again loaned money to Langley, with Gammon as cosigner, in the amount of £51 5ˢ for three months on a bond for £100. Langley later insisted that on December 28, 1591, the due date, he "did well and truly pay unto the said Richard Renching the sum of twenty pounds, parcel of the said fifty-one pounds five shillings, and the said Richard was then contented to continue the loan of the residue . . . for further time upon use of ten pounds the hundred for the forbearing."[24]

Langley and Renching continued this loan for a number of years, for in 1598, when Renching "for certain treasons [coin clipping] by him committed was lawfully attainted and executed," the unpaid bond passed to the Crown with all of Renching's other possessions. In due course the bond was forwarded to the Exchequer for collection, and a writ of *levari facias* was issued against Langley, directing the sheriff of Surrey to collect the amount of the debt from the profits of Langley's land or from the sale of his chattels. Langley, when confronted with the writ, claimed that he had already paid part of it and that he only owed £31 5ˢ; the sheriff claimed the bond was for £51 5ˢ; Langley had no proof of payment for the earlier £20. He entered a plea in the Exchequer Court for relief in which he "did make offer to satisfy the residue of the said principal debt of fifty-one pounds five shillings, but for want of proof of the payment of the said twenty pounds or an acquittance under the hand and seal of the said Renching of the receipt thereof, your suppliant could not be discharged of the said obligation without payment of the said whole principal debt, whereof in truth he hath paid twenty pounds as aforesaid." Langley asked the Court to examine witnesses on his behalf. There is no record of any further proceeding in this matter, so the outcome must remain in doubt. This is, to the best of my knowledge, the only instance of Langley's appearance as a litigant in the Exchequer Court. He may well have capitulated.[25]

XIV

Exit the Alnager

I have done some offence
that seems disgracious in the City's eyes.
RICHARD III

Other matters were beginning to press on Langley at
this time. In the early spring of 1598 the Queen's attorney general, Edward Coke, presented a bill of complaint in the Court of Star Chamber in which he
charged that the four alnagers of the City of London,
"John Leake, [*blank*] Langley, Nicholas Chapman and
George Martin" had engaged in unnecessary harassment and illegal extortion of the clothmakers of the
realm. The alnagers, said Coke, were notorious for
seeking only to "compass their own private . . . gains"
and "to extort and draw by divers indirect and unlawful means from your Majesty's true and faithful subjects great and large sums of money" in violation of
their trust, "nothing regarding their oaths" and without any "regard of the due execution of their said office." [1]

The alnagers, Coke continued, were in the habit of
lying in wait "in the high streets of the said City"
where they regularly "assaulted your Majesty's said
clothiers, and unless your said subjects would forthwith give them great and large sums" the alnagers
would follow the clothmakers to "their usual unloading places within the said City," and had often

"beaten, maimed and wounded divers of your Majesty's said loving subjects," killed or maimed their horses and "taken their packs from off their horses and carried them into strange places and houses, pretending there to search and view the same." The alnagers had also regularly "taken and received of your Highness' subjects . . . several sums of money . . . pretending to take the same for the viewing, searching, trying and sealing" of their cloths brought to market, "but in truth without viewing, searching, trying or sealing of the same cloths."

The details of these charges hardly come as a surprise. The occasion is significant, however, for it demonstrates the readiness of the Queen's Attorney General to bring formal charges against the alnagers in the Court of Star Chamber, where the Privy Councillors themselves sat as judges. Coke concluded that Langley and his fellow alnagers "have not only contemned their duty to your Majesty and abused their said office, but also have committed manifest corrupt and wicked perjury, contrary to their said oaths taken as aforesaid, for that they have not well and lawfully behaved themselves in their said office as alnagers"; he asked that writs of subpoena be issued to the four, "commanding them . . . to appear before your Highness and Council in your Majesty's most honorable High Court of Star Chamber."

The alnagers must have been astonished that their conduct had been noticed, much less challenged, in such high places. On June 3, 1598, the four of them jointly answered the bill in Star Chamber, making a pro forma denial of all the allegations, and shortly afterwards it was decreed by the Court that witnesses were to be called. A preliminary set of interrogatories was drawn up to be answered by Langley and his fellows; the questions were straightforward, and the four alnagers responded to them at the beginning of July. Langley's deposition was taken on July 2. He identified himself as "Francis Langley of Old Paris Garden within the County of Surrey, Gentleman." He affirmed that he had been made an alnager "about twelve years now past . . . by the then Lord Mayor of London and the aldermen his brethren." He denied having taken "any sum or sums of money . . . for any such cause or causes as are mentioned in this interrogatory," but on many occasions, he claimed, having been "informed that great store of faulty and insufficient cloths would . . . be brought into the City," he had taken it upon himself to "watch and attend for the coming" of the said "insufficient and faulty cloths," to seize them and "bring the same . . . to a house next adjoining unto Blackwell Hall." He denied any attempt to "assault, wound or hurt" any clothiers or carriers. When asked if he or his associates had "erected an office" where impounded cloths had to be redeemed, he claimed that "neither he this deponent nor any of the other defendants have erected any such office."[2]

These answers were not adjudged fully satisfactory, and on July 21 a writ was issued from Star Chamber directing John Higham and three others to interrogate the aggrieved clothmakers themselves. This was done towards the end of Michaelmas term. Forty-seven clothmakers and carriers were interrogated, and their stories were the very ones we have come to expect. Robert Colborne affirmed that the alnagers "used to watch carriers and clothiers coming to London for sale of their cloths." They were so relentless in this practice that "no carrier or clothier could come to the City by night or day but there were spies deputed by them lying continually in taverns or alehouses to watch them." Colborne himself "was enforced always to come very late in the night for fear of them, and many times at one o'clock at night to give the porters at the gate sometimes 3^d, sometimes 4^d, to let him in."[3]

Jerome Burman affirmed that the alnagers "have used forcible means against divers carriers, and have cut their wantles to the end to take away their cloths . . . and that there have passed blows betwixt them

226

and the carriers." William Bradley declared that George Martin, one of the alnagers, had stayed the horses of one Nelson and tried to unload them, "whereupon there was a fray, and much blood was drawn, in so much that it grew to a great disorder." Martin and his fellows pursued Nelson to his inn, the Cross Keys in Gracechurch Street—one of the great playing inns before the suppression—and there, "assisted by two of the Lord Mayor's officers," they "violently did break open the door of a chamber and committed a great outrage."[4]

John Curtis claimed that "about Christmas last, Langley, one of the defendants, with four or five other, came to this deponent in a street near Aldgate leading towards the Tower, and there violently in the open street took from off one of the horses of this deponent a pack of cloth . . . and saith further that within one month after, the said Langley, with six or seven in his company, did in the same place in the open street violently take from him six other cloths." Thomas Giles said that "in Lent last or thereabouts the said Langley and Chapman came into the White Hart without Bishopsgate, where this deponent was, and there, with a crow of iron, broke in this deponent's warehouse door there and took away certain cloths which this deponent brought of his neighbors, and did cut the lines of other packs which they had nothing to do with; and another time before, they came and broke open this deponent's chamber door where he lay and fetched out the cloths that were there and carried them away."

Henry Petteward remembered that "in June 1596 Langley and Chapman broke a chamber door, being locked, where this deponent had eleven cloths, which they carried away to their office, and before he could have them again they had of him eight pounds." But door-smashing was not the worst of their offenses. Henry Vintener claimed that "upon the eighth day of March last they took from this deponent's servant one pack of cloths, packcloth and all, about ten of the clock

227

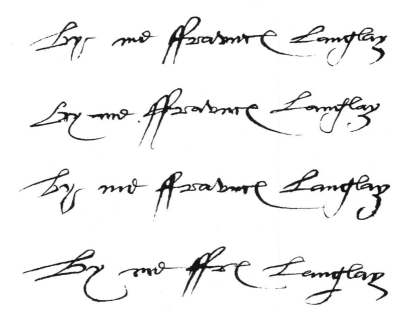

PRO, C.24/134/16 (1578). *The signatures of the heir—* "Francis Langley of London, draper"—*affixed to the four sheets of his deposition in Lady Ursula Langley's suit.*

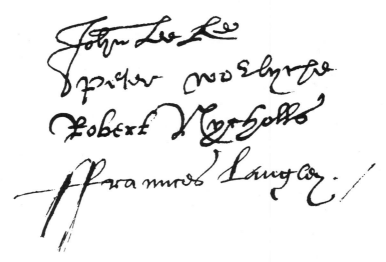

PRO, S.P.12/187 (1586). *Signatures of the alnagers, including the one forged for Langley.*

228

PRO, C.54/1277 (1587). *The signatures of the money-lender*—"*Francis Langley, dwelling in Goldsmiths' Row in West Cheap*"—*affixed to the enrolled copies of two recognizances.*

PRO, Sta.Cha.5/A.8/4 (1598). *The true signature of the alnager*—"*Francis Langley of Old Paris Garden, gentleman*"—*affixed to his deposition in the suit brought by Sir Edward Coke.*

PRO, Sta.Cha.5/S.13/8 (1600). *The signature of the Boar's Head entrepreneur*—"*Francis Langley of St. Saviour's, gentleman*"—*affixed to his deposition in Richard Samwell's suit.*

in the night within Aldgate, cutting the wantle rope and putting his servant in danger of his life, smiting him with naked swords and halberds, and bound him and robbed him and took away his purse and his money." Joseph Alston and Thomas Hammond came into the City together, and Alston recalled that Langley and his fellows "came upon them most violently, and one of them with a sword cut this deponent's head through his hat, and if Hammond had not been by and borne off the blow with his whip and his cloak, it is very like this deponent had been slain."

Such scenes as these, with their mixture of absurdity and pathos, might almost be mistaken for the invention of a Middleton or a Dekker. But they were real enough, and serious enough, at least as far as the Court of Star Chamber was concerned. The alnagers were found guilty of gross abuse of their office and were severally fined. The experience was apparently sobering and chastening to them. Thenceforward they were known to all their associates as fraudulent men, publicly certified as fraudulent by the Star Chamber. The general knowledge of their censure no doubt also emboldened the clothiers to a more spirited resistance when the old tactics were tried again, and the unauthorized seizures may soon have stopped. The embarrassment seems to have destroyed Langley's taste for the office; from that time forward his zeal in apprehending clothiers began to abate, and before long he had turned himself quite away from his former pleasures. His absence did not go unnoticed. On April 17, 1599, the Court of Aldermen determined "that present notice be given to Francis Langley, draper, one of the alnagers, searchers and sealers of woolen cloths at Blackwell Hall, that unless he do from henceforth three days every week execute his said office in his own person, as in right and duty he doen ought, that this Court is minded to displace him and place some other fit person for the execution thereof." [5]

The warning was ineffectual, and before long the aldermen took the inevitable step. At a special session of the Court held on August 8, 1599, Langley's performance as alnager was measured and weighed, and he was found wanting; he was therefore sealed with the F of aldermanic disapproval, and his post confiscated. The aldermen found that Langley "hath not of long time executed his said office as in duty he ought, but wholly neglected the same, contrary to his duty in that behalf." And even though Langley had been "divers times sent for and summoned by the officers of this Court to make his personal appearance here to answer his misdemeanors," he "hath not yet appeared, but in contemptuous manner always made default." The judgment of the aldermen was therefore that "the said Francis Langley shall be presently dismissed and discharged from the said office and the execution thereof forever." He was replaced by the ranking reversioner, one Thomas Normecote, clothworker.[6]

As both the pleasure and the profit had abruptly disappeared from Langley's activities as alnager, his loss of the post may not have unduly distressed him. But some of his other failures must have been more galling. By this time there was neither pleasure nor profit to be had in the Swan playhouse, but here Langley had lost neither his taste for the social diversions nor his appreciation of the monetary benefits that came with the ownership of a usable playhouse. He was certainly not depressed by the contemplation of renewed activity in this arena. He might yet become an entrepreneur if the opportunity should arise to buy or build another playhouse—somewhere else, perhaps under another man's name, away from the parish of St. Saviour's and the accumulated hostilities of the past five years. Indeed, these five years had wrought real alteration in the direction of his life. In 1594, ensconced in the manor house, burgeoning as a moneylender and intrepid as an alnager, beginning the erection of a new playhouse, he could hardly have dreamed that five years later his plans would be in such disarray. Even the manor of

Paris Garden was increasingly a flawed treasure, and Langley's joy in his lordship, in being a seigneur, was by now quite tempered by his incessant encounters with copyholders, sewer jurors, churchwardens, tax assessors, and the local Justices of the Peace. Beginning in about 1599, Langley's thoughts began turning away from Paris Garden.

Such a development was distressing to his wife, Jane, who had grown accustomed to the comforts of ladyship. But Francis was not to be deterred. He asked Jane to query her brother Sir Anthony Ashley about buying the manor for £2,000; she did so, albeit with reluctance. Jane often took into her confidence an elderly widow named Alice Pattenson who lived in the Langley household at the time, perhaps as a servant; and on this occasion Mrs. Pattenson was not left uninformed. As she recalled some years later, Jane Langley had complained to her "that her husband Francis Langley had caused her to go to her brother Sir Anthony Ashley, knight, and to offer the sale of the said manor unto him, for that she said it was to be sold." The encounter between brother and sister must have been a sad one. Ashley "did demand of her the price of it, and . . . she did answer him that her said husband would sell it for two thousand pounds." And then Jane learned the sad state of her own brother's finances. He too was in debt; he too was forced "to sell a piece of land for to pay his debts." The best advice Sir Anthony could give his sister was "to make the best of her land and to sell it to whom they would"; for himself, he said, the price "was too much . . . he would not buy it nor any more land till he was out of debt."[7]

The news was scarcely calculated to cheer, and Langley must have received it glumly. But Mrs. Pattenson was ready with a suggestion, or so she remembered. Mr. Browker had always been interested in the manor, she said, and on this occasion she suggested his name as a likely purchaser. Indeed; but Langley could hardly bring himself to approach Hugh Browker with

such a confession of insufficiency. Browker was a man
of uprightness and substance in Southwark. He was an
officer in the Court of Common Pleas and had represented his borough in the Parliament of 1592. But he
was no friend of Langley's. As executor of the estate of
the elder Thomas Cure, he had watched Langley ensnare the younger Thomas and make off with much of
his substance. As a churchwarden of St. Saviour's, he
had later confronted Langley about the matter of the
tithes, and as one of the sewer commissioners for Surrey he had periodically fined Langley for his negligence. No, Langley could not do it. But Mrs. Pattenson
could; accordingly, she was furnished with the details,
and told "to acquaint Mr Browker herewith, and that
he should buy it if it pleased him." Mrs. Pattenson did
so at once; she "went to the said Mr Browker's house
in Southwark, and did there acquaint him with it in
his garden."

And there, in Hugh Browker's garden, the seed was
planted that would soon grow to fruition. Thereafter
he and Langley warily began staking out their respective bargaining positions, and cultivating one another;
but many months were to go by before a firm agreement
was reached. By an odd coincidence the two men found
themselves joined together on a royal commission in
the summer of 1599, for collection of the lay subsidy in
Southwark, and this may have given them a readier
pretext for meeting. And in the meantime Langley
found himself involved in yet another venture. In the
spring of 1599 he met one Oliver Woodliffe, haberdasher, who was engaged in the remodeling of an inn in
Whitechapel. Woodliffe and an associate, Richard
Samwell, had converted the inn to a playhouse. Woodliffe was now short of capital, and was looking for
someone to buy into the venture. He wondered if Langley might be interested.[8]

XV

The Boar's Head

Thou most beauteous inn, why should
hard-favour'd grief be lodg'd in thee?
RICHARD II

In practice, Oliver Woodliffe was no more a haber-dasher than Francis Langley was a draper. He had served a conventional apprenticeship and had been made free in 1572, but thereafter, like Francis Langley, he disappears from the records of his company. Wood-liffe's livelihood lay elsewhere, in an assortment of speculative dealings. In November 1594, at about the time Langley was commencing the erection of the Swan playhouse, Woodliffe invested in an inn called the Boar's Head, just outside the City bars in White-chapel. Like Langley, he intended to build a playhouse. The inn was owned at that time by Jane Poley, a widow, and her son Henry; Woodliffe's investment took the form of a lease of the premises for twenty-one years, at a cost to him of £40 a year. The terms of the lease were straightforward, but there was one condi-tion that was to prove troublesome: Woodliffe had to agree to spend £100 within seven years on the erecting or refurbishing of certain parts of the inn on the west side of the innyard. If he failed in this expenditure, then he was to forfeit his lease and a bond of £300 be-sides. Woodliffe's lease became effective on Lady Day 1595, and at some time after that date he began various of his projects on the west side of the yard; they included, as he later recalled, the "building of the larder, the larder parlor, the well parlor, the coal house, the oat loft, the tiring house and stage."[1]

During the first two or three years of his lease Woodliffe apparently made little more than token progress on these structures. The ordinary business of running the inn may have been a hindrance to him, and perhaps an expense as well. Except for certain upper rooms on the west side of the inn reserved as living quarters by the widow Poley and her son, the entire remainder of the inn was in Woodliffe's charge. He had not invested in the Boar's Head in order to become an innkeeper, however, and on April 13, 1598, he contrived to free himself of this burden by leasing most of the inn to one Richard Samwell for a period almost equal to the remaining years of his own lease. Woodliffe retained control of the buildings on the west side of the inn upon which he still had to expend money, but conveyed to Samwell the buildings on the other three sides (except for an upper room in which Woodliffe and his wife still lived), and also granted Samwell the right of "ingress, egress, and regress" to the great central innyard. For this conveyance Samwell paid Woodliffe £40 a year. Woodliffe, in turn, passed the money to the widow Poley as the full amount of his own rent. Samwell moved his family into some rooms in his own portion of the inn, and he and Woodliffe then undertook the project that was to consume much of their energy and capital over the next few years—the construction of the Boar's Head playhouse.[2]

The surviving descriptions of the Boar's Head inn are remarkably circumstantial, enabling us to identify with a fair degree of certainty even the individual rooms of the establishment and their relation to one another. But these descriptions are all quite innocent of any measurements or dimensions, and furnish no clue whatever about the size of the yard. Sisson conjectured, on the basis of an analogy with the Fortune playhouse, that the yard of the Boar's Head inn was at least 90 feet by 75 feet. This is a perfectly legitimate conjecture, but nothing more. Those who described the inn seemed uniformly to believe that the yard was large; it is invariably referred to as the "great yard." As no one mentions a small yard, we may perhaps assume that "great" is intended to be descriptive rather than distinctive. Sisson's dimensions conjure up a yard large enough to contain the entire Fortune playhouse; and indeed, as the Boar's Head playhouse was built within the yard of the inn, some such size would have been necessary if the playhouse was to have any capacity. But a large playhouse means a large investment; hence Woodliffe's need to come to terms with Samwell.[3]

The details of their negotiations are difficult to reconstruct. The evidence comes from subsequent claims and counterclaims at law, in which each party took occasion to recall or interpret matters differently. But it appears (thanks to Herbert Berry's painstaking research) that the original plan had been for Samwell and Woodliffe each to construct galleries against the buildings over which he had control. Samwell's galleries were to extend over the yard, on posts, from the northern, southern, and eastern buildings of the inn; Woodliffe's would extend from the west and would be part of the rebuilding which he was required to do there. Woodliffe was also to build the stage and tiring house. These matters were settled and construction was well underway when, in the summer or autumn of 1598, Woodliffe had to go on an extended trip abroad. Samwell agreed to oversee all the construction, including Woodliffe's gallery, during his absence. When Woodliffe returned in the spring or summer of 1599, he found the playhouse in operation and all the essential structures completed except for a second, or upper, gallery on the east side which Samwell was just commencing.

But Woodliffe's sense of the proper size for the playhouse had undergone a change, either during his year's absence or immediately on his return. The finished galleries did not strike him as sufficiently ample. He persuaded Samwell that they should pull them down on all four sides and rebuild them to extend out over the yard an additional four feet. The added profits, he argued, would more than repay the added expense. Samwell assented, and new construction began. Woodliffe was still bound by his covenant with the widow Poley to expend £100 within seven years, and four of those years had already passed; he therefore set to work again on the refurbishment of the various rooms on the western side of the yard as well as on the reconstruction of his long gallery over them. For Woodliffe as for Samwell, the project was costly. Samwell soon found that he did not have the capital to finish the structural work to which he had committed himself, and Woodliffe was apparently unable to muster up even enough money to complete his £100 investment. Both men began to look elsewhere for funds.

Samwell found financial assistance available from Robert Browne, a player, with whom he may have been in contact from the time of his first involvement with Woodliffe in the projected playhouse. Browne was quite willing to help Samwell by lending money for the completion of the galleries, in return for certain concessions about the use of the playhouse. Browne advanced £100, or perhaps even £200, toward the payment of the carpenters. But Samwell soon found that these loans were only short-term remedies. He was unable to repay them, and before long, certainly by the autumn of 1599, he found it necessary to surrender to Browne his entire interest in the inn, excepting only the quarters in which he and his family lived. Browne paid a total of £360 for the lease, less the money already advanced, and moved his company of players into the playhouse.

Woodliffe's own share in the new playhouse was similarly destined to dwindle. His holdings were already reduced to the western buildings, with his additions to them; the profit came from the earnings of the long gallery, which were divided between him and the players in the customary fashion. Samwell's arrangement with Browne had proven a fortunate one, at least for Browne, and the prosperity of the venture was reflected in the steady earnings that Woodliffe realized from his gallery. But Woodliffe still needed money. He had been introduced to Langley in the spring of 1599, almost immediately on his return from abroad; one result of that meeting may have been Woodliffe's decision that the Boar's Head galleries were too small. Woodliffe may also have tried to get some money from Langley at that time. But Langley must have been hard to deal with in the spring of 1599, smarting from his confrontation with Coke in Star Chamber, resenting the curt order of the aldermen to do his job as alnager, and depressed at the prospect of having to find a purchaser for Paris Garden manor. Langley may have turned Woodliffe's request aside, and Woodliffe may have sensed that a later time would be more propitious. In any event, he undertook the rebuilding of his western gallery on his own resources that summer. But Samwell's subsequent leasing of the remaining portions of the inn and theatre to Browne may have been an unexpected development that drove Woodliffe to seek out Langley once again to discuss his troubles, his need for cash, and his half-interest in a long gallery. By this time Langley was himself again, and ready to listen.

Langley knew from past experience what a popular gallery in a good playhouse might be worth. Woodliffe's description must have interested him; indeed, later estimates of the takings from the western gallery of the Boar's Head suggest that Woodliffe's half eventually amounted to four pounds or more a week. Langley was interested. He offered to "buy the whole interest of the said Woodliffe and his wife of the said Inn" for £400, as he later deposed. At this time Woodliffe's whole interest ostensibly consisted only of the western

buildings and of the gallery profits; but there may also
have been some sort of understanding between the two
men that Samwell's (and therefore Browne's) tenure of
the yard might be called into question, as it was not
founded on any documentable evidence. The new galleries built by Samwell and Browne stood upon posts
set into the yard, thereby offering opportunities for
endless dispute about who really owned them. Either
Woodliffe and Langley agreed to collude in an effort to
defraud Samwell and Browne of their rightful interest
in the yard, or else Woodliffe consciously defrauded
Langley by misrepresenting the matter to him. Either
way, Langley's offer of £400, a higher price than
Browne paid to Samwell for the whole remainder of
the inn, suggests that Langley had in mind more than a
mere half-share in a gallery.[4]

Whatever the explanation, Woodliffe and Langley
formally concluded their agreement, and Woodliffe
gave Langley a lease dated November 7, 1599, for his
entire interest in the inn. Langley paid £100 in cash
and gave Woodliffe three bonds for £100 each (double
if forfeit, as usual), borrowed from his nephew Richard Langley. Langley in turn extracted a bond from
Woodliffe in the amount of a thousand marks (£666 13^s
4^d) for the "security of the same lease." It is difficult to
infer from this latter bond whether Langley was taking
his normal precaution in the completion of what he
thought was a straightforward agreement, or whether
the bond represents a covert contract between him and
Woodliffe to sustain jointly the costs of the legal harassment of Samwell and Browne. In view of Woodliffe's
impecuniousness, the latter is perhaps the less likely.

The stage was therefore set for a confrontation between Langley and Woodliffe on the one hand, and
Samwell and Browne on the other. Langley's position
would be that Samwell had no rights in the yard other
than those of normal traverse—"ingress, egress, and
regress"—granted him by Woodliffe in the original
lease. Any other activities by Samwell in the yard were

to be regarded as trespass, and no acknowledgment was to be made that any further understandings existed between Samwell and Woodliffe. And, of course, Langley would refuse to recognize Browne's claim, for his position assumed that Samwell had nothing in the yard to convey to Browne. Langley and Woodliffe would begin, therefore, by focusing their attention on Samwell, even though at that time Samwell no longer had any active interest in the premises.

Samwell, meanwhile, was not oblivious to what was taking place. Indeed, Woodliffe may already have approached him demanding rental for the yard. As soon as Samwell learned that Woodliffe and Langley were negotiating a lease he divined its purpose, and went to law. In Michaelmas term 1599, probably at the time of Langley's acceptance of the lease, Samwell brought an action for trespass against Woodliffe in the Court of Queen's Bench, and presented a bill in Chancery against both Woodliffe and Langley. But Langley was unimpressed; in a later suit in Star Chamber, Samwell maintained that Langley, "nothing regarding the penalties and forfeitures" involved, ignored the Chancery proceedings against him. Samwell claimed that Langley was interested only in "unlawful maintenance, champerty, and buying of pretensed rights and titles"; these terms constitute a virtual indictment of Langley's activity. "Maintenance" is covert assistance, usually in the form of money, given to one of the parties in a lawsuit by a nominally uninterested third party to enable him to keep the suit going. "Champerty" is a bargain between one of the parties in a lawsuit and an outside third party to divide between them the land or other matter sued for in the event that the litigant wins his suit. Champerty is an aggravated form of maintenance, and both are illegal by common law; but cloudy or obscure titles invite such activities on the part of unscrupulous men, and Langley well knew by now that all such actions could be turned to profit with a little skill and patience.[5]

Langley's insolence went beyond the mere ignoring of Samwell's suit. Langley promptly filed a complaint in the Marshalsea Court against Samwell, and when Samwell refused to appear Langley took steps to have him arrested. On Friday December 13, 1599, Langley and Mrs Woodliffe, accompanied by two bailiffs of the Marshalsea, their two servants, and Owen Roberts, a carpenter, entered the inn "most forcibly with bills, staves, swords and daggers," as Samwell later recalled. On this occasion the visitors probably did no more than serve a summons and an admonition, but the tone had been set.[6]

Three days later the little group returned, at about seven in the evening, armed with "swords, daggers, rapiers, pistols and other weapons." They entered "most riotously and forcibly . . . into the said dwelling house of your said subject [this is Samwell again] called the Boar's Head, and then and there with their weapons drawn did assault your said subject, and Richard Samwell your subject's only son and child, and did then and there very sore beat and hurt [the two of them] in their arms and legs and divers parts of their bodies." But the intruders had more than simple mayhem on their minds, according to the elder Samwell; they intended nothing less than "to murder and kill" Samwell and his son. To achieve this discreditable goal, "they, the said riotous persons, did in the dark throw divers daggers and other weapons at [them], which weapons, hardly missing [them], did stick in the walls of the said house, so as [they] hardly escaped their lives by shifting and flying away from their assaults." The "riotous persons," having failed in their effort "to kill and murder" the Samwells, thereupon took yet another despicable course and had them forthwith arrested.[7]

Langley's own view of these later events was more ingenuous. He remembered none of the offences laid to his charge by Samwell; he "did not to his remembrance" engage the bailiffs to "enter into the said messuage or Inn upon or about the 16th day of December last past," though he thought that Woodliffe might have; nor did he or any of the others, "to his knowledge, assault or hurt the complainant or Richard Samwell his son." On the contrary, Langley recalled hearing quite the opposite, that "Richard Samwell [the younger] and others his servants . . . did shrewdly beat the said Marshal's men and their servants." Nor, indeed, did Langley or any other to his knowledge "throw any dagger" at anyone; Langley "had not any weapon at that time nor doth usually carry any weapon at all." The truth rests somewhere in the middle, of course. Langley and the bailiffs had come to the inn with a warrant of Woodliffe's for the arrest of the elder Samwell, and after a brief scuffle Samwell had agreed to accompany them. But he changed his mind when his son appeared with some of the servants; another affray ensued, in which the younger Samwell succeeded in rescuing his father from the bailiffs. The arrest was therefore not completed, and the day's activities resulted in a stalemate.[8]

It was clear to Samwell by now that Langley and Woodliffe were "intending by vexation to oppress" him; he could find no other explanation for "the malice of Langley conceived against your said subject." But Langley was not finished. On December 24 he and his entourage arrived at the playhouse with another writ, this time for the arrest of young Richard Samwell for his assaults on the bailiffs. Young Richard was not in, and his father had managed to lock the door to the galleries before Langley's arrival. But Owen Roberts, Langley's carpenter, was along, and recalled that he and Langley "did set their hands to the said door and did thrust it open." Anthony Strayles, another of their company, was then set at the stair foot to gather money "of such as came then hither to hear the play." In the absence of young Richard, the bailiffs took his wife Winifred, she "having a young infant then of the age of three weeks . . . sucking at her breast," and held her prisoner in Southwark until the elder Samwell posted bail for her.[9]

The matter of the locked gallery door must have provoked Langley, for when he returned yet again two
days later with Roberts and the others he proceeded to
cut open a section of the wall in Woodliffe's upper
room—where the Woodliffes still lived, even though it
was in Samwell's (now Browne's) part of the inn—to
make a passageway into the gallery that was built along
that side of the innyard. Samwell and Browne, of
course, would claim that gallery as their own; but
Langley was not to be deterred. He later recalled the
incident: "Owen Roberts did, by the commandment of
this deponent, cut down certain quarters in the end of
the said galleries with such tools as carpenters do use
in such cases, and made a doorway into the said galleries." Langley wanted access to the galleries, he explained, "for that they, the said galleries, do stand
upon this deponent's ground, as this deponent hopeth
to prove." Roberts's recollections were in agreement.
He remembered that as he "was cutting down the said
wall the complainant's son [young Samwell] came unto
them and did forbid this deponent to work there; and
thereupon the said Langley willed this deponent to go
forward in his said work, and he would bear him out in
it." [10]

Langley's visits to the inn were frequent, either for
structural alterations or for the serving of warrants.
There was method behind this steady harassment.
Each time Langley or Woodliffe contrived to have Samwell arrested, it cost Samwell at least ten shillings in
fees in addition to the payments to the Marshal's men
and the cost of getting his bail bond drawn up and
sealed. In December, at about the time he began his
harassment of Samwell, Langley leased a part of the
innyard to one Thomas Wollaston, and Wollaston in
turn leased a part of his part to one Richard Bishop.
Both these men were Langley's creatures, and the purpose of the new leases was simply to multiply the occasions for litigation. Wollaston, Bishop, and Langley
could then each sue each of the Samwells for trespass
on his particular portion of the yard; they and Langley

together then harassed the Samwells without letup. During the Christmas season alone, for example, Langley recalled that young Samwell "was arrested two several times, whereof one was at the suit of Richard Bishop and the other at the suit of Thomas Wollaston, upon action of Trespass committed upon such grounds as this deponent had let unto the said Bishop and Wollaston."

There were similar arrests of the elder Samwell by both Wollaston and Bishop, and of both Samwells by Langley; a few arrests were made in Woodliffe's name also. Samwell's servants Edward Willis and Rowland Rose were arrested too. But the arrests were simply harassing measures; no suits were ever prosecuted against those arrested, despite the constant threats of action for trespass. Langley denied "that he did bring the said actions of purpose to vex the complainant or his family, or to charge them with the fees of arrests," and stoutly maintained "that he did never say that he would undo the complainant by arrests, nor did use any words to such effect." [11]

In this fashion Langley spent the Christmas season of 1599, harassing the Samwell family, even as two years earlier, at Christmastide 1597, he had intensified his harassment of the hapless clothiers. Perhaps the seasonal festivities at the turning of the year inspired him to a renewal of his own energies, leading him to seek those outlets most congenial to his own tastes. The harassment of the Samwells eased abruptly, however, at the end of December. The holiday season was traditionally one of high receipts for playhouses, if Henslowe's records may be taken as typical in this respect, and Langley's interest in the Boar's Head playhouse was largely founded on its potential profitability; but excessive disruptions might soon begin to drive away the patrons, and Langley's love of disorder had to be tempered by his concern for steady profits from the galleries. Browne, too, was concerned about the patrons; but he may soon have realized that

Langley's disruptions were carefully confined to the Samwells, and not expanded to include himself and his troupe. From this he may have deduced that Langley was trying, in his own way, to maintain the operation of the playhouse despite the incessant forays and arrests. For indeed, Langley brought no suit against Browne, nor arrested any of his men, so far as I can determine; they were allowed to trespass freely in the yard as they went about their profitable business.

The tormenting of Samwell was for other ends. As long as Langley could maintain the position that he was the rightful lessee of the yard, he could continue to trouble Samwell until the latter agreed to some sort of composition in the matter. Samwell could buy his way out of further trouble, if he wished, by settling with Langley out of court, though such a settlement was bound to be costly to him; or he could insist on his rights, and continue to endure Langley's equally costly vexations. Langley hoped for the former, of course; it meant less effort on his part. But Samwell was doggedly tenacious, and after a few months of quiescence Langley found it necessary to commence harassing him again. The arrest of young Samwell on April 4 was but one of many such instances inflicted on Samwell that spring, but it seems to have been the final straw for him. He had already gone to Chancery against Langley in the previous November; but the course of judgment in Chancery was slow, and Samwell's fury was mounting. He could hardly endure Langley's vexations through the entire course of a Chancery decision. A speedier and more potent remedy lay at hand, and Samwell took it. He brought a new bill of complaint into the Court of Star Chamber.

In his new bill he rehearsed all his new grievances, which had not as yet transpired at the time of his earlier plea in Chancery. He described the riotous arrival on December 13 to serve a summons; the nighttime assault in his own quarters, complete with dagger throwing, on December 16; the forcing of the gallery door and the taking of money on December 24; the cutting of a doorway on December 26; the arrests made on himself, his son, his son's wife, and his servants; and the implacable malice of Langley, which underlay all these actions. He sought also to remind the honorable judges in Star Chamber that Langley had been before them on another charge not long before: "the said Francis Langley [is] a man heretofore questioned and convicted in your Majesty's High Court of Star Chamber for many unlawful offenses." The reference is of course to the alnager case, heard in the previous year. Samwell also reminded the Court that Langley was "well known to be a barrator and a common disturber of your Majesty's subjects, by prosecuting suits, by sinister vexation of your subjects." Samwell may have felt uneasy about the term "barrator," for he lined it through before submitting his bill. The deletion is puzzling. A man guilty of champerty and maintenance is clearly a barrator, and Samwell shrank from neither of the former terms. We may never know why he hesitated at "barrator." [12]

The Court of Star Chamber wasted no time. Samwell entered his bill on April 11, 1600, and the defendants were contacted immediately. Langley and Owen Roberts brought in their answers on April 17; Foxley and Johnson, the two Marshalsea bailiffs, answered on April 24; Woodliffe brought in his answer on May 10, and felt constrained to apologize for his inordinate delay. And indeed, by Star Chamber standards he was late. The judges had by that date already evaluated the earlier answers, found Langley's and Roberts's to be insufficient, drawn up interrogatories for them to answer, and taken their depositions. Langley deposed on April 30, Roberts on May 1. By the end of May the proceedings were complete. As all the records of decrees and orders from Star Chamber are missing from this period, there is no evidence that a judgment was actually rendered. Samwell's grievances were grounded more in humanity than in law, and Langley and Woodliffe stoutly maintained that Samwell had no rights in the yard. Langley may well have been reprimanded by the Court, but it is not certain that the Court's judgment, if rendered, would have gone against him. Samwell may have withdrawn the suit. Whatever the ultimate outcome, it must have been over by the summer of 1600. Samwell endeavored to keep his earlier Chancery suit moving, and as late as October 1600 was still arranging for depositions to be taken on his behalf. But he had clearly lost his spirit, and after November 1600 he disappears from litigation. He and Langley no doubt reached some sort of an understanding. As a last fling, Samwell brought suit against Robert Browne, but soon withdrew it, went home, and died before the following summer.[13]

The seventh of November, 1600, marked the anniversary of Woodliffe's assignment of the lease of the Boar's Head to Langley. It had been a vigorous and interesting year. Browne and his players continued to use the playhouse, and Samwell had finally bowed out under the pressure of Langley's arguments. Langley and Woodliffe had survived a Star Chamber suit, and apparently outlasted Samwell's Chancery suit. All seemed to be going well. But November 7 was also the due date of the first of the three bonds that secured the balance of Langley's debt to Woodliffe for the lease. Woodliffe could hardly have anticipated that Langley would default on the bond; the playhouse was at last free of encumbrance, Browne's troupe was proving popular, and the premises represented a steady source of income for Langley. But Woodliffe had underestimated his partner. Just a month earlier Langley had managed to reach an agreement with Hugh Browker about the terms of the sale of Paris Garden, and his mind and spirit were elsewhere. The due date for the bond came and went, and no payment was made.

But if Langley had lost interest, he had not lost his shrewdness. A year earlier, Woodliffe had bound himself in a thousand marks to convey a secure lease to

Langley, and the experience of the ensuing year had amply demonstrated that the lease that Woodliffe had conveyed was anything but secure. The evidence of Samwell's intransigence was incontrovertible. Langley might quite properly renege, and even demand that his original £100 be returned. He might then force payment of the thousand marks as well. Woodliffe stood in some peril. Accordingly, he sought to make the first move, and brought suit against Langley at the common law early in 1601.[14]

But this was a game that Langley had played before. An action for debt brought into a court of law could often be stayed by the defendant by the simple expedient of bringing into a court of equity a plea for relief from the suit. This was a tactic that Langley had used in the past; Pembroke's players had even used it against Langley in 1597. Woodliffe's suit presented no new difficulties, and Langley, with his nephew Richard, promptly entered a counter suit in the Court of Chancery. Their plea was found to be a "billa vera," or true bill of complaint, and Woodliffe was ordered to abstain from all proceedings at the common law until he had defended himself satisfactorily in Chancery. And there the matter ripened and mellowed. The deliberate pace of proceedings in Chancery, so vexing to Samwell, was a source of balm to the Langleys. Woodliffe had been stopped, and thereafter they might prove as dilatory as they pleased, for they were in no hurry to have their delaying tactic terminated by a judgment.

More important, Langley was perhaps uncertain about the entire Boar's Head venture. In the early stages of his Chancery suit against Woodliffe he seriously entertained a proposal to withdraw. Woodliffe offered to deliver up to him the three bonds, including the forfeit one, and to return his original payment of £100 as well, in return for Langley's giving back the lease and the bond for a thousand marks. Langley responded that he was "likewise content" with this arrangement "so as he may have up . . . such costs and charges as he hath been at in and about the building and repairing of the said house." It is perhaps difficult at this stage to suspect Langley of straightforward dealing, but it is quite possible that at the moment he was weary of the whole enterprise. Their tenant, Robert Browne, was not slow to capitalize on the disaffection between Langley and Woodliffe. He promptly withheld all his payments from the western gallery, on the reasonable grounds that he could not determine who was the rightful owner of the proceeds. But it was Woodliffe, not Langley, who complained of this in Chancery. "One Browne, who is tenant of part of the house or Inn in question, taketh the profits of the whole house and payeth nothing either to the plaintiffs or defendant for the same."[15]

Had matters remained as they were, Langley and his nephew Richard might well have extricated themselves from the playhouse and left Woodliffe and Browne to confront one another. But Browne, in an effort to secure his own substantial investment in the Boar's Head, chose this juncture to bring a suit in Chancery against both the Langleys and Woodliffe. The timing was ironic; Langley and Woodliffe had just settled comfortably into their adversary roles when Browne forced them to become united as defendants. More dilatory litigation was clearly in store, but one effect of Browne's intrusion may have been the reawakening of Langley's interest in the playhouse. The simple exchange that he and Woodliffe had perhaps been on the verge of making was now put into the background, and new argumentative positions staked out. But during all this time, the main business of Langley's life was taking place in another sphere. His arrangements with Hugh Browker were never far from his thoughts, and the complications attendant on the settling of the Paris Garden estate, though not nearly so dramatic as the complexities of the Boar's Head playhouse, were far more intricate.

249

XVI

Exit the Lord of the Manor

Let all my land be sold.—'Tis all
engag'd, some forfeited and gone; and what remains
will hardly stop the mouth of present dues.
TIMON OF ATHENS

The manor had to be sold. Langley's debts were
mounting and the Boar's Head playhouse, for all its adventure, was at last only a diversion and ultimately not
profitable. By the autumn of 1600, at about the time
that Samwell was capitulating, Langley had reached
an accord with Hugh Browker about the terms of the
sale. It had been just one year since he first took possession of the Boar's Head, and in that brief span of
time Langley had been sued for debt by a great many of
his creditors. Most of the debts were straightforward,
and should have been paid. The suits at the common
law were fair, and could not be stayed by counter suits
in equity because of a general lack of extenuating circumstances on which to build a case. Langley no doubt
tried to enter blocking suits, but I have been unable to
find any, which might argue that his bills were thrown
out of court. Thomas Harrison, a merchant of the City
who had lent money to Langley by means of his agent,
one Blage, sued Langley in Queen's Bench in Easter
term 1600 for a defaulted bond, now worth £500; Richard Langley and Hannibal Gammon were named in
the suit as cosigners of the bond. The Court awarded
its judgment to Harrison, who moved to collect. In the

250

same term Langley, along with his nephew and Gammon, were sued by Thomas Hassould in Common Pleas on another defaulted bond, this one worth £100. Hassould also won his suit, and moved to collect.

The two Langleys and Gammon were also sued during this period by one Henry Fermor, gentleman, who held a forfeited bond worth £100; by John Jaques, a merchant, also for £100; and by Tidsley Monk, a country gentleman from Hornchurch, Essex, for the same amount. Langley was also sued "on his sole bond," that is, without cosigners, for £200 by John Wells, a clerk; for £40 by John Guy, an attorney in the Court of Common Pleas; for £200 by Oswald Durant, one of the new alnagers for the City; for £200 by Christopher Hill, a draper; and for a modest £7 by William Kympe, a Paris Garden neighbor. The records show that in five of these latter suits as well, the Court awarded its judgments to the complainants, at a total cost to Langley of almost a thousand pounds. The records are inconclusive in the remainder of the cases, perhaps suggesting settlements out of court; but had they come to trial, and been lost, they would have cost Langley an additional £400. In all but three of these cases, Langley was arrested by a bailiff of the Marshalsea at the commencement of litigation. This was normal procedure, of course, but there were so many suits pending against Langley in 1600 that he may well have begun to feel almost as harassed as Richard Samwell by the constant threat of arrest. Life must have been wearisome on those terms, and Langley's lack of enthusiasm at the end of the year may be explained in part by his own sense of growing persecution. A settlement with Browker was all the more imperative.

Langley's plan for the sale of the manor to Browker was quite simple, but it was a simplicity born of desperation. The price the two men finally settled upon was £2,500, a substantial improvement over what Langley had earlier asked of Ashley. Once the agreement had been struck, in September or October of

1600, a schedule of payments was devised, requiring Browker to pay quarterly sums of money to Langley or to his assigns. Browker was to pay £400 at the time of the agreement, that is, in Michaelmas term 1600; £300 in the Hilary term next following; and thereafter £200 in each of the four yearly law terms until the full sum had been paid. If uninterrupted by external considerations, this schedule would have kept Browker paying until Easter term 1603.[1]

But an agreement to buy and sell was not the same as a sealed indenture. Langley and Browker had struck a bargain, but there was nothing binding in Langley's offer and Browker knew it. But Browker also knew Langley, and perhaps was able to detect the early signs of fatigue in his bearing or demeanour. Langley was being pressed by debts. Browker might relieve the pressure, by paying the purchase money for the manor not to Langley but directly to Langley's creditors. Langley would simply sign bonds for the appropriate amounts, as security for Browker's outlays; the bonds would be canceled when the title to the manor was transferred to Browker. Langley might, if he wished, change his mind at any time about the sale of the manor; should he do so, all his bonds to Browker would be automatically forfeit. Browker might in this fashion convey the whole £2,500 to Langley, or to his creditors; but if Langley then failed to complete the transaction, he would owe Browker £5,000. The arrangement must have seemed secure enough to Browker, for he proceeded with it; and Langley's intentions appear to have been equally serious, for he did indeed begin using Browker's money to clear his debts.

Browker of course wanted a sound conveyance, a tenure unencumbered by obligations; so it was in his own best interest to clear Langley's debts before effecting a transfer of title. But he soon discovered that the process would take longer than he had anticipated, Langley's debts being so extensive. Browker remembered that when he and Langley "went to his counsel to get his assurances drawn, there were many lets and hindrances thereof by means of the said Francis Langley and his dealings, so that [Browker] could not get such good conveyance and assurance of the said manor and bargained premises according to the said bargain as was fit until about the month of January [which] was a twelvemonth after the said bargain made," that is, until January 1602. Browker would, in other words, have to pay some £2,200 to various of Langley's creditors before the manor could be cleared of all encumbrances. The news was apparently upsetting but not disabling, for the two men agreed to go on with their bargain.[2]

Gammon later recalled the events in a different sequence; to his remembrance, it was Browker's discovery of the true extent of Langley's debts that led him to propose his method of payment. As Gammon saw it, "between the time of the said bargain-making" between Langley and Browker "and the passing of the assurance," there had grown up "divers sums of money due and payable by the said Langley upon bonds to sundry his creditors." As a means of allaying these debts, "divers sums of money were, by the said Langley's consent, received of [Browker] to discharge the same bonds, which sums of money [Browker] was then contented to disburse and to let them be for and towards the sum of money which he was to pay for the said purchase." Hence the need for the bonds: "because the assurances for the purchase were not then made, the said Mr Browker for his own security took bonds for the repayment of the said sums of money, if in case the assurances should not be perfected as was agreed upon."[3]

Gammon remembered several of the bonds, for he had been a cosigner in many cases. In the first term of the agreement, Michaelmas 1600, Gammon remembered being present on two occasions when Langley gave bonds to Browker; Gammon cosigned both of them "as followeth (viz), one bond wherein this depo-

253

nent and the said Langley stand bound in four hundred pounds for the payment of two hundred pounds, dated the 13 of November anno 42 Elizabethe Regine; one other bond of one hundred pounds wherein this deponent and the said Francis Langley stand bound to [Browker] for the payment of fifty pounds, dated 24 November anno 43 Elizabethe Regine." There were other payments as well in that term, though apparently not up to the full amount bargained for. Browker himself later recalled that in that first Michaelmas term he paid out only "three hundred and fifty pounds, part of the said sum of four hundred pounds." No explanation is offered for his failure to pay the balance, nor does his failure appear to have caused any friction; but the amount that he did pay went in its entirety, so far as I can determine, to Langley's creditors.[4]

Gammon remembered that during the course of the next dozen or sixteen months Browker made several payments on Langley's behalf, Langley furnishing bonds to secure the payments. Of the bonds that were cosigned by Gammon, "all and every the said sums of money were received of [Browker] and paid to the creditors of the said Francis Langley, to whom they were due"; and these payments were all effected "before such time as [Browker] had the said manor conveyed to him by deed in writing." Gammon was also present at some of the payments, and was able to affirm that "in the presence of this deponent" Browker paid "to Mr Blage of the Temple, to the use of the said Thomas Harrison, £20; To John Audley or his assigns, for charges of suit for [Browker] of a hundred pounds, £16; to one John Leake [the alnager], £20 in part of fifty pounds . . . To James White, the sum of fifty pounds, with interest for the same and costs of suit," and so on.[5]

Browker was not always able to satisfy Langley's creditors with payments in cash, however; much of the time he was constrained to offer them his own bonds in order to redeem Langley's. This arrangement may even have been advantageous for Browker, as it enabled him to defer for six months or a year the payments that would otherwise have been due at the time. But it also complicated the accounting. Richard Langley remembered quite clearly how Browker had to "satisfy divers of the creditors of the said Francis Langley . . . by giving his own bonds for payment of the several sums of money to them owing by the said Langley." But he also remembered the cash settlements, and described how he "did receive of [Browker] the sum of twenty pounds in money to pay unto one Mr Pyncheon, mercer, in Cheapside, to whom the said Francis Langley stood indebted for a more sum."[6]

John Turner, a scrivener, was Langley's agent in many of the original bonds; for the most part they were of his own making, and like all competent scriveners he kept his own records of the issuance and payment of these negotiable instruments. As he himself explained, "he being a dealer for the said Langley was acquainted with all and every the said payments." Turner confirmed all of Hannibal Gammon's recollections and was able to add to them. His records showed that Browker had made cash payments to several of Langley's creditors, most such payments being in part rather than in full: "to Thomas Playne, £24 . . . To Thomas Geram, servant to the said Francis Langley, £10 . . . To George Turfett, £20 . . . To Mr Lewis Lewkenor or to his use, fifty pounds; To Thomas Walker, forty-two pounds; To Francis Kemp to the use of Edward Archer, fifty-two pounds ten shillings . . . All which he knoweth to be true."[7]

Turner also remembered that "as part of the money which he was to pay for the said manor," Browker "became bound severally" to other of Langley's creditors. Turner had a record of many of these new bonds as well. By his reckoning, Browker had become bound to Thomas Squire of Clement's Inn for £80; to Richard Littler for £120; to Robert Smith of the Inner Temple for £52 10ˢ and again for £105; to Henry Palmer for £55 16ˢ; to Nicholas Satterley for £52 10ˢ; to Edward Harvest for £105; to Edward Archer for £51 5ˢ and again for £52 10ˢ; and to James Pemberton, goldsmith and now alderman, Langley's old associate from the time of the purchase of the manor, in three bonds for £20 each. These assurances alone, as the methodical reader will have calculated, amount to nearly a thousand pounds.[8]

Langley was not slow to appreciate the possibilities inherent in this new arrangement. If Browker intended to guarantee his debts, there was no reason why he should not continue to borrow money where he could. Langley soon began to enjoy the process of disposing of the manor even as he had earlier enjoyed the process of acquiring it. He would manage Browker as he had managed young Thomas Cure, and make the selling as profitable to himself as the buying had been. He approached Thomas Squire of Clement's Inn for a loan, and Squire recalled Langley telling him "that Mr Browker was to buy of him, or had bought of him, the manor of Paris Garden, and was in respect of that bargain to pay and discharge many of the debts of him the said Francis." Nor did Langley hide these practices from Browker. Through the agency of Richard Johnson, a scrivener, Langley arranged a loan of £100 from one George Barkley, and Browker himself, along with Thomas Emerson, cosigned the bond. Johnson, the scrivener, recalled Langley explaining to him "that notwithstanding that he the said Francis was principal in the bond, yet Mr Browker would discharge the money at the day, in regard of certain moneys which was behind for the purchase of the said manor of Paris Garden."[9]

Thomas Jadwin, another scrivener, made a bond for Langley for £100 borrowed from Nicholas Satterley, with "the said Francis Langley as principal debtor and the said Mr Browker as his surety"; and, indeed, just as Langley had predicted, "afterwards the said Mr Browker . . . did pay." Another of Langley's credi-

256

tors, George Turfett, demanded of Langley twenty pounds on one occasion, and Langley responded by penning a note to Browker which Turfett recalled as follows: "Mr Browker, I pray you do me that favor as to pay my good friend Mr George Turfett twenty pounds, which I owe him, and it shall be allowed you of the moneys which I am to have paid upon the purchase; by that token that you left the book with me. Written the 7th of August 1601, yours, Francis Langley." And afterwards, as Turfett affirmed, Browker "did pay unto this deponent the full sum of twenty pounds."[10]

One can only marvel at Browker's patience in the face of these impertinences. But his funds were not inexhaustible, and after a time his equanimity wore thin. He personally delivered £42 to old Thomas Walker, the royal housekeeper at Whitehall, in settlement of one of Langley's bonds; Walker recollected Browker's sighing "that he had paid more money for the debts of Langley by £200 . . . than the purchase of the manor of Paris Garden was worth, and wished that he had never dealt with the said Francis Langley for the said purchase, for he might have had a far better bargain for his money, or words to that effect." Browker himself recalled his distress at finding "the premises far more encumbered than he did think of"; and how, "being weary of following the said Francis Langley," he began to wish himself out of the arrangement. He asked Langley at one point to find another purchaser, "to get any other to repay [him] his money and damages and to take the premises."[11]

Browker's fatigue was not caused by Langley's monetary excesses alone; there were also legal complications. The reader will recall that when Francis Langley purchased the manor of Paris Garden there was some difficulty about a thousand-year lease to part of the property. Browker, who was one of the executors of the elder Cure's will, claimed to have sold the lease to his friend Michael Smalpage, while the widow Cure confidently sold it to Hannibal Gammon. Of the two

257

supposed purchasers, Michael Smalpage has the shorter history, for he was dead by the autumn of 1594; at his death the thousand-year lease became once again a topic of discussion. Richard Bury, a country squire from Bedfordshire, was a friend of Smalpage's; he could vouch for Browker's conveyance of the lease to his friend, for he "was a witness to the said deed of assignment, and did subscribe his name as a witness to the same." He further affirmed that the deed was dated "the eight day of June in the thirtieth year of the reign of our . . . sovereign Lady Queen Elizabeth," that is, on June 8, 1588, a date well in advance of Langley's claimed purchase of the lease for Gammon. Bury was also present at the deathbed of Michael Smalpage in 1594, and signed his name to Smalpage's will "as a witness." Smalpage had appointed his brother Thomas Smalpage to be the "full and whole executor" of his will, and it was Bury's considered judgment that Michael Smalpage's whole interest in the thousand-year lease had thereby passed to his brother Thomas Smalpage.[12]

William Haydock of London was also with Michael Smalpage in 1594 "when he lay on his death bed," and recalled Smalpage saying at that time, "I have settled my estate and have made my brother Thomas Smalpage my executor, because I am assured of his faith and love to my wife and children." Haydock "was a witness and did subscribe his name thereunto," and approved Thomas Smalpage's appointment of Hugh Browker as "executor therof." In due course Thomas Smalpage died, though Haydock insisted that he was "in good and perfect health" at the time he made his will. One must assume that the Smalpages were a sickly family, else this sequence of events begins to sound a bit melodramatic. On the death of Thomas Smalpage the thousand-year lease came once again into the hands of Hugh Browker.[13]

Browker's annoyance with the widow Cure in 1589 had been increased by her insistence "that she did convey the said term of one thousand years unto the said Hannibal Gammon." For a variety of reasons, Browker forbore to take issue with this new development. He might easily have gone to law, but he hesitated to do so "for the love he did bear to the said Thomas Cure the younger, [Browker's] wife's brother," who "unprovidently was wrapped into very hard covenants and great bonds to the said Francis Langley . . . wherewith he might have been endamaged if [Browker] had entered." Browker nevertheless had his opinions "concerning the insufficiency of the right" whereby Langley "did take the profits and use the possession of the capital house and other things part of the said manor."[14]

Further complications were still in store for Browker. Among Langley's creditors was one Robert Allison, who at the time of his death was in possession of unpaid bonds of Langley's. Allison's executor, Edward Harvest, a brewer, went to law upon the unpaid bonds, and apparently threatened to attach a part of the manor in lieu of satisfaction. He and Langley, with Gammon's assistance, thereupon reached an agreement whereby the thousand-year lease would in effect be pawned to him as security for the payment of the bonds. The actual procedure was a bit more complex. Gammon began by conveying "his interest in the said lease of 1000 years to the said Edward Harvest." Then, with the understanding that "the interest of the said lease was tied for the payment of forty pounds yearly by the said Francis Langley during the term of 21 years," Harvest "did regrant and convey again the residue of the said term of one thousand years to . . . Hannibal Gammon." The thousand-year lease, then, was encumbered by a twenty-one-year claim for forty pounds a year.[15]

Langley, as might be expected, said nothing of this to Browker during the course of their negotiations. The payment of the annual £40 to Harvest had been further secured by binding Langley "in a recognizance in nature of a statute staple of six hundred pounds for payment of the said forty pounds per annum." Browker might at some point have become aware of this bond; Gammon thought it wiser to tell him outright, but Langley was opposed. The encumbrance on the lease was to be kept secret. Langley, as Gammon later recalled, did not have "any intent to advertise [Browker] thereof"; but Gammon took matters into his own hands, and "of his own accord informed" Browker of the circumstances, apparently in the early spring of 1601. John Turner knew of Gammon's action in telling Browker, and also remembered that "the said Langley was very angry with the said Gammon for so doing." As Browker finally understood the transaction, Gammon "had conveyed his interest under the said lease unto one Edward Harvest and had taken an assignement back again by which the interest of the lease was tied for the payment of forty pounds by the year by Francis Langley during the term of one and twenty years."[16]

This meant, of course, that even after Browker took title to the lease he would still be obligated to pay an annual premium to Harvest. Over the full term of the encumbrance these payments would amount to some eight hundred pounds or more, and Browker was quite properly angered about having been kept in the dark. Langley attempted to shrug off the matter as of no consequence, but Browker was adamant, and the two men finally reached an agreement whereby Browker "should from thenceforth take upon him to pay the said forty pounds yearly"; and, "in consideration thereof," Langley would rebate from the total purchase price "the sum of three hundred pounds, part of the money which [he] was to pay unto the said Francis Langley." The settlement appears, on the surface, to have worked to Langley's advantage, as indeed do many of the other arrangements in which Browker engaged himself as part of the procedure for the purchasing of the manor. But in this instance we may see that

Browker was shrewder than Langley supposed; for there could be no encumbrance on Gammon's thousand-year lease if Gammon had never owned the lease. Browker's acknowledgment of a debt to Harvest was a convenient means of getting Langley to reduce the purchase price; and Browker could at any time produce his own evidence about the lease to quash Harvest's claim. But Langley did not know this, and was probably beginning to think that Browker was soft, unable to deal shrewdly or with rigor. Langley, accordingly, soon contemplated even further excesses.[17]

Gammon remembered calling upon Langley at a time (as he put it) when Langley had been paid by Browker "to the sum of twelve hundred pounds or thereabouts," which must mean in the summer of 1601. Gammon was himself among those people who were creditors of Langley's, and on this occasion he had come to ask Langley "about moneys that were due" to him, money which Gammon "had paid for him upon arrests and executions." But a forthright answer was not to be Gammon's lot that day; instead, "Langley fell to persuading of him . . . to leave his trade and to bring his wife and children and to dwell with him the said Langley" in Paris Garden. Gammon was no doubt touched by the sentiment, but he felt obliged to ask Langley "how he would satisfy Mr Browker . . . for those moneys which he had received of the said Mr Browker in part of the said bargain."[18]

The consideration was of no moment, said Langley; "he would repay the said Mr Browker as he was able the moneys which he had received of him." Gammon must have seen that it was a foolish boast, but he was not prepared for what followed. Langley urged that if Gammon "would come unto him," he would see to it that "the said Mr Browker should never have his bargain, and that he the said Langley would never sell the said manor to the said Mr Browker or any other." Gammon was left speechless by this suggestion, "whereby [he] gathered that the said Langley had a mind both to defraud the said Mr Browker and other creditors to whom he the said Langley was indebted." The details of Langley's proposed stratagem are not clear, but it seems on the face of it an extreme notion even for him, and the appeal of the plan to Gammon must have been minimal. Gammon's trade as a goldsmith was a comfortable one. He still lived in Cheapside with his wife, Frances, and their four surviving children; their eldest son was nineteen, their youngest only a year and a half. He was rising in the esteem of the Company of Goldsmiths, and had been chosen that very summer to participate in the Trial of the Pyx, an annual assay conducted by the Company of Goldsmiths at the direction of the Government to certify the quality of coins issuing from the Mint. Gammon had no need to throw all this over to live with Langley on the Bankside.[19]

Gammon left Langley that afternoon without his money, without even the promise of his money, but surely with increased misgivings about his participation in the entire affair of the manor, and perhaps also with growing doubts about his friend Langley's realistic assessment of his own limitations. Not very long after that, Gammon and Browker were in contact with one another, and Gammon signed over to Browker his entire interest in the thousand-year lease. The formal assignment from Gammon to Browker took place on July 20, 1601, and was witnessed by Thomas Emerson, another associate of Browker's from the Inner Temple who was also known to Langley. Browker was quite businesslike about this transaction. On the following day, July 21, he sold his entire interest in the lease to William Howpill and Thomas Harvey, two gentlemen of Lyons Inn, an Inn of Chancery attached to the Inner Temple. Emerson witnessed this transfer as well, and also the assignment which took place on the following day, July 22, when Howpill and Harvey redemised their interest in the lease to Browker again for a period of one hundred years, retaining the subsequent term of the lease to their own use. These exchanges of title were intended to strengthen Browker's claim to an entire interest in the lease, and to prevent Langley's filing a subsequent complaint.[20]

It is uncertain whether Langley viewed this transaction with equanimity. When challenged on this point some years later, both Emerson and Browker maintained that the various assignments of the lease had been done "with the privity and consent of the said Francis Langley," and Browker even insisted that all three transactions were sealed "in the said chief mansion house of the said manor in the presence of the said Francis Langley." These statements are no doubt technically true, but they tell us little of Langley's reaction to the events. The withholding of Gammon's lease from Browker may have been the final trump that Langley was hoping to play; but Gammon had played a cooling card that would have destroyed any hopes along this line, and Langley had no recourse but to acquiesce. Langley and Gammon had known one another ever since the latter had been taken in as an apprentice in alderman John Langley's shop. The two men had shared much, and in their own way they had been close; but I have found no evidence that they ever saw one another after this date, except as the exigencies of the law might bring them together in court. Both men were in their early fifties.[21]

Thereafter Langley found little solace in his erstwhile companions. Sir Anthony Ashley's own disaffection with Langley antedated Gammon's; indeed, it dated from the diamond misadventure, but one may assume that Ashley had been loath to go to law against his own sister's husband. The extremity of his debts must have become intolerable, however, for in July 1601, the very month of Gammon's treachery, Ashley brought suit in the Court of Queen's Bench to collect the six hundred pounds that he claimed Langley owed him from the diamond. Langley evaded the issue; he was not to be found when Henry Anderson and William Glover, the sheriffs of the City, arrived with their writ. Langley was then ordered to appear before the Queen's Bench at Westminster on October 17, 1601, and again he was not to be found, though Ashley and the Justices awaited him there. The judgment was accordingly awarded to Ashley by default, with damages of £6 10ˢ in addition. But Langley did not pay then, nor did he ever pay.[22]

Had the sheriffs of London (who were also sheriffs of Middlesex) known of Langley's claim to an interest in the playhouse in the Boar's Head Inn, they might have attempted an attachment of the premises. Instead, they found themselves obliged to report to the Court that Langley "had nothing in their bailiwick." This was just as well, surely, for the whole question of title in the playhouse was the subject of lawsuits in both Common Pleas and Chancery between Langley and Woodliffe. It was not even in Langley's interest to win his case, for so soon as he might establish a legal claim to any of the profits of the playhouse Ashley would be enabled to sue forth a writ of *fieri facias*, ordering the sheriff to take all the subsequent proceeds up to the amount of the judgment. Langley was required therefore to maintain an active opposition to Woodliffe in the courts, but not to allow matters to proceed to a judgment either way. The entry of Robert Browne into the affair, with his Chancery suit against both Langley and Woodliffe, altered the picture somewhat. Should Browne win his case, thereby establishing the validity of Samwell's original claim to have rights in the yard, then the suits of Langley in Chancery and Woodliffe in Common Pleas would both be terminated, and neither party would be advantaged thereby.

Browne had in fact taken his company into the provinces in the early autumn of 1601, leasing the Boar's Head playhouse to the Earl of Worcester's company during his absence. The new players did not realize that they owed fealty to Langley, and Langley, despite his weariness, could not let pass the opportunity to introduce himself. He arrived at the playhouse on the morning of a playing day. John Mago, who was Browne's carpenter, was working in the yard with his assistant John Marsh at the time; he remembered that Langley "by force with some rude company" got "possession of the said stage and tiring house and galleries, swearing and protesting to kill or slay any that should resist them." Mago and Marsh were "working in the said great yard" at the time of this invasion, "and one of the said Langley's company with a halberd or such like weapon struck at this deponent's servant, then working there, and almost wounded him, but as God would he hurt him not." The assistant, John Marsh, concurred that Langley "got the possession of the said stage and tiring houses [*sic*] . . . and with a company of rude fellows kept the same, some of them swearing and vowing that they would kill or murder any that should resist them; and this he hath cause to remember, for that one of the said company with a halberd or such like weapon had almost maimed this deponent in the thigh."[23]

Despite the fatigue of other business, it seems, the prospect of some profitable rowdyism could always move Langley to action. Worcester's players—Will Kempe, John Lowin, Christopher Beeston, Thomas Heywood, and their fellows—had intended to use the playhouse that afternoon for a performance; but they were intimidated by the armed rout on their stage and had to come to terms with the intruders. Langley's terms were the predictable ones; the players could continue to use the stage, tiring house and galleries for their plays, but they were to acknowledge Langley as their rightful landlord and bond themselves to pay him £3 a week for their continued privilege. Mago, the carpenter, remembered hearing that "some of the company of the players" were "forced to enter into bond to pay £3 a week" to Langley, "which they were constrained to do" because Langley claimed to own the playhouse and "the players for that winter had no other winter house licensed for them to play in"; Mago thought that "the said weekly payments began at Michaelmas time or thereabouts and were to continue until Shrovetide then next following," earning for Langley, in all, some sixty pounds for his morning call, and perhaps persuading him that some good might yet come of the Woodliffe business.[24]

But still another spectre hung over the Boar's Head. By the terms of his original lease from the widow Poley, Woodliffe was obligated to expend £100 in the building or refurbishing of certain features on the west side of the innyard. The term allowed for these expenditures was seven years, and that term would expire on Lady Day (March 25) 1602, now only a few months away. If Woodliffe failed to make good on this expenditure, he would forfeit his own lease, and of course all the leases depending from it. It was imperative that he finish his building on the west side of the yard. Unfortunately, the yard was no longer his; Langley claimed it, and so did Browne, and he would lay himself open to further suits for trespass if he attempted to do the work under those conditions. Browne was not inclined to help; he seems to have looked on Woodliffe as the source of all his troubles, and if Woodliffe lost his lease it might be just as well. Perhaps then the Poleys would undertake to resume landlordship themselves, or, better yet, lease the premises to someone with a clear interest in the theatrical operation, someone like Robert Browne perhaps. Browne might even find it useful to obstruct actively any attempt by Woodliffe to complete the building on the west side. After all, the stage and tiring houses were also on the west side, and any building activity in that area might arguably disrupt the playing.

All the more reason, therefore, for Woodliffe to combine with Langley to defeat Browne's claims. Langley's views about the construction were more genial; it was in his interests to keep Woodliffe in the Boar's Head, and he even seems to have offered to lease sufficient room in the yard for Woodliffe to finish his work—contingent, of course, on their prior success in defeating Browne's suit. Accordingly, Langley drew up a lease demising to Woodliffe "certain romeths [that is, open spaces] part of a messuage called the Boar's Head." But the lease was not sealed; it was shown to Woodliffe, who approved it, and then given to Hugh Browker for safekeeping. Browker later recalled that the lease was "delivered by the said Woodliffe to [Browker's] custody to be kept to the use of the said Francis Langley." In return for this enabling step, Woodliffe gave Browker a bond for £8, representing perhaps (as Herbert Berry suggests) the cost of the repairs made by Langley in the Boar's Head. Browker also gave Woodliffe a bond for £12, which he remembered as being the price of the lease; it was probably an assurance to Woodliffe of Browker's good safekeeping of the document.[25]

Whatever the exact details of the arrangement, they must have been ultimately successful, and Woodliffe must have completed his expenditure of £100; for Lady Day 1602 came and went, and Woodliffe retained his tenure in the Boar's Head Inn. The process would have been expedited if Browne had withdrawn his Chancery suit; but in any event, Langley and Woodliffe promptly returned to their adversary positions, with Woodliffe appealing to Chancery to allow his Common Pleas suit against Langley to proceed once more. Langley, he claimed, was stalling unconscionably in the Chancery proceedings. And so he was; so they both were, probably by unspoken common agreement, at least till Woodliffe's expenditures were completed, his lease secured, and Browne's claim held at bay. So the opening months of 1602 saw the Boar's Head enterprise mired yet again in the courts, where it would continue for the foreseeable future. The opening months of 1602 also saw another important event in Langley's career; the formal sealing, in January, of the indentures by which Browker at last took the manor of Paris Garden from him.[26]

267

XVII

Cardigan

It is not so good to come to the mines.
HENRY V

Francis Langley's fortunes had passed their peak,
and were tumbling downhill. A judicious observer
might have discerned this a year or so earlier; by the
beginning of 1602 it must have been apparent to the
world at large. He had lost Paris Garden; he had been
discharged from his post as alnager; his theatrical en-
terprises were at a standstill, stalemated at the Boar's
Head and stopped entirely at the Swan. Even his holdings in Cheapside, the Saracen's Head and the Horse
Head—long mortgaged to Giles Simpson—finally had
to be sold, and Langley and Simpson had jointly conveyed them to Robert Lee, alderman. For Langley,
there was now nothing of any substantial value left.
Not since the early years of the 1580s had he been so
bereft of worldly goods. Then, however, his prospects
had been bright; now there was little to await him but
old age. But he was not the sort to resign himself; he
still had enough energy and enough capital for another
gamble, and he decided to risk it. He could hardly have
known it was to be his last venture.[1]

The enterprise that he now contemplated was of uncertain value and had a dubious history. We might best
begin the story a year earlier, with a familiar incident.

268

In January 1601 the Earl of Essex's household steward Sir Gelly Meyrick—Ashley's nemesis from the Cadiz voyage—had approached the Lord Chamberlain's players at the Globe playhouse and offered them forty shillings if they would present the play of King Richard the Second on Saturday February 7. The players had been reluctant, arguing that it was an old play and not likely to appeal; but Meyrick was insistent, arguing the special desire of the Earl of Essex, and the players finally acceded to his demand. The performance was duly given, and attended by Meyrick along with Sir Christopher Blount, Lord Mounteagle, Sir Charles Percy and a number of others. Fortified in this fashion by the tale of a deposed monarch, these followers of the Earl lent their support on the next day, February 8, to Essex himself as he attempted to raise an insurrection in the City of London. The attempt was a failure, though it had its moments of high tension; certain Privy Councillors, who had called upon Essex at Essex House and been allowed entry, were subsequently imprisoned there by Meyrick, and for some hours their fate was uncertain. But the calmer heads—that is to say, the Cecil faction—carried the day, and by nightfall the leaders of the uprising were in submission. The Essex rebellion was over, having lasted only one afternoon; but it had indeed been a rebellion, and therefore treasonable. As a consequence, the fate of the chief participants was sealed.[2]

Sir Gelly Meyrick was among the first to suffer censure. He was attainted for treason on February 9, tried on March 5, and hanged at Tyburn on March 13. All his goods were confiscated to the use of the Crown. As with most men of property or standing, a certain portion of his goods belonged to the Crown to begin with; and he, as a tenant in chief with regard to these items, would therefore be subject after his death to an *inquisitio post mortem*, that is, an enquiry by a jury to determine which Crown leases or patents he was seised of at his death, and who his heir was. In Meyrick's case, as a result of his attainder, there was no permissible heir for his Crown holdings; all these chattels were forfeit. Among those properties that Meyrick held *in capite*, and which therefore returned to the Crown, were the leases to certain mines in Wales, reputed to be the source of great wealth.[3]

Meyrick had purchased his leases to these mines some five years earlier, perhaps on his return from Cadiz. The leases had been granted originally by the Queen to John Hopwood on November 6, 1595, and Hopwood in his turn had demised them to Meyrick. The acquisition of wealth had always been one of Meyrick's ambitions, and in looking westward to the mines of Wales for the fulfillment of these aspirations he perhaps typified a characteristic attitude of his time. Fanciful tales about the silver mines of Cardiganshire had been current in London throughout the 1580s and 1590s, and men of a speculative turn of mind sought for ways to go west and make their fortune. The characteristic industry of the sixteenth century was mining, and rumors of the fabled mines of the Indies had not hindered this development. A new technology, men hoped, might now reveal the secrets of the earth; a new industry would bring affluence within reach. The discovery in 1545 of the silver mines at Potosí, high in the hills of Peru, had not only brought astonishing wealth into the royal coffers of Spain, but had also awakened the imaginations of men throughout Europe. The name of Potosí became a synonym for limitless wealth, and the exploration of older mines was resumed with vigor. In England, barely two years after Elizabeth's accession, the Company of Mines Royal was chartered, and the fair hills of Albion were surveyed with new eyes by an enterprising breed of investors.[4]

Rumors reached London by the late 1580s that a mining operation financed by Thomas Smythe, the collector of import customs for the Port of London, had been gratifyingly successful. Smythe's chief miner,

Charles Evans—so the report went—had discovered silver in the mountains of Cardigan in unprecedented quantities. Later communications tempered this rumor for the judicious; Smythe had admittedly undertaken to mine in Wales, under a lease from the Company of Mines Royal, but the mines that he was putting back into operation were ancient (some said Roman) lead mines at Cwm Symlog in the hills east of Aberystwyth. Some of the lead ore did indeed contain silver—as is often the case, in varying amounts—but it was unlikely that an undiscovered British Potosí lay hidden in the crags of Cardigan. Popular enthusiasm dies hard, however, and the rumors of Smythe's silver mines gained new currency when he did in fact discover a lode at Cwm Symlog whose silver content was unusually high.[5]

Sir Gelly Meyrick's mines were at Cwm Ystwyth, a barren holding on the Ystwyth river only a few miles from Customer Smythe's operation. There is no evidence that Meyrick actually tried to work the mines, but one must assume that he did; avarice and dilatoriness seldom go hand in hand. News of the richness of Smythe's mines at Cwm Symlog must have spurred all the neighboring entrepreneurs to renewed activity, and those who were not fortunate enough to be in on the action must have cast covetous glances. Among those whose eyes had been attracted to Meyrick's holdings at Cwm Ystwyth were Lewis Lewkenor and his uncle Sir Richard Lewkenor, members of a conventionally ambitious Sussex family. Sir Richard was the new Chief Justice of Chester, having been appointed to that office by the Queen just two days before the execution of Sir Gelly. His seat was at Ludlow Castle. His nephew Lewis Lewkenor lived in London, and was attached to the Court in a minor capacity. In 1601 he was a creditor of Francis Langley's, and Hugh Browker paid £50 to him as part of the purchase of Paris Garden manor.[6]

The news of Sir Gelly Meyrick's attainder, and con-

THE MINES OF CARDIGAN

sequent forfeiture of his leases, moved the Lewkenors to action. The leases would once again be in the Queen's gift, and they began to entertain the hope of securing them for themselves. One needed more than a mine to engage in mining, however; the appurtenances could be costly, but could not be forborne. Near the mines at Cwm Ystwyth, on land held by Edward Vaughn, stood a mill for smelting ore. Meyrick had no doubt used it. Lewis Lewkenor leased it from Vaughn, at a rental of £8 yearly. At the mines were some tools and implements belonging to Sir Henry Guildford. Meyrick had probably leased them from Guildford, and offered to pay in lead ore or refined lead, for Guildford claimed to own certain quantities of both that stood near the mines. Sir Richard Lewkenor bought the lead, lead ore, tools, and implements from Sir Henry Guildford for £100. The Lewkenors then had the Cwm Ystwyth mines effectively bracketed between them, with Lewis holding the smelting mill and Sir Richard the tools. The Queen might now award the leases of the mines to whomever she wished; the Lewkenors hoped that it might be themselves, but even if the leases went to someone else, the new grantee would have to treat with the Lewkenors if he expected to profit from his venture.[7]

On August 21, 1601, the Queen granted the leases to Sir John Morley, to run from the previous March 25 for twenty one years. The rental, as with Hopwood and Meyrick, was to be £5 yearly. Morley accepted the leases with humble thanks, but was more interested in them as commodities than as licenses to dig. He soon made contact with Lewis Lewkenor in London, and the two men combined to find a purchaser for their several leases. They settled upon one John Dallender, who seemed genuinely interested in working the mines, and signed articles with him whereby he was to acquire Morley's lease of the mines and Lewis's lease of the smelting mill for £250. The first payment, in the amount of £50, was to be made on Christmas 1601, and a default clause was written into the articles whereby Dallender's failure to make the first payment would be grounds for canceling the whole agreement. Dallender would be allowed, in the meantime, to work the mine, extracting and refining the ore as he wished, but he might not take any profit thereby until the perfecting of the articles.

Dallender still needed tools, however, so he journeyed to Ludlow Castle to call upon Sir Richard Lewkenor. Sir Richard was using the tools and implements that he had purchased from Sir Henry Guildford in a small mining operation of his own; he had acquired an interest in mines at Cwm Penllydan and Llwyn y Coed, and was extracting and refining ore as he could from those two sites. Dallender might have the tools, Sir Richard said, if he would agree to carry on Sir Richard's enterprise at these two sites, and also to reimburse him for his expenses to date. Dallender was willing enough to work, but had no more money. He struck an agreement with Sir Richard whereby the profits of the Cwm Ystwyth mine would be divided equally between the two of them until Sir Richard's asking price (which was now £250) was met. The profits of the other two sites, which belonged wholly to Sir Richard, were not to be reckoned into this account. Both men were satisfied, and Dallender went off to Cardigan and set the miners to work.

The extraction of the lead ore was tedious, and the refining was slow. The lease of the smelting mill had carried with it some adjoining woodland to furnish timber for the smelting fires, and Dallender's men spent an inordinate time cutting firewood. Christmas approached, and the mine showed little profit. Dallender, "after he had bestowed some three or four weeks or thereabouts" in "the felling of trees," and setting his workmen "as well to smelt and make lead," found that his money was once again gone. He could not pay wages. The operation was not so prosperous as he had been led to believe. (Sir Gelly Meyrick may well have learned the same lesson at an earlier date.) He began to seek means to extricate himself. His "money . . . being then spent, he went from thence to London . . . to supply the same . . . pretending and promising . . . to return again thither"—this is Sir Richard's recollection. But Dallender never returned. He called upon Lewis Lewkenor in London on December 26, the day appointed for the payment of his first £50, and confessed that he did not have the money. Lewis reminded him that, by the terms of their agreement, the articles were thereby canceled. Dallender agreed, and departed.[8]

The Lewkenors and John Morley had not fared badly in this exchange. Sir Richard had his mining operations at Cwm Penllydan and Llwyn y Coed managed for him for a month or so; Lewis had a quantity of timber cut by his smelting mill; and Morley had gotten some ore dug out and perhaps even refined. None of this had cost them a penny. They might now begin to look for another client. But, unexpectedly, John Dallender returned to Lewis late in January 1602 asking "to recontinue his former bargain for the said mines." As earnest of his renewed intentions, Dallender "did not only pay unto the said . . . Lewis the sum of fifty pounds" which had been properly due on Christmas, but he "did also faithfully promise to bring one Mr Hugh Browker" to Lewis "to be bound to him . . . for payment of the residue."

We may be reasonably certain, I think, that Hugh Browker was not interested in buying a lead mine in Wales. But someone had managed to obtain £50 for Dallender, and had assured him that Hugh Browker would furnish more. There is only one candidate. Yet we have no evidence to suggest how, in December 1601 or January 1602, Langley and Dallender might have met. Lewis Lewkenor knew Langley, of course, and he might have suggested casually to Dallender that he was a money broker; but Langley already owed money to Lewis Lewkenor, and his financial plight could hardly inspire confidence in a creditor. Nevertheless, Dallender had reappeared with money and an offer. Lewis was uncertain what to do. Dallender insisted that Browker would not only bind himself to Lewis, but would also sign bonds to Sir Richard for the full amount. Lewis wrote to Sir Richard at Ludlow, inquiring whether he ought to require Browker to sign bonds to Morley as well. And, in the meantime, "Lewis Lewkenor was content to allow the said John Dallender his former bargain and to accept of him the fifty pounds which he before had made default of payment of."[9]

Sir Richard Lewkenor, ensconced in Ludlow Castle, was somewhat cut off from these negotiations, and was dependent on his nephew's correspondence for his information. He was therefore quite unprepared when, "at or about the first day of March" 1602, someone named "Francis Langley . . . came to [him] to Ludlow." His visitor had a marvelous if ingenuous tale to tell. He had met a man in London named John Dallender, he explained, and had bought from him the leases to several mines in Cardigan, at Cwm Ystwyth, at Cwm Penllydan, and at Llwyn y Coed, along with a smelting mill and certain quantities of lead ore and refined lead at the mineheads. Dallender had sold him all these leases for £100, which Langley had paid to Dallender's agent Lewis Lewkenor. Dallender had also assured him that Sir Richard Lewkenor would sell him all the necessary tools and implements for working these three mines for only £100 more. He and Dallender had just come from Cardigan, Langley told Sir Richard, and the mines themselves were satisfactory; Langley had come to Ludlow, therefore, to see about the tools.

Sir Richard hardly knew how to respond. He began by explaining to Langley that the mines at Cwm Penllydan and Llwyn y Coed belonged to him, not to Dallender; that Dallender had leases only to the Cwm Ystwyth mine and to the mill, and that even these leases had been forfeit on December 26 last for non-payment. Langley was astonished; he insisted that he had had "speech and conference" with Lewis Lewkenor in London, and Lewis had "avowed the interest of the said Dallender to be good and indefeasible." Sir Richard then explained that Dallender's claim had been reinstated by Lewis on the tardy payment of £50, and the assurance of bonds to come; but those bonds had not come, and in the meantime Sir Richard had been required to pay wages to the miners and to meet other expenses as a result of Dallender's decamping in December. At this news, "the said Francis Langley, seeming to be much disquieted and discontented, told the said John Dallender that he had very greatly abused him." Langley was "the more troubled" in that he had already paid "one hundred pounds or thereabouts" to Lewis in London, "for which the said Francis Langley . . . had little or no assurance more than the bare words of the said . . . Lewis Lewkenor and John Dallender."[10]

Sir Richard was appropriately sympathetic, but it was clear that Dallender had misrepresented himself to Langley and that Langley had not been careful. Sir Richard agreed that Dallender had not dealt "truly or plainly with . . . Francis Langley, but went about . . . to deceive him." Perhaps Lewis Lewkenor had been disingenuous as well, but it was not for his uncle to suggest so much. Langley might indeed be in the process of purchasing leases to the Cwm Ystwyth mines and the smelting mill; but Sir Richard was not at all certain whether Langley was purchasing them from Dallender or from Lewkenor and Morley. He professed himself sanguine about the ultimate outcome of the negotiations. It was equally clear to Langley that he had taken a misstep and that his venture was suddenly to be more costly. But he determined to go forward; as Jane Langley later described it, he "had already entered so far into the said bargain for the said mines, and had already disbursed so much money thereabouts, that he could not without his great loss and hindrance relinquish the same."[11]

Accordingly, he began to treat with Sir Richard

about the tools and implements. Dallender had earlier
assured Langley that Sir Richard would convey the
tools to him "for the same price and at the same rate
that they stood him in, and would only desire to have
his own money repaid him." Sir Richard concurred
amicably with the latter part of this sentiment, but
pointed out that Dallender's disappearance in December
had been costly to him, and he would expect to re-
coup those costs in any agreement about the tools.
Langley persevered, perhaps obstinately by this point,
and Sir Richard agreed to cast up his accounts and furnish an exact figure. Langley and Dallender retired,
but "the next day (according to appointment)" they returned, and Sir Richard "affirmed that by such notes
and remembrances as he then found, the [new costs]
amounted in the whole to more than three hundred
pounds." Sir Richard proposed a price of £305 in
money and three tons of lead; Langley acquiesced, but
when Sir Richard pressed for immediate payment of
the money Langley protested "that he was not then
furnished with money sufficient to satisfy or pay the
same, neither had he (being a stranger in those parts)
any acquaintance with any men of worth or value in
those parts that he could desire or require to enter into
bond with him." Some other arrangement would have
to be found.

After some negotiating, an agreement was reached
whereby Langley could defer his payments. An indenture was then drawn up, committing Langley to the
payment of £200 "upon the twelfth day of May then
next ensuing at or in the hall of Serjeants' Inn in Fleet
Street." At the same time, Langley was to deliver a
bond for the remaining £105, cosigned by Hugh
Browker, and containing a payment date of October 28,
1602. The three tons of lead were to be delivered before Michaelmas "at or in the town of Aberystwyth in
the said county of Cardigan." Langley agreed that the
articles of conveyance were not to be perfected until
all these conditions had been met, and that his failure

278

to appear on May 12 as appointed would constitute forfeiture of the whole agreement. In the meantime, he was free to work the mines as he wished, provided that he did not attempt to make any profit on his labor before the perfecting of the articles. All these conditions were drawn up in proper form, and Langley and Sir Richard "did severally and interchangeably put their hands and seals" to it on "the sixth day of March." [12]

Langley then returned to Cwm Ystwyth, and there, among the wild and barren crags, he expended what remained of his energy and enthusiasm in a last futile search for wealth. He "did smelt and convert much of the ore" and disbursed "some sums of money" before returning to London, but the price he paid for these modest achievements was great. The harshness of the land and the drudgery of the labor dispirited him even more than it had depressed Dallender. He was ill when he returned home. His wife told him that in his absence William Gresham had entered a suit against him in Chancery, and that he was expected to appear soon to make his answer. He did not appear. Jane later explained "that by reason of sickness and of other troubles which he was fallen into, it had been very dangerous for him to have gone to put in his answer at that time"; Jane thought it preferable "that he deferred his answer till his recovery." But he remained ill. On May 12, as agreed, Sir Richard Lewkenor was "in London, and in the hall there, expecting the payment" of the money and the delivery of the bonds, but "Francis Langley failed in performance of both." Sir Richard sent for Hugh Browker, but Browker "absolutely denied to enter into any bond" on Langley's behalf. [13]

Sir Richard then resigned himself to a default, even as he had on an earlier occasion with John Dallender. But Langley managed to convey word to Sir Richard of his illness, and as Sir Richard's business in London would keep him there for several days he agreed to see Langley at a later time. It was "about the latter end of the said month of May, or the beginning of June" when finally they met; Langley begged Sir Richard's indulgence for his tardiness, pleading illness as the only cause. As an earnest of his good intentions in the matter, Langley paid Sir Richard £150, and promised him the remaining £50 of the first installment within a few days, with "interest for the forbearance thereof," because he would rather "not trouble any his friends for entering into bond for him." And indeed there was no longer anyone who would accommodate him. Hugh Browker had signed his last bond for Francis Langley some months earlier and refused to engage himself. Hannibal Gammon and Richard Langley had both turned away to their own interests and were not sympathetic. Sir Anthony Ashley no longer trusted Langley and would advance him no money. Giles Simpson, James Pemberton, Thomas Chapman—all were disaffected. Langley had nowhere to turn, but for some obstinate reason he refused to abandon the purchase. He held his ground before Sir Richard Lewkenor, clutching at the chimera of a silver mine in Wales. Sir Richard finally offered to continue the agreement with Langley, even though it had been technically forfeit. And then Langley returned home.

Langley never saw Wales again, nor did he pay any more money to Sir Richard Lewkenor. His illness was terminal. Early in July he died, and the parish clerk of St. Saviour's recorded in his register that "Francis Langley," without any pomp or ceremony worthy of remark, was "buried in the church" on July 9, 1602. He was fifty-four years old. He left a wife and six children, and innumerable unresolved lawsuits and debts. He had neglected to make a will.[14]

XVIII

Exit Langley

If a man do not erect in this age
his own tomb ere he dies, he shall
live no longer in monument than
the bell rings and the widow
weeps.—And how long is that?
MUCH ADO ABOUT NOTHING

On July 24, 1602, the Prerogative Court of Canterbury granted to Jane Langley the administration of her husband's goods in lieu of a will. Jane continued to live in the manor house, "a poor desolate widow charged with six children," as she described herself a few months later. As administratrix of her husband's goods she of course became the heir to all his litigation, for his creditors continued to sue his estate for payment of the money owed them. Jane had no alternative but to seek relief in equity. Her husband had told her that Hugh Browker's purchase of Paris Garden would clear up all their debts, but Jane soon found that this was not so; accordingly, she brought suit against Hugh Browker for dealing fraudulently with her husband's estate. Sir Anthony Ashley, who had earlier won a judgment in Queen's Bench against Langley for £600, now sued his estate. The consideration that he was now at law against his own widowed sister seems not to have deterred him. Hannibal Gammon, John Terry, and Richard Langley sued the estate on the grounds that their leases to the Saracen's Head and the Horse Head (now the Nag's Head) in Cheap had been fraudulently terminated by Langley's sale of the properties to

281

Robert Lee. They retained Sir Francis Bacon as their counsel in this proceeding. The suits brought against the Langley estate by strangers, such as Grace Darrell, must not have been nearly so painful to his widow as those brought by Langley's associates of a lifetime.[1]

Her brother's claim for £600 appears to have touched Jane most closely, for she did endeavor to accommodate him. She conveyed to Sir Anthony all her late husband's interest in the leases of the mines, lead ore, smelting mill, tools, and instruments at "Cwm Ystwyth . . . in the parish of Llanfihangel y Creuddin in the county of Cardigan." Jane had assumed that the value of these leases would amply cover her late husband's debt to her brother, and she did not foresee that it would involve Sir Anthony, many years later, in a series of lawsuits with the Lewkenors. She ought not be blamed for any impercipience; in the months immediately following the death of Francis Langley, her energies must have been exhausted in parrying the multitude of claims made upon her, most of them about matters of which she had little or no knowledge.[2]

In 1605 the St. Saviour's token collectors found Jane Langley still in the manor house, and listed her for four tokens. In the autumn of that year the jurators for the sewer commission found that she and Hugh Browker were jointly responsible for repairing the mill bridge, though neither of them seems to have complied. In 1606 Jane bought only two tokens, but a "Mr Justin Delahaye" appears to have moved into the manor house with the Langley family, or perhaps to have lodged nearby; his name is inserted in the token book for that year immediately above Jane's. Justin's relation to George Delahaye is unclear, but on June 4, 1606, "Mr George Delahaye and Mris Jane Langley" were married "with license" in St. Saviour's church. A license from the bishop was required because Jane had been formerly married. George Delahaye was either elderly or sickly; he endured the joys of connubiality with Jane and her brood for some two or three years, and

282

then died. His beloved wife Jane is mentioned in his will, but the bulk of his estate was left elsewhere. None of Jane's children is mentioned.[3]

With the death of George Delahaye, Jane and her family returned to the manor house. In 1607, while she was presumably living in Reigate, Surrey, with her new husband, the token collectors found Justin Delahaye still on the premises, and sold him four tokens. As he had purchased only one in the previous year, one must assume that he had suddenly acquired a household. In the following year, 1608, the token collectors found a widow Delahaye back in the manor house, and sold her five tokens. There is no sign of Justin Delahaye in this list, unless he has been subsumed into the household as the extra token. Widow Delahaye's name is listed in the 1610 token book, but she bought no tokens; perhaps she wasn't even there. Her name does not appear in any of the subsequent books. The St. Saviour's parish register shows no marriage involving a widow Delahaye, and no burial; Jane and her dependents must simply have moved away.[4]

If she went to live with her brother Sir Anthony she has left no trace of such a move. I frankly doubt that he would have been hospitable. Sir Anthony Ashley's own career took a marked turn for the better with the accession of King James to the throne. Out of that new monarch's largess Ashley was able to secure himself a baronetcy, and he seems to have ingratiated himself in Court circles. His wife died some years before him, and he was married a second time, to Philippa Sheldon. The wedding was in the chamber of the Countess of Buckingham at Court, and the dinner was in the Duke of Buckingham's chamber with the King and Prince present. Anne, Sir Anthony's daughter by his first wife, married Sir John Cooper, and Ashley agreed to settle his estate upon them on condition that their heir be named after him. They assented, and their first son was duly christened Anthony Ashley Cooper, later to become the first Earl of Shaftesbury. Ashley made his will in 1625; neither his sister Jane Langley nor any of her children are remembered in it. He died in 1628.[5]

Lying on his death bed in the early years of King Charles' reign, Sir Anthony Ashley probably had no more than a fleeting memory of the man of whom he had spoken, thirty years earlier, as his "bad brother-in-law." Ashley had outlived all of Langley's other confederates; Gammon and Browker had both been dead for twenty years and even Richard Langley was dead in 1625. By the time of Ashley's death there were few people who even remembered Francis Langley, and before much longer his memory had quite faded from the common consciousness. And there it would have remained, in the limbo of oblivion, not quite lost because of its survival in too many documents, yet not at all remembered; but a quirk of fate brought Langley's name up into the light in the nineteenth century, as students of English dramatic history began to reconstruct the principal features of the Shakespearean theatre. Langley was found to have been the builder of the Swan playhouse, and in that capacity a part of him was resurrected for posterity to muse upon.

Yet the "Francis Langley" presented to our view by the theatrical researchers of the nineteenth and early twentieth centuries is a strange transfiguration of the historical Langley. The commonly available evidence suggests that he was a man of some standing and influence, with connections in high places. This is a harmless enough misconception, but it has done us a disservice on two counts: first, it was used by certain Victorian apologists for the theatre as proof that men of respectability might be associated with the craft; and second, it became the ground for unjust vilification of Philip Henslowe as an unscrupulous and unworthy adventurer in the same arena. Fortunately these abuses are being redressed. Foakes and Rickert, in the introduction to their edition of Henslowe's *Diary*, went a long way toward restoring Henslowe's credit, and in this they have been followed by others; and recent studies of the Boar's Head playhouse have quite deflated the myth of Langley's respectability. We are now in a position to see him in something much nearer to his true original shape.

One advantage of this new perspective is that it enables us to understand a little better the various impulses that might lead to the erection of a playhouse, and the various relationships that might exist between companies of players and the owners of playhouses, though even under these rubrics Langley must be seen as an extreme case. His career as a playhouse builder was cautionary in the sense that no one again ventured, as Langley had done, to build a playhouse purely on speculation and on anticipation of profit, without benefit of any prior theatrical experience and with no resident company in mind. The next several playhouses to be built in London—the Globe, the Fortune, the Red Bull, the Hope—were built by men either already associated with the professional theatre or with assured arrangements for tenants. This sober and pragmatic approach might have obtained in any event, but Langley's spectacular failure surely gave it added force.

Langley's relations with his tenants were perhaps also cautionary. Philip Henslowe's concern for the welfare of the Admiral's men appears almost paternalistic when set beside Langley's attitude toward Robert Browne and his players in the Boar's Head, or toward Pembroke's men in the Swan. The precarious tenure that players must have felt under Langley is quite different from the assurance of the Admiral's men at the Rose, and utterly different from the autonomy of the Chamberlain's men in the Globe. The punitive bonds, the lawsuits, the constant harassment and threat of arrest, must have made Langley the last choice of every playing company in London for a landlord.

But one must avoid the temptation to make a facile judgment about Langley. "Who calls me villain?" asks Hamlet in a moment of self-deprecation, and Langley may well rise before us with the same indignant question if we bring our own morality to bear on him. That he was unscrupulous and opportunist few would deny; the danger is in conceiving of him as somehow different from his contemporaries in this regard. Langley was not, so far as I am able to tell, very much worse than most of his colleagues in the attitudes and activities that engaged them all. His fellow alnagers were not models of rectitude, and one of them, John Leake, may well have been the most unscrupulous of the lot. His acquaintances who dealt in moneylending, such as Giles Simpson, James Pemberton, Thomas Chapman, or Robert Brooke, did not at all shrink from using the same tactics that Langley used; Simpson, indeed, may have been his mentor in this regard. Richard Humble had been as eager as Langley to ensnare the younger Thomas Cure. Hannibal Gammon, Robert Howe, and John Terry had been yet more eager than Langley to turn an illegal profit on their diamond, and even Anthony Ashley's hopes were aroused by that prospect. Oliver Woodliffe had shared Langley's pleasure in extracting profit from a playhouse at the expense of a company of players and a putative owner. John Dallender had sold an unprofitable lease to Langley in the full knowledge that he was misrepresenting matters. And Justice William Gardiner went beyond them all in the sheer breadth of his fraudulence, as Leslie Hotson has amply demonstrated.

It was not, in short, an age likely to engender confusion between the actual and the ideal. Langley's London was the brazen world, the historian's world (as Sidney would put it), and we must bring it to account with all its imperfections on its head. This is not to say that Virtue had no triumphs; but they were, like all other triumphs in the sublunary world, mutable. No doubt Hugh Browker viewed his acquisition of Paris Garden as a triumph of sorts; of patience over avarice, perhaps, or of godliness over contempt. Browker brought a commendable sobriety to his new position, and proved a conscientious manorial lord. The drainage sewers were cleaned, the wharves were repaired, the millstream was banked, tithes were paid, and money was collected and given to the poor. Browker had settled the manor on his eldest son Thomas almost immediately after his purchase, as a precaution to secure the title, but as Thomas was only a youth Hugh continued to take the responsibility of the manor upon himself. He grew ill, however, at the end of 1607; he made his will on December 31, and was buried at St. Saviour's, "in the church," on January 5, 1608.[6]

Browker's godliness manifested itself in other ways as well. From the time of his purchase of the manor until his death, there is no record of any plays being performed at the Swan playhouse (though Richard Vennar's fraudulent *England's Joy* was scheduled for November 6, 1602). Browker's steadfastness in this regard must have gratified his fellow vestrymen, but even this moral triumph was to be shortlived. On his death, his place as vestryman at St. Saviour's was filled by the election of Edward Alleyn, one of the sober pillars of the parish despite his earlier years as a player. And a few years after Browker's death, perhaps in 1611, we have evidence that the Swan was once again in use as a playhouse, presumably with young Thomas Browker's assent. Most of the Swan's life, in fact, still lay before it; its future was destined to be more active than its past, though perhaps not so fraught with excitement. That, however, is part of another story.[7]

Abbreviations

APC	*Acts of the Privy Council of England,* ed. J. R. Dasent. London, HMSO, 1890–1907, 32 vols.
Brit. Lit.	The British Library
Cal. S.P.Dom.	*Calendar of State Papers, Domestic,* ed. R. Lemon and M. Green. London, Longmans, 1856–1872, 12 vols.
CLRO	The Corporation of London Record Office
GLRO	The Greater London Record Office
HMSO	Her Majesty's Stationery Office
Hist.Mss.Comm.	The Historical Manuscripts Commission
PCC	The Prerogative Court of [the Archbishop of] Canterbury, the premier testamentary jurisdiction in England. Its records are now in the PRO
PRO	The Public Record Office
SKCS	The records of the Surrey and Kent Commissions of Sewers, now in the GLRO
STC	*A Short-Title Catalogue of Books Printed in England, Scotland, & Ireland, and of English Books Printed Abroad,* 1475–1640, comp. A. W. Pollard and G. R. Redgrave. London, Bibliographic Society, 1926

Notes

I The Youth

1. PRO, C.24/254/53.

2. Thomas Langley's will is preserved in the collections of the Lincolnshire Archives Committee, the Castle, Lincoln; the reference is Stow Wills 1531–1556, no. 4. See *The Index Library*, lvii,102 (London, British Record Society, 1930).

3. The advanced entry into the Freedom is unusual, but probably not extraordinary. The most probable explanation is that John Langley, being of slender means on his arrival in London, was obliged to indenture himself initially for a longer term than he subsequently wished to serve. I think there is no suggestion that John Langley served less than the conventional minimum term. For the circumstances of his freedom, see the Wardens' Accounts and Court Minutes of the Goldsmiths' Company, vol. E, p. 106. The records of the Goldsmiths' Company are preserved in Goldsmiths' Hall, Foster Lane, London.

4. Trappes was elected for Tower Ward on March 3, 1534, but subsequently declined the office; he was discharged on March 19 and fined £300. He observed at the time that he "would be very well contented to pay £300 to be discharged of all manner of offices to be exercised within this City forever." The relevant documents are in the Corporation of London Record Office, Guildhall, London. For his election, see Repertory 9, fol. 47b; Journal 13, fol. 400; Letter-book P, fol. 32b. For his discharge, see Repertory 9, fol. 50b; Letter-book P, fol. 34 (the source of the above quotation). The details of John Langley's own career as a goldsmith may be found among the records of the Company.

5. This quotation and those that follow are from the edition of Henry Machyn's *Diary* edited by John Gough Nichols in 1848 (Camden Society, o.s., vol. xlii).

6. Ibid.

7. Timothy Tapwell's speech is from sig. B2r of the 1633 edition of Philip Massinger's *A New Way to Pay Old Debts*. Seagull's speech is from J. H. Harris's edition of *Eastward Ho*, by George Chapman, Ben Jonson, and John Marston (New Haven, Yale University Press, 1926), where it is lines 1530–33. The need for temporal wealth as a prerequisite to public office was clearly understood. Simon Eyre's public career, as described by Thomas Dekker in *The Shoemakers' Holiday*, begins when his disguised workman "Hans" offers him instant affluence in the form of "a bargain in the commodities," i.e., the contraband lading of a merchant ship. For fuller details about these and related matters, see John James Baddeley, *The Aldermen of Cripplegate Ward from AD 1276 to AD 1900* (London, 1900), which contains an excellent general introduction to the office of alderman; and Alfred B. Beaven, *The Aldermen of the City of London*, 2 vols. (London, Corporation of the City of London, 1908, 1913). Margaret Kollock, *The Lord Mayor and Aldermen of London during the Tudor Period* (Philadelphia, J. C. Winston, 1906), is less reliable.

8. Full details on all aldermanic elections will be found in Beaven, *Aldermen*.

9. I conjecture that Thomas Langley was indentured in 1559, though no records of bindings exist for so early a date among the Haberdashers' archives. The Register of Freedoms of the Haberdashers' Company (Class II, vol. 1, 1526–1641) show Thomas Langley gaining his freedom from Brendholme on November 4, 1569, an appropriate term of servitude. The records of the Haberdashers' Company are kept at Haberdashers' Hall, Staining Lane, London. John Langley and Ursula Beresford were married in St. Lawrence Jewry, the church next to Guildhall. See Harleian Society *Registers*, lxx,82 (London, Harleian Society, 1940). Ursula's two sons, George and Rowland, are mentioned in John Langley's will. In other documents their surname is variously spelled Bashford, Basford, or Basforth. John Langley's ventures with his new friends were manifold. For example, Langley, Bowyer and Hayward in 1569 bought several manors in Norfolk (PRO, C.66/1059, memb. 15); Langley and Hayward in 1570 bought a manor and other lands in Kent and Middlesex (PRO, C.66/1072, memb. 23). One can get a sense of the activities of the four men and their business colleagues by examining the indices of the *Calendars of Patent Rolls* (London, HMSO) for these years. The speculations that required letters patent for their execution probably formed but a small part of the regular commerce of these men. Rowland Hayward in particular involved himself in financial speculation on

a large scale. For John Langley's function as a speculator and moneylender, see Hist. Mss. Comm., *Rutland Papers*, i,432–433, iv,378–379 (London, HMSO, 1900, 1905). Duckett and Hayward, along with George Beresford and forty-seven others, were named as free of the company of Merchant Adventurers in the Grant of Incorporation on July 18, 1564. Duckett was the first Governor of the Company of Mines Royal, incorporated by royal charter on May 28, 1568.

10. John Langley's return to aldermanic candidacy had actually begun two months earlier. He had been nominated for the vacancy in Portsoken ward in late August, and for the vacancy in Bassishaw ward in late September, but was unsuccessful. Less than two months after his election for Billingsgate he was nominated for translation to Farringdon Within, but he declined. All details are in Beaven, *Aldermen*.

11. Eyre's speech is from sig. F1v-2 of the 1600 edition of *The Shoemakers' Holiday*. The subsidy list for 1571 is preserved in the Guildhall Library, where it is MS 2942.

12. The seriousness of the decline in the cloth trade is suggested in part by the details of a report sent to Sir Thomas Egerton (Huntington Library, MS Ellesmere 2334). "There are growing yearly within this realm 1,500,000 tods of wool at least: wherein the loss is upon every tod, [from] what it was usually about 6 years past, 6^s 8^d per tod, which in all amounteth yearly unto £500,000." A loss of nearly seven shillings per tod is a serious decline. Shakespeare's shepherd in the *Winter's Tale* (1611) tells us that "every tod yields pound and odd shilling" (IV.iii.33). For the relationship between the Drapers' Company and the various venturing companies, see A. H. Johnson, *The History of the Worshipful Company of the Drapers of London*, 5 vols. (Oxford, Clarendon Press, 1914–1922). For the larger picture, see T. S. Willan, *Studies in Elizabethan Foreign Trade* (Manchester, Manchester University Press, 1959), and Ralph Davis, *English Overseas Trade, 1500–1700* (London, Macmillan, 1973).

13. Further details on Hobbes are in Johnson, *History*, vol. ii. The reference to offenders is from ii,225. The customary period of apprenticeship at this time was for ten years, and by general ordinance the freedom of the company could not be given to anyone under the age of twenty-four; see Tom Girtin, *The Triple Crowns: A Narrative History of the Drapers' Company 1364–1964* (London, Hutchinson, 1964), p. 165 and passim.

14. The record of Francis Langley's correction (not reproduced in Johnson) is cited from Repertory E (+256), fol. 88b. The records of the Drapers' Company are preserved in Drapers' Hall, Throgmorton Street, London. Thomas Metcalfe was a friend and associate of John Langley's.

15. Langley described the trip to Surrey many years later in his deposition, on September 11, 1589, in the suit of Edward Peacock vs. Richard Alwell. He described himself at the time of the deposition as "of the age of 40 years or thereabouts." PRO, C.24/211/92.

16. For the confrontation with Hobbes, see Repertory E (+256), fol. 149b. For the freedom, see the Freedom Lists (+278 and +279) and the Wardens' Accounts (+176/16).

17. The ordinance requiring service as a sheriff is in Liber Albus, fol. 241b, and may conveniently be found in *Munimenta Gildhallae Londoniensis; Liber Albus, Liber Custumarum, et Liber Horn*, ed. Henry Thomas Riley (London, 1859), i,464. As John Langley was not elected for a full term, but was chosen at an odd time of year, one can still find accounts of London government that single him out as an instance of a man becoming Lord Mayor without having been sheriff. But Langley was indeed sheriff, though only for a few months.

18. Firk's speech is from sig. E4v of the 1600 edition.

19. For Hannibal Gammon's certification, see the Wardens' Accounts and Court Minutes, Book L, p. 177: "Received of Mr Alderman Langley for the presentment of Hannibal Gammon his apprentice," the fee of 2^s 6^d. For the oath, Book L, p. 221: "Received of Hannibal Gammon late the apprentice of Mr Alderman Langley for his oath," the fee of 3^s.

20. Shortly after taking on Hannibal Gammon, Thomas Metcalfe died; in his will, dated March 13, 1576, he left memorial legacies to "Mr Alderman Langley" and his wife, and also "to Hannibal Gammon my late servant one black cloth coat" (PCC 3 Carew, now PRO, Prob.11/58). For the defaulted bond, see PRO, Req.2/233/11, in which Francis Langley, in 1581, pleads for relief in the Court of Requests from the Common Pleas suit of Francis Griffin, the bondholder. The quotations are from Griffin's answer.

21. John Langley's brethren in the Company of Goldsmiths made him a handsome presentation on the occasion of his election: "Forasmuch as before this time of old and ancient custom there hath been granted by the Wardens and Assistants of this Company to him of the said Company that hath been chosen to be Mayor of this City of London the sum of £30 towards the trimming up of his house," the livery determined on Tuesday, October 2, 1576, to grant John Langley "not only the said benevolence of £30 but also (having regard to the great charge that Mr John Langley Alderman, now elected Lord Mayor of the said City, shall be at, and to the end that he may the better do things to the honor of the Prince and the estate of this City) have granted unto him more the sum of £70 in full of one hundred pounds" (Wardens' Accounts and Court Minutes, book L, p. 281).

22. *APC 1575–1577*, pp. 250, 375.

23. These and the following instances may conveniently be found in *APC* 1577–1578, pp. 4, 5, 22, and 40. The Theater was probably in operation during the summer of 1576, before John Langley's election. For the likelihood of the playhouse at Newington Butts also being in operation that year, see *Shakespeare Quarterly* 21, no. 4 (Autumn 1970), pp. 385–398.

24. Fleetwood's letter is in the Brit. Lib., MS Lansdowne xxiv, fol. 196, art. 80; it has been reproduced in Malone Society *Collections* i, pt. 2, p. 153 (Oxford, Malone Society, 1907), and in E. K. Chambers, *The Elizabethan Stage*, iv,277 (Oxford, Clarendon Press, 1923). The guests were Sir William Cordell, the Master of the Rolls; John Southcote, Justice of the Court of Queen's Bench; Sir William Damsel, Receiver-General of the Court of Wards; Sir Owen Hopton, the Lieutenant of the Tower; Sir Rowland Hayward; Thomas Pullyson, draper, alderman of Vintry ward. I have been unable to identify "Mr Justice Randoll."

25. Langley's letter is summarized in the *Analytical Index to the Remembrancia*, ed. W. H. and H. C. Overall (London, 1878), p. 276.

26. The records of the Court of Aldermen for this period are preserved in a series of Repertories in the keeping of the Corporation of London Record Office at Guildhall. This citation is from Repertory 19, fol. 251v.

27. Sir John's burial was the occasion of a calamity in the church, as recorded in the minutes of the vestry. The entry is worth quoting in full: "A brief remembrance written by Samuel Gray 1605, being then younger churchwarden, to supply the want of such things as happened in the year 1577 in the time of Thomas Sherman not written by the Churchwardens then living and yet worthy to be committed to memory for the great damage which the parish sustained that year, a thing well known to this writer, for that both his own father was a committeeman . . . and Thomas Sherman his wife's father was then younger churchwarden and himself being an eyewitness thereof. The executors of Sir John Langley craved leave of the parish to make a vault in the south aisle, in that space of ground which lieth between the most easterly pillars and the east end of the chapel, between the tomb and the pillar in the very passage as we go out of the chapel into the choir; in the digging of which—what by the negligence of the digger and Middleton the bricklayer, the ground being digged too near the pillar—immediately after Mr Crowley had ended his lecture between the hours of 8 and 9 o'clock in the morning (then being in the church Lawrence Garret the clerk, and in the grave the workman) the clerk being in the choir heard the glass windows on the south side of the choir in the very top of the chancel give a great crack, and casting up his eyes toward the place, perceived manifestly the ruin; and coming away called very hastily to the workman in the grave, who sud-

denly followed, and all the ceiling of that aisle with all the wall and windows over the two pillars even to the very roof of the chancel, even to both ends thereof, fell immediately down and broke in pieces; all the pews, the great organs and the loft wherein they stood (which was over the stairs going down into the vestry) and whatsoever else was in that chapel, the repairing whereof was a very great charge to the parish; and the great trouble which the younger churchwarden Mr Sherman sustained thereby was the cause that the parish chose 2 new churchwardens next year for the ease of Mr Sherman and dispensed with him for the next year's service" (St. Lawrence Jewry vestry minutes, Guildhall MS 2590.1, p. 56).

II The Heir

1. The circumstances surrounding the making of Sir John's will, as described in this section, are taken from the depositions in the suit of Ursula Langley vs. Thomas Langley (PRO, C.24/134/16). Francis Langley and Sir Rowland Hayward were among those deposing in this suit. Mark Eccles came upon these documents more than forty years ago during his researches on Christopher Marlowe, as a result of tracking down the references to Rowland Hayward, who was one of the Aldermen who sat at the Gaol Delivery in December 1589 at which Christopher Marlowe appeared in the matter of his duel with William Bradley. Eccles cited the reference, albeit incompletely, and dealt in a few sentences with the matters more fully set forth here. See Eccles's *Christopher Marlowe in London* (Cambridge, Massachusetts, Harvard University Press, 1934), pp. 17–18.

2. The record copy of Sir John's will is in the Public Record Office (PCC 1 Langley, now PRO, Prob.11/60).

3. Lady Ursula's comments are from her plea in the suit against Thomas Langley (PRO, C.2.Eliz/L.11/10).

4. Sir John's deathbed aphorism (Job I:21) is an Elizabethan commonplace; see, for example, Margery Eyre's observation (*Shoemakers' Holiday*, London, 1600, C4v, or III.iv.120 in modern editions) that "naked we came out of our mother's womb, and naked we must return, and therefore thank God for all things."

5. Crowley had been vicar of St. Lawrence·Jewry at the time of Sir John's death, but had resigned the post by the time he made his deposition. He therefore preferred to style himself on that occasion as the vicar of St. Giles Cripplegate. This was indeed a position that he had held at one time, but he had been deprived of the living by Archbishop Parker a decade earlier; for further details see the Introduction to *The Select Works of Robert Crowley*, Early English Text Society, extra series 10 (London, 1872). Crowley's narrow and rigid Puritanism may give us a clue to Sir John's own doctrinal leanings.

6. Again, the comments are from Lady Ursula's plea.

7. These are the depositions referred to in note 1 above; extracts from them have appeared in the narrative.

8. The indenture between Thomas and Francis is enrolled in Chancery (PRO, C.54/1034).

9. The actual exchange is a bit more complicated than this. On July 17, 1578, Lady Ursula sold to her son Rowland Beresford for £300 "all those two houses and tenements with the appurtenances in Cheapside in London . . . in the possession or occupation of one Ballett . . . next adjoining to the house called the Horsehead in Cheapside." On December 28, 1580, Lady Ursula and Rowland Beresford jointly conveyed the same property to Rowland Hayward. The Whittington College properties were sold to Richard Warren, Esq., for £600. All these transactions were enrolled in the Court of Hustings: see Hustings Rolls 264/7, 264/49 and 265/32 in the Corporation of London Record Office.

III The Moneylender

1. "The Usurer Reformed," an undated essay from the period (Huntington Library, MS Ellesmere 2468, fols. 5v–6), dilates on these relationships: "It is questionable whether the scrivener be the master or the man, the substance or the shadow, of the usurer, but certain it is, that he is the agent of the usurer, and the familiar spirit that putteth his avaricious designs into execution; and therefore when I am to entreat of the scrivener for the most part, I have directly or indirectly a relation unto the usurer as being a mixed body, with his sweet soul the scrivener; and under his name comprise the broker also."

2. At the baptism of Thomas Chapman's son Thomas, in the church of St. Pancras Soper Lane, Cecily Cyoll stood as godmother and Francis Langley as godfather. The register of this church is preserved in Guildhall (MS 5015), and has been reprinted by the Harleian Society. In the lay subsidy assessment of August 1, 1582 (PRO, E.179/251/16, memb. 106), Hannibal Gammon was rated at £3, and assessed 3^s. He was living at the time in the parish of St. Matthew Friday Street. For his loan of £100 in that year, see PRO, C.P.40/1435, memb. 2005d, and C.P.40/1438, memb. 1709. The quotation is, again, from "The Usurer Reformed."

3. In more modern usage, usury has come to mean an immoderate or excessive rate of interest; but in the sixteenth century the term was used to denote interest of any amount. The Act prohibiting usury is 5&6 Edw. VI, Cap. 20; the Act of 1571 is 13 Eliz., Cap. 8.

4. For men whose need of money is desperate, the allowed rate of interest is but a fiction; the amount they are required to pay will always be excessive. This was true long after Langley's time: Burgo Fitzgerald, in Anthony Trollope's *Can You Forgive Her?* (1864), found that the rates steepened as his need grew. He tells his friend

George Vavasor, "I asked him for two hundred and fifty. He says he'll let me have one hundred and fifty on a bill at two months for five hundred,—with your name to it" (Oxford World Classics edition, p. 374).

5. Langley's suit against Mervyn was in the Court of Common Pleas (PRO, C.P.40/1442, memb. 1454).

6. Percy's bond to Langley is enrolled in Chancery (PRO, C.54/1335). "Save him harmless" is a stock phrase; see Thomas Middleton's *Michaelmas Term* III.iv.102 (University of Nebraska Press edition).

7. My readings are not entirely conjectural; in Langley's answer to this plea the charges are rehearsed again, and all the lacunae in the bill of complaint can be quite accurately filled from the answer. Only the bill and answer survive. The suit was filed in the Court of Chancery (PRO, C.2.Eliz/P.8/37).

8. William Gresham's plea for relief from the importunities of Francis Langley was filed in the Court of Chancery. The bill and answer are PRO, C.2.Eliz/G.2/28; the depositions are PRO, C.24/304/16.

9. Ashley apparently borrowed £300 for a year for a total indebtedness of £330, which sum he claimed to have paid when due, though he received no acquittance for it. The resultant lawsuit got as far as the taking of depositions, though no judgment is recorded. One of the deponents, Edward Hancockes, recalled in 1588 that Ashley spoke of Langley as "brother Langley," suggesting that by this date Langley had already married Ashley's sister Jane (PRO, C.24/201/2).

10. The original indenture was dated September 22, 1588, sealed on October 2, 1588, and enrolled in Chancery on February 19, 1589 (PRO, C.54/1323). The indenture was also enrolled in the Court of Hustings on November 20, 1588 (CLRO, Hustings Roll 269/41). The property had obviously increased in value during the decade Hayward held it.

11. Ballett's wealth can be roughly ascertained. In the same lay subsidy assessment in 1582 in which Hannibal Gammon was rated at £3 (PRO, E.179/251/16, memb. 106), John Ballett was rated at £100. Among their near neighbors in that year, Nicholas Herrick, goldsmith, father of the poet, was rated at £40, and Nicholas Hilliard, goldsmith, the celebrated miniaturist, at £5.

IV   The Alnager

1. Stafford's conflict with the City is documented in the Remembrancia, letters I.126 and I.128, and in the aldermen's discussion of August 30, 1580 (CLRO, Rep. 20, fol. 101v); for his ultimate capitulation, see Remembrancia I.127. Summaries of all letters are in the *Analytical Index to the Remembrancia*, ed. W. H. and H. C. Overall (London, 1878), p. 68.

2. CLRO, Rep. 20, fol. 116.

3. CLRO, Rep. 20, fol. 207.

4. CLRO, Rep. 20, fol. 207.

5. CLRO, Remembrancia I.439; summarized in the *Analytical Index*, p. 277.

6. CLRO, Remembrancia I.443, summarized in the *Analytical Index*, p. 277.

7. Hatton's letter is in the Remembrancia I.241, summarized in the *Analytical Index* p. 69. The decision of the aldermen is CLRO, Rep. 20, fol. 383.

8. CLRO, Rep. 20, fol. 383.

9. In the 1582 assessment, in which Hannibal Gammon was rated at £3, "Francis Langley, belonging to Blackwell Hall" was rated at £6. He was living at the time in St. Peter's parish, Cheap ward. PRO, E.179/251/16, memb. 106.

10. CLRO, Rep. 21, fol. 119.

11. CLRO, Rep. 21, fol. 207.

12. The statute (39 Eliz., Cap. 20) directs that the alnagers "shall fix unto every kind of the cloths aforesaid, a Seal of lead, containing the length and the weight of every such cloth, together with this word, *searched.*"

13. This wording is from 39 Eliz., Cap. 20, where it is clear and unambiguous, but it can be found in earlier forms. Penalties for the counterfeiting of seals are also spelled out in all the relevant statutes.

14. For Thompson's suit, see PRO, K.B.27/1297, memb. 114.

15. The letter from the alnagers has somehow found its way into the State Papers, where it is PRO, S.P.12/187, fol. 55. The forged signature, along with various authentic signatures by Francis Langley, is reproduced in Chapter 14.

16. For the bonding of the alnagers, see Rep. 21, fol. 283v. News of the City's involvement in musters and subsidies was relayed by the Antwerp correspondent of the House of Fugger; see *The Fugger News-Letters*, second series, ed. V. von Klarwill, tr. L. S. R. Byrne (London, Bodley Head, 1926), pp. 83, 85.

V The Lord of the Manor

1. Langley's need to turn elsewhere for funds was genuine, as evidenced by the bonds; but usurers who lent their own money pretended the same need. The device became a cliche. Shylock tells Bassanio: "I cannot instantly raise up the gross / Of full three thousand ducats: what of that? / Tubal, a wealthy Hebrew of my Tribe, / Will furnish me."

2. Goddard filed suit in Chancery in 1598; his plea and the answer of Langley survive. See PRO, C.2.Eliz/G.6/56.

3. In 1570 Thomas Cure the elder presented a large folio volume of empty pages to the churchwardens of St. Saviour's parish for

their use as a register. On the first page of this volume, which now contains the records for the period under consideration, is written the following: "A Register Book Given by Thomas Cure unto the parish church of St. Saviours in Southwark of all such weddings, christenings and burials as hath been celebrated in the same church from the first of March in the year of our salvation 1570 in the 13th year of the reign of our sovereign Lady Queen Elizabeth." Cure's own burial is appropriately recorded in the volume. He was buried in the church, and his epitaph speaks punningly of his care (*cura*) for the saddles of three monarchs—"Respublica Curae Semper erat Curo," and so on. See Concanen and Morgan, *The History and Antiquities of the Parish of St. Saviour's, Southwark* [Deptford-Bridge, 1795], p. 103.

4. The elder Cure's will is PCC 43 Rutland, now PRO, Prob.11/72. Humble's recollections are from his suit against the elder Cure's two sons, PRO, C.2.Jas I/H.26/69. Thomas Cure the younger continued in his father's office as Queen's Sadler; see PRO, C.24/207/29, where he describes himself as the Queen's Majesty's Sadler in 1589, he then being 28, and PRO, L.C.9/83, the Great Wardrobe account for 1592, where his expenses for saddles and coach harnesses are noted.

5. The indenture of transfer is PRO, C.54/1323.

6. Cure was obviously not taking his lordship seriously. His manor was soon "leas'd out (I die pronouncing it) / Like to a tenement or pelting farm . . . With inky blots, and rotten parchment bonds." Cure's profligacy was not so great as Richard II's, but it quickly ran the course just described, and continued with further leases of parts of the manor given to various creditors, until one appeared to "redeem from broking pawn" the failing fortunes of the manor's lord.

7. The decision to sell was reached earlier than this, for Cure had gotten a license to alienate on April 2, 1589 (PRO, C.66/1327). The final concord is dated June 9, 1589 (PRO, C.P.25(2)/227/31 Eliz/Trinity/memb. 9). The details of the foregoing pages were pieced together from various documents as follows: C.54/1354, the indenture of sale from Cure to Langley, 1589; C.2.Eliz/C.19/13, George Chute's suit in Chancery against Francis Langley, 1592; Req.2/34/73, Richard Humble's suit in Requests against Giles Simpson and Francis Langley, 1596; C.2.Jas I/L.13/62, Jane Langley's suit in Chancery against Hugh Browker, 1603; C.24/305/1, depositions in the foregoing suit. All these documents are in the Public Record Office.

8. The early history of the manor is set forth more fully in *Bankside*, vol. xxii of the *Survey of London* (London, London County Council, 1950), pp. 94–96.

9. The matter of tenure is not simple, and I err if I make it seem

so. A useful discussion of the problems may be found in R. H. Tawney, *The Agrarian Problem in the Sixteenth Century* (London, Longmans, 1912), supplemented by Charles M. Gray, *Copyhold, Equity, and the Common Law* (Cambridge, Massachusetts, Harvard University Press, 1963).

10. The other lands were to be held "de nobis . . . in libero & communi soccagio & non in capite nec per servitium militare"; this was to be facilitated by granting the lands as of the manor of East Greenwich ("ut de manerio nostro de East Greenwich in comitatu nostro Kancia"), a Tudor device designed to facilitate the holding of lands from the Crown other than in chief. Paris Garden, however, was to be held in chief, that is, by knight service, according to the formula: "in capite per servitium militare, videlicet per servitium quadragesime partis unius feodi militis." Forty days' knight service per year was the traditional fee; hence, one day of service was exacted from Newdigate and Fountayne, or more likely its equivalent in cash. For the burdens of tenure in chief, and exploitation of the manor of East Greenwich as a means of avoiding those burdens, see Joel Hurstfield, *The Queen's Wards* (London, Longmans, 1958), especially pp. 18–24. The grant to Newdigate and Fountayne is enrolled in the Patent Rolls (PRO, C.66/1165); the above quotations are from memb. 22.

11. The "total annual value" of the manor is of course difficult to define; after Jane Seymour's death Henry VIII had farmed the manor to William Baseley for twenty-one years at an annual rent of £52, which is perhaps a close enough estimate. Francis Langley later claimed that his profits were much higher, as a result of his investment in the property. Newdigate and Fountayne's license to alienate portions of the manor is enrolled in Chancery (PRO, C.66/1175, memb. 43).

12. The indenture to Taylor and Platt is GLRO, M.92/111. For copyholders buying their freedom, see G. O. Sayles, *The Medieval Foundations of England* (London, Methuen, 1952); the practice is called *commutation*.

13. GLRO, M.92/113.

14. The sale to Thomas Cure the younger is enrolled in the Close Rolls (PRO, C.54/1079). Hunsdon, Newdigate, and Fountayne had received permission from the Queen earlier (March 1, 1580) to alienate the manor, on payment of 66^s 8^d (PRO, C.66/1194). The bond from Hunsdon is also enrolled (PRO, C.54/1096). The last of the transactions, the Final Concord, was executed on May 30 ("crastino sancti trinitatis") 1580 in the Court of Common Pleas (PRO, C.P.25(2)/226/22 Eliz/Trinity). A thousand marks is £666 13^s 4^d. The exact nature of the younger Cure's tenure is spelled out in the enrollment of sale; Hunsdon, Newdigate, and Fountayne conveyed to him "their lordship and manor of Paris Garden in the

county of Surrey, with their rights members and appurtenances whatsoever . . . And also all and singular messuages, houses, edifices, barns, stables, gardens, orchards lands, tenements, meadows, leasows, walls, ways, banks, waters, fishings, fishing places, rents, reversions, services, court leets, view of frankpledge, with the profits and perquisites of court leets and all things to the court leets and views of frankpledge belong[ing] and appertaining . . . in as large and ample manner and form as our said sovereign Lady the Queen's majesty, by her highness' letters patents bearing date the tenth day of July in the twentieth year of her Highness' reign, did give and grant the same amongst other things to the said Robert Newdigate and Arthur Fountayne . . . except and always reserved out of this present bargain and sale all such lands, tenements, meadows, pastures and hereditaments with their appurtenances which are holden of the said lordship and manor by copy of court rolls according to the custom of the said lordship and manor and being worth unto the lord or owners of the said lordship and manor in yearly rents to the sum of eight pounds five shillings and four pence . . . And also except the court baron belonging to the said manor and all other things to Thomas Taylor, Esquire, and Richard Platt, brewer, demised by the said lessors by indenture dated the day of the date of these presents . . . And also except one indenture of lease bearing date the day of the date of these presents made of the premises by these presents bargained and sold or of parcel thereof unto the said Thomas Cure the elder by the said Lord of Hunsdon, Robert Newdigate and Arthur Fountayne for the term of one thousand years, whereupon the yearly rent of ten shillings is reserved . . . And also all estates and grants by copy of court roll and leases heretofore made of the premises or of any part or parcel thereof by any copyholder or copyholders of any part of the premises, and all licences from the lord or lords of the same manor made to the customary tenants or any of them to make leases or grants of the premises or any parcel thereof."

15. These recollections are from the depositions in the suit of Jane Langley vs. Hugh Browker (PRO, C.24/305/1). Loans from the Orphans' Court were desirable because the interest was moderate; see Charles H. Carlton, "The Administration of London's Court of Orphans," *Guildhall Miscellany* 4, no. 1 (October 1971), pp. 22–35, esp. p. 32.

16. Nicholas Herrick was the father of Robert Herrick the poet. The records of the several indentures to the Chamberlain were discovered by Betty R. Masters, Deputy Keeper of the Records in the Corporation of London Records Office. They are recorded in Letter Book &c (*sic*), fols. 252b, 253, 253b, and 254. The order directing Elizabeth Walter, widow, to bring to the Chamberlain an inventory of her deceased husband's goods is in Rep. 21, fols. 567v–568,

dated June 25, 1588. Nathaniel Walter, the orphan, apparently did not live long, and his death necessitated further financing on Langley's part. Gammon recalled that "after the orphan to whom the said money was due was dead, the said Langley being urged to pay in the said money, this deponent & one Richard Langley of London, haberdasher, became bound to several men with the said Francis Langley for the same" (PRO, C.24/305/1).

17. Wase's recollections are from his depositions in the suit of John Pasfield and Richard Veale vs. Francis Langley (PRO, Req.2/256/19).

18. Browker's recollections are from his answer to Jane Langley's complaint against him in 1603 (PRO, C.2.Jas I/L.13/62). The Latin citation that includes Pemberton is from the final concord of June 9 (PRO, C.P.25(2)/227/31 Eliz/Trinity/memb. 9); the citation which omits him is from the license to alienate of April 2 (PRO, C.66/1327).

19. Browker's recollections are from his answer to the complaint of Jane Langley in 1603 (PRO, C.2.Jas I/L.13/62); Bury's recollections are from his deposition in the same suit (PRO, C.24/305/1).

20. Also from PRO, C.24/305/1.

21. Fleetwood's letter is PRO, S.P.12/125, fol. 42 (July 13, 1578). He must have meant that the willows were in clusters or clumps; a *virgultum* is a thicket, and by "eight" he probably meant *ait* or *eyot*, an islet.

22. Brit. Lib., MS Add. 34,112A. GLRO, SKCS 22, memb. 3; SKCS 28, memb. 5v. In 1571 the water went all the way to St. George's fields; see the account of the manor in *The Survey of London*, vol. xxii, *Bankside*.

23. The Auditors of Land Revenue operated out of the Exchequer. For the Paris Garden entries, see PRO, L.R.2/190, fol. 103ff.

24. The St. Saviour's token books are annual lists of the residents of the parish, compiled some time before Easter in each year. Attendance at Easter communion was mandatory throughout the realm, under penalty of law, for all persons over sixteen years; at St. Saviour's, admission to Easter communion was by token only, purchasable in advance from the churchwardens at 3^d each. Every year, in February or March, the wardens or their delegates would go from door to door through the parish, carrying with them a book prepared by the parish clerk in which were listed in order the names of the parishioners who were heads of families, and the number of persons over sixteen in each household. In the course of their rounds the collectors made additions, deletions, and changes in the book as warranted, and it then became the basis of the following year's book. The number of adults in each family was recorded, and also the number of tokens purchased, which two numbers would not necessarily correspond. Most of these token books have

somehow survived, and they constitute a unique resource. The Corporation of Wardens of St. Saviour's has deposited them with the Greater London Record Office in County Hall, S.E.1.

25. Browker's recollection is from PRO, C.2.Jas I/L.13/62, the answer. Smith's recollection is from PRO, C.24/304/16.

26. Young John Langley apprenticed himself in 1586; his statement of indenture, and his signature, are in Apprentice Book 1, p. 71, at Goldsmiths' Hall; interestingly, he spelled his name "Langlay," even as his uncle Francis did.

27. The Horse Head enjoyed a reputation of sorts. Sir John Throckmorton, describing events of November 19, 1536, says that he "met Sir John Clarke at Paul's . . . and after the sermon he and I went and dined at the Horse Head, in Cheap, with the goodman of the house in a little low parlour" (*Letters and Papers of Henry VIII*, xi,557, London, HMSO, 1888). The ill-fated Thomas Arden is portrayed as staying at "the Nag's Head" on his visit to London (*Arden of Feversham*, 1592, sig. D1r). Thomas Nashe, in *Have with You to Saffron-Walden* (1596), says of Thomas Watson the poet: "A man he was that I dearly loved and honoured, and for all things hath left few his equals in England; he it was that, in the company of divers gentlemen one night at supper at the Nag's Head in Cheap, first told me of his vanity, and those hexameters made of him" (R. B. McKerrow, *The Works of Thomas Nashe*, Oxford, Blackwell, 1966, iii,126ff). Richard Langley would have been the host at this latter gathering.

28. Chute's lawsuit is PRO, C.2.Eliz/C.19/13; Humble's is PRO, Req.2/34/73. Though they both knew Langley as a goldsmith, there is no danger of confusion here; Paris Garden was purchased by "Francis Langley, Citizen and Draper of London" (PRO, C.54/1354). There is no question that the draper, the goldsmith, and the alnager are all the same person.

29. The words of Massinger's Sir Giles Overreach are to the point:

These trespasses draw on suits, and suits, expenses;
Which I can spare, but will soon beggar him.
When I have harried him thus, two or three years,
Though he sue *in forma pauperis,* in spite
Of all his thrift and care he'll grow behind-hand . . .
Then with the favor of my man of Law,
I will pretend some title: want will force him
To put it to arbitrement: then if he sell
For half the value, he shall have ready money,
And I possess his land.

(*A New Way to Pay Old Debts,* 1633, sig. D2r)

30. Langley's suit against Wood is recorded in the Court of

Queen's Bench, PRO, K.B.27/1319, fol. 342, Michaelmas 33-34 Eliz.

31. *APC* 1591–92, pp. 179, 255.

VI The Carrack

1. The most detailed recent account of this scandal is in A. L. Rowse, *Ralegh and the Throckmortons* (London, Macmillan, 1962).

2. Sir John's name is variously spelled *Borough*, *Burrowes*, or *Borrowes* in the documents, a clue perhaps to the way others heard it pronounced, though he himself always wrote his name as *Burgh*. Modern scholarship has usually followed his preference. I am perhaps being recalcitrant in insisting on *Burroughs*, though it is consistent with my use of *Langley*, despite Francis's regular practice of signing his name *Langlay*. For an early contemporary account of the sea fight, see *The Sea-mans Triumph*, 1592 (*STC* 22140). Partisanship engendered its own accounts: the Queen's interest is laid forth in the account printed in Hakluyt's *Principal Navigations* (Hakluyt Society, vii,105–118); the Earl of Cumberland's side is put forward in *Purchas his Pilgrims* (Hakluyt Society, xvi,13–17). The account of Francis Seall, one of Cumberland's men, and the accounts of Sir John Burroughs, Captain Thomas Thompson of the *Dainty*, and Captain Robert Cross of the *Golden Dragon* are reproduced (from MS Lansdowne 70) in *The Naval Miscellany*, vol. ii (Navy Records Society, vol. xl), 1912.

3. These statements are from a bill of grievances forwarded to Cecil, and are now among the Cecil Papers at Hatfield House (Cecil Papers 21/110).

4. Details will proliferate as this narrative proceeds; I trust the reader will not think me derelict if I suggest that it would be burdensome to cite individual page references to the printed calendars for each of them. Anyone wishing to pursue the matter further need only consult the indices of the following volumes, all of which are generally available: Historical Manuscripts Commission, *Salisbury Papers*, vol. iv; *Cal. S.P.Dom.* 1591–1594; *Acts of the Privy Council* 1592–1593; and the published catalogue of the Lansdowne MSS (London, 1819) for the contents of vol. lxx.

5. For Middleton's letter, see Cecil Papers 22/1. For the formal account of the carrack's lading, as assessed at Leadenhall on September 15, 1592, see Brit. Lib., MS Lansdowne 70, item 89; of the full value of the cargo almost half, or £70,280, was for 648,744 pounds of pepper rated at $2^s\ 2^d$ the pound. But profits in such mundane commodities could not make up for the evident losses in gold and precious stones. By the latter part of September the plunder was recognized to be so extensive that a royal proclamation was deemed necessary. "The Queen's most excellent Majesty being cer-

tainly informed of divers great spoils made of the goods laden in a Spanish Carraque lately brought to Dartmouth in Devonshire, & the same conveyed secretly on land to certain parts of the realm, as well in Devonshire as to the City of London . . . and there dispersed and unlawfully bought by sundry merchants and brokers, to the manifest breach of her Majesty's laws . . . her Majesty chargeth all merchants, goldsmiths, jewellers, seamen, and all other persons that have bought or received any of the said goods . . . to discover & deliver the same" (Proclamation of September 23, 1592; STC 8222).

6. Favell's deposition (Cecil Papers 21/111, September 29, 1592) is but one of many documents relating to the carrack that may be found among the Cecil Papers at Hatfield House.

7. Cecil Papers 22/11.

8. Cecil Papers 21/115. Terceira, in the Azores, was the carrack's last Spanish contact before her capture.

9. This is Michael Germyn's account; as the mayor of Exeter he assisted in the interrogations. Cecil Papers 21/116. In the calendar (Hist. Mss. Comm., *Salisbury Papers*, iv,232), *pearell* (pearl) is misread as *pemell* in one instance.

10. Fonseca's testimony is in Cecil Papers 21/98; his estimate is in Brit. Lib., MS Lansdowne 70, item 36. The letter of the commissioners to Burghley, September 14, 1592, is Brit. Lib., MS Lansdowne 70, item 42.

11. Bradbank's confession was taken on October 9, 1592 (Cecil Papers 22/3); Merick made his denial on November 7. Merick is identified as the captain of the *Prudence* in *The Sea-mans Triumph* (STC 22140).

12. For Burghley's prohibition, see PRO, S.P.Dom. ccxliii,14. For Shory's list, see Cecil Papers 22/13.

13. Cecil Papers 27/5; 28/7; 33/38.

14. Cecil Papers 28/7; 28/19; 29/31. The following is from 28/19: "I, Robert Brooke, goldsmith . . . did lend unto Bartholomew Gilbert & Robert Howe, by the means of Giles Simpson, goldsmith, the sum of one thousand pounds."

15. Cecil Papers 28/6; 28/19; 29/28; 29/30; 29/31.

16. The surviving evidence about these negotiations will prove, in the end, intractable to any scholar determined to make all the pieces fit. I have imposed a structure of my own on such facts as are available, in an attempt to make sense of them. In so doing I have been careful not to distort or misrepresent anything, but I would be hesitant to ask the reader to accept my version of the events as the inevitable one. Anyone wishing to track me through the evidence will see the points at which I had difficulty. The problems are all in the details, not in the substance.

VII   The Swan

1. Henslowe's letters are preserved at Dulwich College. For the texts of these and other letters, see *Henslowe's Diary*, ed. R. A. Foakes and R. T. Rickert (Cambridge, Cambridge University Press, 1961), pp. 274ff.

2. The letter to Burghley is in the Remembrancia, ii.73, and summarized in the *Analytical Index to the Remembrancia*, ed. W. H. and H. C. Overall (London, 1878), pp. 353–4. There is a transcription in E. K. Chambers, *The Elizabethan Stage* (Oxford, Clarendon Press, 1923), iv,316–17. The letter reads in part: "I understand that one Francis Langley, one of the Alnagers for sealing of cloth, intendeth to erect a new stage or theater (as they call it) for the exercising of plays upon the Bankside."

3. For a fuller discussion of the geography and tenancy of the copyhold lands next to the playhouse, see my "'Neere the Playe Howse': the Swan Theater and Community Blight," *Renaissance Drama*, n.s. 4 (1972).

4. The rental figure for the Horse Head, or Nag's Head, is taken from the deposition of Sir Robert Lee in 1604 in the suit which Hannibal Gammon and Richard Langley brought against Jane Langley, widow (PRO, C.24/307/29). The mortgage to Simpson was enrolled in the Court of Hustings (CLRO, Hustings Roll 274/26). The specific properties are not named in this indenture, but from the list of tenants it is clear which messuages are meant. Richard Langley was in the Horse Head; Terry, Howe, Gammon and Cornwall were in the Saracen's Head; and widow Clarke was in one of the messuages next to the Horse Head. Her late husband Thomas had shared the two adjoining messuages with John Ballett, who was presumably still a tenant also. Ballett, who was unsuccessfully nominated as alderman for Aldersgate ward in October 1594, died in September 1595; his will (PCC 62 Scott, now PRO, Prob.11/86) was witnessed by Hannibal Gammon, William Herrick and Rowland Barker. Robert Lee was in possession of all of these messuages by September 1597. His purchase was not enrolled in Hustings, and I have not been able to find a record of it elsewhere. But from his deposition above, and from the indenture by which he in turn transferred the property to his son Henry (CLRO, Hustings Roll 276/64, September 30, 1597), it is clear that he purchased the properties from Francis Langley and Giles Simpson. On this latter date the tenants were Richard Langley, haberdasher, Hannibal Gammon, goldsmith, John Terry, goldsmith, John Cornwall, goldsmith, Nicholas Hooker, goldsmith, and Katherine Clarke, widow.

5. For a fuller discussion of these dates, and of the costs, see Joseph Quincy Adams, *Shakespearean Playhouses* (New York, Houghton Mifflin, 1917), esp. pp. 44, 144, 162, 249, and 260. For

still further particulars, see the lawsuits reproduced by C. W. Wallace in "Shakespeare and His London Associates" and "The First London Theatre" (*University of Nebraska Studies*, 1910, 1913).

6. F. T. Rickert, in "That Wonderful Year—1596" (*Renaissance Papers*, 1963, pp. 53–62) thinks that Langley spent "between 500 and 600 pounds" in erecting the Swan, but offers no argument to support his estimate; to me it seems low.

7. The token books for 1594, 1595, 1596–1597, 1598, and 1599 are, respectively, GLRO, P.92/SAV/242, /245, /246, /247, and /248.

8. For a fuller discussion of the tenements near the playhouse, see my "'Neere the Playe Howse'."

9. The long plague also marked a watershed in the literary history of the stage. By the summer of 1594 Greene and Marlowe were both dead; Kyd would be dead by the year's end. Chapman and Jonson were just appearing on the horizon. Few playwrights of any consequence can be found who wrote both before and after the plague; Nashe and Munday are perhaps exemplars. The great exception is of course Shakespeare, the only writer in evidence in June 1594 with real talent and with prior service. See E. K. Chambers, *William Shakespeare* (Oxford, Clarendon Press, 1930), i,47.

10. During the Lenten break Henslowe refurbished his playhouse, "painting & doing it about with elm boards & other reparations," at a cost of over a hundred pounds. This may represent a normal year's wear and tear on the building; or it might represent Henslowe's attempt to modernize the Rose in anticipation of Langley's competition. See Foakes and Rickert, *Henslowe's Diary*, p. 6.

11. Rickert, "That Wonderful Year," p. 56.

12. Foakes and Rickert, *Henslowe's Diary*, p. 9.

13. Ibid., p. 7. Greg's notes are in his own earlier edition of the *Diary* (London, A. H. Bullen, 1904–1908), ii, 240, 299, 312. For further discussion of Nichols and Smith see Mary Edmond, "Pembroke's Men" (*Review of English Studies*, n.s. 25 [1974] pp. 129–136), and Scott McMillin, "Simon Jewell and the Queen's Men" (*Review of English Studies*, n.s. 27 [1976] pp. 174–177).

14. The Bankside token books referred to here are GLRO, P92/SAV/245/30, /246/34, /247/35, and /248/32. Henslowe recorded a further loan to his nephew in the year of his disappearance from Langley's rents: "Lent unto Francis Henslowe the 15 of December 1597 when he went to take his house on the Bankside called the Upper Ground the sum of £6." Greg, in his edition of the *Diary* (ii,277), says "the house was doubtless the Upper Ground, which gave its name to the modern Upper Ground Street." But this is surely too fanciful; the Upper Ground was simply the name of that stretch of the Bankside which lay within the manor of Paris Garden. Henslowe probably meant "on that part of the Bankside called

the Upper Ground," and not that the house itself was so named. The note in the Foakes and Rickert edition is not much help.

15. Chambers, *Elizabethan Stage*, ii,300. The token books for the Boroughside are numbered differently from those for corresponding years from the Bankside. The references for these citations are GLRO, P92/SAV/188/21, /189/22, /190/23; not listed in /191/11; listed in /192/19 and /193/21; not listed subsequently.

16. Some clues about other playing companies are already available. In the spring of 1594, for example, the Countess of Warwick was treating with the Lord Mayor and aldermen "concerning plays" (see Chambers, *Elizabethan Stage*, iv,315); she may have wished to continue the patronage of a company after the manner of her husband, who had died in 1590.

17. For the *Samaritan*, see *The Fugger News-Letters*, second series, ed. V. von Klarwill, tr. L. S. R. Byrne (London, Bodley Head, 1926), p. 269.

VIII   Cadiz

1. The letter was written "from my house in London" on April 28, 1596. Cecil Papers 40/36.

2. Cecil Papers 40/80.

3. Cecil Papers 40/80.

4. Cecil Papers 40/88. One must infer from this that Terry and Gammon, and perhaps Howe as well, were temporarily out of the Saracen's Head, perhaps as a result of Langley's mortgage to Simpson. They shortly returned, however, and were still on the premises in 1602. I have tried to read the manuscript *horshew* as *horshed*, but the final letter is clearly a *w*. There was a messuage in Cheapside called the Horseshoe; it was one of the shops in Goldsmiths' Row, next adjoining to Sir John Langley's old shop, the Adam and Eve. But there is no evidence of Gammon's occupancy; the Goldsmiths' records show the Horseshoe as leased to one Robert Forrest at this time. It is unlikely, however, that Ashley would misrepresent the matter to Cecil. Nearly a decade earlier Langley had lodged "at the Gilt Horseshoe in Cheapside"—Ashley had corresponded with him there—and Ashley may have been inadvertently recalling that name (*Calendar of State Papers, Foreign, 1585–1586*, London, HMSO, 1921, p. 406).

5. Cecil Papers 40/89. The letter is dated from Hartford Bridge, some thirty-five miles west of London, near Basingstoke, May 16, 1596.

6. Cecil Papers 41/6.

7. Cecil Papers 41/31.

8. Cecil Papers 42/23 for Carew's letter. The knights are listed in Brit. Lib., MS Lansdowne 81, item 73, fol. 188, "the names of the

Knights made at Cales [Cadiz] 1596." The prohibition against looting was reported even on the Spanish side; see Hist. Mss. Comm., *Salisbury Papers*, vi,226. For a fuller general account of the raid on Cadiz, see Robert W. Kenny, *Elizabeth's Admiral* (Baltimore, Johns Hopkins University Press, 1970), pp. 167–202.

9. Cecil Papers 42/103 for Ashley's early departure from Plymouth.

10. For the letters from Drake and Gorges see Hist. Mss. Comm., *Salisbury Papers*, vi,320–322. Ashley's letter to Burghley is Brit. Lib., MS Lansdowne 82, item 84, fol. 170 n.f. (172 o.f.).

11. For the text of the letter, see *APC* 1596–1597, pp. 84-89.

12. Cecil Papers 43/70, Ashley to Meyrick, August 10, 1596; 43/81, Ashley to Meyrick, August 12, 1596; 44/5, Ashley to Cecil, August 23, 1596. Ashley's adventure with the shipload of oil did not prosper either; Meyrick wrote him about the "shipwrack of the oil prize," and Ashley wrote back to inquire "what order you have taken for the disposing of the oil that was saved from wrack." In a postscript, Ashley cautioned Meyrick, "I pray conceal all for fear of the worst, nor be not known I have writ to you" (43/70, 43/81). But Meyrick did not conceal all. In his articles against Ashley (PRO, S.P.12/260, item 28) he claimed to have heard Ashley state "we must have wealth, we will have wealth in this journey by what means soever." He claimed that Ashley also said "I will make this commission worth a good manor to either of us," and Meyrick asserted that Ashley "did gain above £3000 by color of that commission," and that he stole "jewels . . . worth a thousand ducats."

13. Cecil Papers 44/21; PRO, S.P.12/259/109.

14. Cecil Papers 45/52. In an earlier essay on this subject (*Modern Philology* 69, no. 2 [November 1971], p. 114) I offered the observation that Ashley was kept in prison for a year. I based this assumption on a comment in a letter from Rowland Whyte to Sir Robert Sydney, dated March 4, 1597: "Sir Anthony Ashley is still in the fleet, and his disgrace continues on all sides; but I hear my lady Rich hath undertaken to appease the Earl of Essex" (Hist. Mss. Comm., *De l'Isle Papers*, ii,244). Ashley was, however, released from the Fleet in October 1596 by his own testimony. It could have been but small consolation to Ashley that one G. Phillips dedicated his book, *The April of the Church*, to Ashley and his wife in 1596; see Franklin B. Williams, *Index of Dedications and Commendatory Verses in English Books before 1641* (London, Bibliographical Society, 1962).

15. Cecil Papers 40/89.

16. PRO, K.B.27/1340/425; see Leslie Hotson, *Shakespeare versus Shallow* (Boston, Little Brown, 1931), for a discussion of Gardiner and especially pp. 322-323 for an abstract of this suit and two similar suits.

IX   Langley and Shakespeare

1. Cecil Papers 42/56 for Cobham's letter, 42/59 for Stallenge's letter.

2. It is often maintained that the suspension of playing on July 22, 1596, was brought about by the death on that day of Lord Hunsdon, the Lord Chamberlain. This is of course possible, for both events did occur on the same day; but the Privy Council, in ordering the justices to "restrain the players from showing or using any plays" at that time, justified its action only on the grounds that "by drawing of much people together increase of sickness is feared." No mention was made of Hunsdon, or of funeral obsequies. Hunsdon's successor in the office of Chamberlain, Lord Cobham, died on March 6, 1597, and no effort was made to suspend playing on that occasion. More likely the occurrence of Hunsdon's death and the restraint of playing on the same date is only a coincidence. If Hunsdon's death was indeed the cause of the suspension of playing in 1596, it was a singular honor, and I see no reason for the Council's pretending in its own minutes that the suspension proceeded from some other cause. Hunsdon's death is first mentioned in the minutes of the meeting of July 24, and there only in reference to his office as Lord Lieutenant of Suffolk.

3. R. B. McKerrow, *The Works of Thomas Nashe* (Oxford, Blackwell, 1966), v,194. Cobham was not anti-theatrical. He maintained his own company of players during the decade of the 1560s, known variously as "Lord Cobham's players" or "the Lord Warden's players"; see J. T. Murray, *English Dramatic Companies* (London, Constable, 1910), ii,82.

4. E. K. Chambers, *The Elizabethan Stage* (Oxford, Clarendon Press, 1923), ii,359.

5. See Chambers, *Elizabethan Stage*, ii,361n for a summary of the arguments in favor of 1596 as the year of de Witt's visit, and ii,362 for the text of van Buchell's notes. The drawing is reproduced on ii,521. De Witt and van Buchell were both born in 1565 and would have been thirty years old or thereabouts in 1596; see K. T. Gaedertz, *Zur Kenntnis der altenglischen Bühne* (Bremen, 1888), p. 57. I suppose the general consensus is that the drawing in van Buchell's book was made by van Buchell himself, copying an original drawing by de Witt, and that de Witt's drawing and the accompanying text reached van Buchell by letter. Gaedertz himself seemed confused on the matter; on p. 63 of his essay he suggested that the drawing was de Witt's own, though elsewhere he named van Buchell. H. B. Wheatley ("On A Contemporary Drawing of the Interior of the Swan Theatre, 1596," *Transactions of the New Shakspere Society*, 1887–1892, pt. 2, series 1, no. 12, pp. 215-225), rejected the idea that de Witt did the drawing on the grounds that it was on a page of van Buchell's book. No one has seriously objected since. But

I see no bar to the alternative suggestion that de Witt communicated his observations to van Buchell on his return, and perhaps even did the drawing for him.

6. Raymond Chapman, in "'Twelfth Night' and the Swan Theatre" (*Notes and Queries* 196 [1951], pp. 468–470), argues for Olivia and Malvolio. Martin Holmes ("A New Theory about the Swan Drawing," *Theatre Notebook* 10, no. 3 [April-June 1956], pp. 80–83) explains the empty seats in the drawing by suggesting that de Witt was present at a rehearsal.

7. Chambers presents his evidence in *William Shakespeare* (Oxford, Clarendon Press, 1930), ii,87ff. More useful, if less accessible, is Evans's *Shakespeare in the Public Records*, Public Record Office Handbooks no. 5 (London, HMSO, 1964).

8. PRO, K.B.29/234. Hotson transcribes and translates both of these entries, and furnishes a photograph of the latter, in *Shakespeare versus Shallow*, pp. 9, 20.

9. It was not uncommon for such writs of attachment to be misdirected. Early in December 1596, during the same law term in which Wayte swore out his writ, William Mosyer was granted a writ of attachment against Francis Langley by the Court of Chancery; the writ was erroneously ordered directed to the sheriff of London, even though Mosyer knew that Langley lived in Surrey. See PRO, C.33/92 "B" 38–39 Eliz, fol. 576v.

10. For the records of Moyerghe's suit against Langley see PRO, K.B.27/1332, memb. 567, Hilary 37 Eliz.

11. The letter is dated January 5, 1597, from Antwerp, new style; the corresponding date in England was December 26. The letter presumably refers to the weather of the preceding week or so. See *The Fugger News-Letters*, second series, ed. V. von Klarwill, tr. L. S. R. Byrne (London, Bodley Head, 1926), p. 287.

X Pembroke's Men

1. The lawsuit is PRO, Req.2/266/23. Wallace did not identify it, but many subsequent researchers have independently rediscovered it and furnished its appropriate reference. Wallace's complete transcription of the documents is in "The Swan Theatre and the Earl of Pembroke's Players," *Englische Studien* 43 (1911).

2. The introduction to the Foakes and Rickert edition of *Henslowe's Diary* (Cambridge, Cambridge University Press, 1961, pp. xxxiii–xxxvi) contains a good summary of the current views on the system. Henslowe's new accounting required five columns of figures; the first two columns seem to correspond to the earlier entries in pounds and shillings (Henslowe stopped recording pence in December 1595), but now Henslowe used arabic notation instead of the earlier roman system. The only numbers that occur in the first column are 0,1,2,3. In the second column numbers 0 through 19 all occur, but no others. The remaining columns are more problemati-

cal. Numbers in columns 3 and 4 go as high as 30; in column five as high as 14. I have taken the first two columns to be pounds and shillings in order to do the computation offered in the text.

3. For Henslowe's letter see Foakes and Rickert, *Henslowe's Diary*, p. 280.

4. Bernard Beckerman, "Philip Henslowe," in *The Theatrical Manager in England and America*, ed. Joseph W. Donohue (Princeton, Princeton University Press, 1971), p. 37.

5. Wallace, "Swan Theatre," p. 358.

6. Chambers (*Elizabethan Stage*, ii,200) prefers to think that the Pembroke's company of 1597 arose "from a combination of discontented elements in [Hunsdon's] company and in the Admiral's," on the grounds that "there is no known evidence, in provincial records or elsewhere, for any continuous existence of Pembroke's between 1593 and 1597." This is surely a reasonable caution, though in order to follow through with it Chambers was constrained to suggest that Shaa, Spencer, Bird, and the two Jeffes all came from Hunsdon's, another presumption for which there is no known evidence. Again, defectors from Hunsdon's are no more likely to have had an independent supply of playbooks with them than are defectors from the Admiral's. One takes one's choice of uncertainties. We must decide at the outset whether we wish to argue, with Chambers, that there were only two companies in London from 1594 to 1597, or (as I prefer) that there were more than two. How the available evidence arranges itself in our minds will be contingent on our response to this first question.

7. See Wallace, "Swan Theatre," p. 363, for Wallace's reckoning of Langley's receipts. His calculations are based on the assumption that the receipts at the Swan were approximately equal to those at the Rose, an assumption not without its risks.

8. George Carey's paternal grandmother was Mary Boleyn, sister to Anne Boleyn who was the Queen's mother. Carey was forty-nine years old when he became Lord Chamberlain in 1597.

9. For further details on these matters, see G. B. Harrison, *The Life and Death of Robert Devereux, Earl of Essex* (New York, Henry Holt & Co., 1937), and P. M. Handover, *The Second Cecil* (London, Eyre & Spottiswoode, 1959). Additional details may be found in E. K. Chambers, *Sir Henry Lee* (Oxford, Clarendon Press, 1936).

10. See William Green's edition of the *Merry Wives of Windsor* (Princeton, Princeton University Press, 1962) for a summary of the Cobham argument, and a rebuttal.

11. *Prothalamion* 147–150. In the disputes that arose between Essex and Cecil, the administrative temperament would no doubt choose to side with Cecil; perhaps the academic temperament does as well. But there is no denying that Spenser, and probably Shakespeare, were in Essex's camp.

12. The kind of arms furnished varied with the worth of the indi-

vidual, as determined by the assessments of the commissioners for the subsidy. Langley was rated at £20 in 1598 and 1599 (PRO, E.179/186/370, /375A); his assessed value for the two prior years has not survived, but it was likely the same. The relevant statute is 4&5 Philip and Mary, cap. 2, sec. 2. For the bonds between Langley and Shaa, and the suit, see PRO, C.P.40/1608, memb. 1856.

13. *APC* 1597, p. 287. The Lord Mayor had earlier protested against the increased levies in London, writing to the Privy Council on December 24, 1596 (Cecil Papers 47/50; Hist. Mss. Comm., *Salisbury Papers*, vi,534–536, London, HMSO, 1892). On that occasion he expressed the City's willingness "to apply ourselves towards the accomplishment of her Highness' pleasure if the present estate of this her City were any way answerable" to her requests. The Lord Mayor recounted "the former service done by this City as well for the common defence of this Realm as for all other extraordinary adventures required by her highness," but also noted that "we may not conceal the great discontentment & utter discouragement of the common people within this City touching their adventure in the late voyage to the town at Cales [Cadiz]." Despite the great victory there, the Lord Mayor went on, the citizens were unhappy because "neither their principal nor any part thereof was restored unto them" of the money they had advanced; as a result, "they are made hereby utterly unfit & indisposed for the like service to be done hereafter." These grievances were nourished over the winter. The City's reluctance to muster troops in the spring was therefore not a sudden new attitude.

14. *APC* 1597, p. 292. Even Falstaff, corrupt muster master though he be, considered the need for apparel. "These fellows will do well, Master Shallow . . . Bardolph, give the soldiers coats" (2 *Henry IV*, III,ii).

15. *APC* 1597, p. 298.

XI   The Isle of Dogs

1. This letter, and the two others subsequently cited, are in the Remembrancia; full transcripts are in E. K. Chambers, *The Elizabethan Stage* (Oxford, Clarendon Press, 1923) iv,316–322.

2. The Polish ambassador's visit is noticed in *Cal. S.P.Dom.* 1595–1597, pp. 474, 476 and *APC* 1597, p. 307.

3. Glynne Wickham (*Early English Stages*, II,ii,11, London, Routledge and Kegan Paul, 1972) proceeds on the assumption that the Lord Mayor received a similar letter. There is no evidence to support this assumption. The Lord Mayor, and all aldermen who have passed the chair, carry the title of Justices of London; but these are emphatically not the same as the Justices of Middlesex. See Remembrancia I.496 (*Analytical Index to the Remembrancia*, ed. W. H. and H. C. Overall, London, 1878, p. 43).

4. *Henslowe's Diary*, ed. R. A. Foakes and R. T. Rickert (Cam-

bridge, Cambridge University Press, 1961), p. 48. See Greg's edition (London, A. H. Bullen, 1904–1908), ii,326, for the discussion of erroneous dates. Chambers, in a moment of weakness, says "it is possible that plays were inhibited altogether during the summer of 1596, although no formal order to that effect is preserved" (*Elizabethan Stage*, ii, 195); further along (iv, 319) he cites the formal order from the minutes of the Privy Council. This is surely a slip of memory, forgivable in a work of such magnitude. He may have had the previous year in mind. Henslowe's diary shows a suspension of playing by the Admiral's men in 1595 from June 27 to August 25; but unfortunately the Privy Council registers for that period are lost, and there is no way to check Henslowe's date of termination against the Council order.

5. Chambers, *Elizabethan Stage*, ii,132; *The Reader's Encyclopedia of Shakespeare*, ed. O. J. Campbell, s.v. "Isle of Dogs"; Wickham, *Early English Stages*, II,ii,12.

6. For Wallace's earlier acceptance of these forgeries, see "The Children of the Chapel at Blackfriars 1597–1603," *University of Nebraska Studies* 8 (1908), p. 155 (269). Collier's interpolations are on pp. 94, 98, and 99 of his edition of Henslowe's diary (*Publications of the Shakespeare Society*, vol. xxvii, London, 1845). Foakes and Rickert discuss these interpolations in notes on pp. 63, 67, and 68 of their own edition. These are not Collier's only forgeries in the *Diary*. For further details of his activities among the papers at Dulwich, see the introduction to George F. Warner's *Catalogue of the Manuscripts and Muniments of Alleyn's College of God's Gift at Dulwich* (London, 1881).

7. Foakes and Rickert, *Henslowe's Diary*, pp. 239, 240. Wallace ("Children of the Chapel at Blackfriars," p. 155 [269]) thought the *Isle of Dogs* was played not before July 28 but "within ten days after the . . . order of July 28." I too once argued (*Modern Philology* 69, no. 2 [November 1971], p. 107) that the *Isle of Dogs* might have been played on or after the twenty-eighth; but I now see that this view is inconsistent with Henslowe's opinion, which must be accepted as a reasonable interpretation of the events. If the *Isle of Dogs* had been played on the twenty-eighth, and the inhibition received that evening, Henslowe would have had to believe that the Council was clairvoyant in order to perceive a connection.

8. R. B. McKerrow, ed., *The Works of Thomas Nashe* (Oxford, Blackwell, 1966), iii,153–154.

9. *APC* 1597, p. 338.

10. Cecil Papers 54/20, Topcliffe to Cecil. The letter is awkwardly summarized, and wrongly attributed to a Robert Topcliffe, in Hist. Mss. Comm., *Salisbury Papers*, vii,343. The earlier calendars of the Historical Manuscripts Commission are of variable quality and are therefore untrustworthy.

11. For Gerard's views see the *Dictionary of National Biography*

article on Topcliffe. For the warrants to the keeper of the Marshalsea, see *APC* 1597–1598, p. 33 or Chambers, *Elizabethan Stage*, iv,323. Both these transcriptions wrongly reproduce the date as October 8; see PRO, P.C.2/23, p. 13. Topcliffe is one of the more interesting excrescences of the period and deserves fuller study than he has yet received. On October 5, 1597, two days after the release of the three players, Langley borrowed £7 from Thomas Downton, one of their fellows, signing a bond in St. Mary le Bow. He defaulted, and Downton sued him for debt in the Court of Common Pleas at the same time that Shaa was suing him for his own debt. Downton's suit is PRO, C.P.40/1608, memb. 1856.

12. McKerrow, *Nashe*, v,33; G. R. Hibbard, *Thomas Nashe* (Cambridge, Massachusetts, Harvard University Press, 1962), p. 236.

13. Wickham has in fact shifted his own ground on this issue. In *Early English Stages*, II,i,279 he states "We do not know why the Privy Council allowed its instructions to be flouted so glaringly." A few years later (II,ii,11) he has decided that the order "cannot be taken at its face value." His argument needs to be read in full. "The Privy Council Order of 1597 for the Destruction of London's Playhouses" is the title of the second chapter in II,ii.

14. *Henslowe's Diary,* ed. W. W. Greg (London, A. H. Bullen, 1904–1908), ii,186–7.

15. The decree of May 29, noticed by Wallace, is PRO, Req.1/19, p. 405. Two earlier entries in the decree book, not noticed by Wallace, are on pp. 299 (May 12, 1598), and 327 (May 26, 1598).

16. PRO, Req.2/266/23.

17. PRO, Req.2/266/23.

18. These suits are all in the PRO. For Benyan, see C.P.40/1588, memb. 1504. For Shepperd, C.P.40/1587, memb. 830d. For Pitchford, C.P.40/1605, memb. 1710, /1601, memb. 3391d. For Hassould, C.P.40/1641, memb. 1646. For Sutton, C.P.40/1620, memb. 420, /1616, membs. 1515 and 1203d. For Lever, K.B.27/1346, memb. 343. For Monk, K.B.27/1360, memb. 1057d, /1364, memb. 476.

19. This and the subsequent depositions are from PRO, Sta.Cha.5/A.25/27.

20. From the Vestry Minute Book of St. Saviour's parish, GLRO, P92/SAV/450, pp. 316 and 317.

21. For Renching, see *APC* 1597–1598, and also PRO, E.112/28/343. Coin clipping or filing must rank among the more tedious ways of accumulating a stock of precious metal, but it was not that uncommon, and many examples of clipped coins from the period have survived.

XII   The Diamond

1. Cecil Papers 57/69.
2. Cecil Papers 57/77.

3. Cecil Papers 57/110. In the printed calendar (Hist. Mss. Comm., *Salisbury Papers*, vii,521), Terry's name appears as *Tinvey*, but in the manuscript it is clearly *Tirrey*. The letters cited above are all paraphrased and condensed in the calendars.

4. These details are from a letter which Ashley wrote to Lord Cobham on January 17, 1598; Cecil Papers 48/102.

5. Cecil Papers 61/3, May 6, 1598. Howe's name is transcribed as *Stow* in the calendar, but in the manuscript it is clearly *How*.

6. PRO, K.B.27/1349, memb. 317 for Gilbert's suit. Howe and Terry's countersuit is Req.2/215/53; the judgment is PRO, Req.1/19, p. 470.

7. Cecil Papers 61/3.

XIII The Community

1. For the Privy Council letters see *APC* 1597–98, p. 327.

2. Exemplification was a common abuse, finally put down in 1616 as a result of the following accumulation of incidents: "Thomas Swynnerton and Martin Slaughter, being two of the Queen's Majesty's company of players having separated themselves from their said company, have each of them taken forth a several exemplification or duplicate of his Majesty's letters patent granted to the whole company and by virtue thereof they severally in two companies, with vagabonds and such like idle persons, have and do use and exercise the quality of playing in divers places . . . William Perrie having likewise gotten a warrant whereby he and a certain company of idle persons with him do travel and play under the name and title of the Children of his Majesty's Revels . . . also Gilbert Reason one of the Prince his Highness' players having likewise separated himself from his company hath also taken forth another exemplification or duplicate of the patent granted to that company and lives in the same kind & abuse; and likewise one Charles Marshall, Humfry Jeffes and William Parr three of Prince Palatine's company of players having also taken forth an exemplification or duplicate of the patent granted to the said company," etc. The warrant for which this catalogue of abuses served as prologue authorized all justices of the peace, mayors, sheriffs, bailiffs, constables and other royal officers to confiscate such exemplifications; the order was signed by the man who was Lord Chamberlain in 1616, William, Earl of Pembroke. See E. K. Chambers, *The Elizabethan Stage* (Oxford, Clarendon Press, 1923), iv,343.

3. GLRO, Vestry Minute Book, P92/SAV/450, pp. 323, 324. Jacob Meade, waterman, was Henslowe's neighbor in Clink liberty and his business partner from about this period.

4. Vestry Minute Book, p. 325.

5. *Henslowe's Diary*, ed. R. A. Foakes and R. T. Rickert (Cambridge, Cambridge University Press, 1961), pp. 76, 77.

6. Ibid., pp. 98, 68, 99.

7. Vestry Minute Book, p. 326. Glynne Wickham (*Early English Stages*, II,ii,14, London, Routledge and Kegan Paul, 1972) states that the churchwardens "were invited to view" Langley's new buildings; but the evidence is clear, even from the source he cites, that the decision was not reached in response to an invitation but rather by the action of the vestry on its own initiative. A bit further on (p. 19), he states that Langley "was busily refurbishing or improving" the Swan playhouse in February 1598, and that the playhouse "was to be inspected by the churchwardens of the parish two months later." There is no documentation to support any refurbishing, and the vestry's inspection was to be of the new tenements, as they clearly stated. Still later (p. 69), he speaks of Langley's "outlay of additional capital in an endeavour to bring the building into line with the Privy Council's new requirements"; this is, again, unsupported by any evidence that I know of.

8. Vestry Minute Book, pp. 331, 338.

9. Vestry Minute Book, p. 339.

10. Vestry Minute Book. For the details of this meeting, p. 343; for Humble's earlier elections to office, pp. 274, 287.

11. Vestry Minute Book, p. 344. For some of Humble's legal entanglements, see the following, all in the PRO: Humble vs. Langley, Req.2/34/73; Humble vs. Browker, C.3/261/34; Humble vs. Cure, C.2/Jas I/H.26/69.

12. For Humble's appointments by and to the Sewer Commission, see GLRO, SKCS 18, fols. 189v, 265v, 290v.

13. The first volume of records, covering several decades, is in the GLRO, SKCS 18; subsequent records are in both the GLRO and the British Library. For further documentation on the Newington Butts playhouse see *Shakespeare Quarterly* 21:4 (Autumn 1970), pp. 385–398.

14. GLRO, SKCS 18, fols. 73v, 63, 71v, 69v, 91.

15. These items were chosen at random; for representative instances, see GLRO, SKCS 18, fols. 30r, 96v, 80v, 23r, 57v.

16. GLRO, SKCS 18, fol. 194v.

17. GLRO, SKCS 18, fol. 252v.

18. GLRO, SKCS 18. For the assessment, fol. 256v; for the presentment, at the Court of June 9, 1958, fol. 279v. Opposite this entry the clerk of the court has written "done."

19. GLRO, SKCS 18, fol. 293v.

20. GLRO, SKCS 18, fol. 300v.

21. GLRO, SKCS 18, fol. 310r.

22. GLRO, SKCS 18, fol. 317r.

23. GLRO, M92/117.

24. For the Council's attentions to Renching see *APC* 1597–98, p. 188. For his apprenticeship see the Wardens' Accounts and Court Minutes of the Company of Goldsmiths, Book L, p. 177. For

Langley's debt to him see PRO, K.B.27/1316, memb. 421. For the Exchequer suit see PRO, E.112/28/343, Trinity term 1598.

25. Of the goods confiscated from Renching, the Queen on January 29, 1599, made a gift of £200 towards the relief of his widow Susan and her three children. See *Cal. S.P.Dom.* 1598–1601, p. 155.

XIV Exit the Alnager

1. PRO, Sta.Cha.5/A.25/27. The inability of the Attorney General's office to determine Langley's given name is curious; one would think that ordinary inquiry would produce the information. Perhaps Langley's sense of dignity required that he be known as Mister to his colleagues, or even as Lord. His given name had perhaps dropped from general circulation by 1598.

2. PRO, Sta.Cha.5/A.8/4.

3. The depositions of the clothiers are all from PRO, Sta.Cha.5/A.25/27.

4. A wantle is a pack or bundle.

5. CLRO, Rep. 24, fol. 393. The Decrees and Orders of the Court of Star Chamber do not exist for this period, but evidence of the decrees can be found elsewhere. In this case, the records of the Exchequer show that John Leake, the senior alnager, was fined £133 6^s 8^d (that is, 200 marks), and George Martin, the most junior alnager, £40 (PRO, E.159/417/Trinity 41 Elizabeth/51). Langley and Chapman seem not to have been fined. It was not unusual for the Star Chamber to levy fines selectively, and no imputations of guilt or innocence ought to be read into these facts. The City had its own interpretation, of course; despite the conviction in Star Chamber, Leake, Martin and Chapman were allowed to continue in their posts; Langley alone was singled out for dismissal.

6. CLRO, Rep. 24, fol. 444. August 8 was a Wednesday; the aldermen normally met only on Tuesdays and Thursdays. This session was recorded as a *curia specialis*.

7. PRO, C.24/305/1, the deposition of Alice Pattenson, August 1, 1604.

8. For the lay subsidy commission, see PRO, E.179/186/375A. Langley was also on this commission in the previous year (E.179/186/370), and had earlier been an assessor for Paris Garden (E.179/186/349, /362). For Langley's encounter with Woodliffe in April, see PRO, Sta.Cha.5/S.13/8, wherein Langley deposed in April 1600 that he "hath known them [Samwell and Woodliffe] for the span of one year or thereabouts."

XV The Boar's Head

1. Two recent works on the Boar's Head treat the subject more fully than I do here. C. J. Sisson left a manuscript on innyard theatres at his death in 1966, which was readied for the press by Stan-

ley Wells and published in 1972 with the somewhat misleading title *The Boar's Head Theatre: An Inn-yard Theatre of the Elizabethan Age* (London, Routledge and Kegan Paul). Herbert Berry is now readying for the press a book that is (as Sisson's is not) exclusively about the Boar's Head, on which subject it is more circumstantial and better documented. Portions of Berry's work have already appeared in print: "The Playhouse in the Boar's Head Inn, Whitechapel," in *The Elizabethan Theatre I*, ed. D. Galloway (Hamden, Connecticut, Archon Books, 1970), pp. 45–73; "The Boar's Head Again," in *The Elizabethan Theatre III*, ed. D. Galloway (Hamden, Connecticut, Archon Books, 1973), pp. 33–65; and "The Playhouse in the Boar's Head Inn, Whitechapel, III," in *Shakespeare 1971*, ed. C. Leech and J. M. R. Margeson (Toronto, University of Toronto Press, 1972), pp. 12–20. Given these circumstances, it may seem gratuitous for me to offer another discussion of the Boar's Head here; I do so, nevertheless, chiefly to provide a balance in my narrative and to indicate the interrelation between Langley's Boar's Head activities and his other affairs. My survey of Langley's involvement is deliberately brief, and the reader will want to consult Professor Berry's work for the fullest account. I was privileged to see portions of his forthcoming book in typescript; my indebtedness to it is far greater than my notes indicate.

2. "But only ingress egress and regress into and from the same great yard"; Woodliffe's answer to Samwell, PRO, Sta.Cha.5/S.74/3.

3. Sisson, *The Boar's Head Theatre*, p. 30.

4. For Langley's deposition see PRO, Sta.Cha.5/S.13/8. For the weekly income from the western gallery see Berry's first Boar's Head article (1970), p. 55 n. 19. Samwell assumed that Woodliffe and Langley engaged in collusion from the start. He described Langley as a man "well known to be a common disturber of your Majesty's subjects by prosecuting suits, by sinister vexation of your subjects, and upon buying of many other pretended rights and titles" (PRO, Sta.Cha.5/S.74/3).

5. PRO, Sta.Cha.5/S.74/3, Samwell's bill of complaint.

6. For Samwell's recollection see PRO, Sta.Cha.5/S.74/3.

7. PRO, Sta.Cha.5/S.74/3, the bill.

8. PRO, Sta.Cha.5/S.13/8.

9. PRO, Sta.Cha.5/S.74/3; C.24/278/71.

10. PRO, Sta.Cha.5/S.13/8.

11. PRO, Sta.Cha.5/S.13/8. Samwell complained in April 1600 that "since Michaelmas last past" he had "been put [to] the expense of forty pounds" in the course of extricating himself and his family from the marshal's men, "and no suit there prosecuted or proved to be good." In another place he complained again of his "arrests in the said Marshal's court without [any] cause of action" ever

presented (PRO, Sta.Cha.5/S.74/3). He was probably right about the costs; Alexander Foxley, one of the marshal's men, affirmed that he had "often arrested the plainant [i.e., Samwell] at many men's suits by writ out of the court of the Marshalsea and hath taken the ordinary fee every time" (PRO, Sta.Cha.5/S.74/3, Foxley's answer). Remedy was theoretically available by Parliamentary Statute (8 Eliz., cap. 2); men were often arrested on various charges, the Statute affirmed, and when they were later "brought forth to answer to such actions and suits as should be objected against them, then many times there is no declaration or matter laid against the parties so arrested or attached, whereunto they may make any answer; and so the party arrested is very maliciously put to great charges and expenses without any just or reasonable cause." All such vexatious charges were henceforth to be recovered from the false plainant, according to the Statute; but enforcement was another matter. The statute was reiterated in 1601 (43 Eliz., caps. 5, 6).

12. Samwell's Star Chamber bill, and the replies, are PRO, Sta.Cha.5/S.74/3. The related interrogatory and depositions are PRO, Sta.Cha.5/S.13/8.

13. Evidence for Samwell's suit against Browne survives in the Chancery Decrees and Orders, PRO, C.33/99, fol. 127v. The bills and answers apparently have not survived.

14. Woodliffe's suit against Langley is PRO, C.P.40/1655, memb. 724, Hilary 1601.

15. PRO, C.33/99 fol. 464v; /100 fol. 452v; /102 fols. 249v, 343r–v.

XVI Exit the Lord of the Manor

1. The manor had also been offered to others. George Smithes, a goldsmith in the City, recollected in 1605 that "the said manor of Paris Garden was offered to be sold unto him . . . by the said Francis Langley . . . the sum of money which [Smithes] then offered and should have given for a good assurance of the said manor, and to have had the same cleared of all encumbrances, was two and twenty hundred pounds or thereabouts, which should have been paid within a short time after the agreement . . . if [Smithes] had gone through with the bargain, as he did not" (PRO, C.24/305/1, Smithes' deposition, item 11).

2. PRO, C.2.Jas I/L.13/62, Browker's answer.

3. PRO, C.24/305/1, Gammon's answer to no. 19.

4. For Browker and Gammon, as in the notes immediately above. The regnal year changed on November 17, so 13 Nov 42 Eliz. and 24 Nov 43 Eliz. occur in the same month in 1600.

5. PRO, C.24/305/1, Gammon's answer to no. 22. I have not exhausted the list of payments cited by Gammon in this answer.

Browker's man, Thomas Rotherham, recalled paying £100 to Thomas Harrison "at a goldsmith's house in Cheapside which was one Mr Herrick's house as he now remembereth" (PRO, C.24/305/1).

6. PRO, C.24/305/1, Richard Langley's answer to nos. 22, 23, and 24.

7. PRO, C.24/305/1, Turner's answer to no. 22. The bond to Archer had been signed by Langley, his nephew Richard, and Gammon, but Robert Howe was a fourth signer. See Kempe's deposition, items 21 and 22, in this same document, and also PRO, C.P.40/1661, memb. 1044.

8. Turner's answer to no. 21.

9. PRO, C.24/305/1; Squire's answer to no. 22, Johnson's answer to no. 21.

10. PRO, C.24/305/1; Jadwin's answer to no. 21, Turfett's answer to no. 22. The "token" is no doubt a privy secret between Langley and Browker, used here to authenticate the letter.

11. PRO, C.24/305/1, Walker's deposition, item 21. The cited passage was subsequently deleted in the deposition, perhaps as not being germane to the issue at hand; but it is still legible. Browker's comment is from his answer in PRO, C.2.Jas I/L.13/62.

12. PRO, C.24/305/1, Bury's deposition, items 5 and 6.

13. PRO, C.24/305/1, Haydock's deposition, item 6.

14. PRO, C.2.Jas I/L.13/62, Browker's answer. The final comment suggests that the manor house was a part of the property conveyed in the thousand-year lease.

15. PRO, C.24/305/1, Gammon's deposition, items 10 and 11.

16. PRO, C.24/305/1, Gammon's answer to nos. 10 and 11, Turner's answer to no. 10. PRO, C.2.Jas I/L.13/62, Browker's answer.

17. PRO, C.24/305/1, Gammon's answer to no. 11. Richard Langley concurred that Browker "had taken upon him . . . to pay an annuity of forty pounds to one Harvest"; see his answer to no. 12.

18. Gammon's answer to no. 18.

19. As above. For the Trial of the Pyx, see Wardens' Accounts and Court Minutes of the Company of Goldsmiths, Book O, p. 181. Giles Simpson was another of the jurors. Gammon continued to live in St. Vedast Foster's parish until at least August 15, 1602, when his daughter Suzanna was christened. He may have continued to live in the Saracen's Head; in the lay subsidy of October 1, 1599, his neighbors are Richard Langley and John Terry. But on December 21, 1603, he described himself as "of the parish of St George in the Borough of Southwark, Goldsmith, of the age of 58 years or thereabouts" (PRO, C.24/305/1); on October 26, 1604, as "of the parish of St Giles without Cripplegate, London, Goldsmith, of the age of 60 years or thereabouts" (PRO, C.24/314/34); on No-

vember 11, 1605, as "of London, Goldsmith, of the age of 60 years or thereabouts" (PRO, C.24/324/109).

20. PRO, C.24/305/1, Emerson's deposition, items 7 and 8; C.2.Jas I/L.13/62, Browker's answer. For Gammon's assignment to Browker, see Surrey Feet of Fines, Hilary 44 Eliz. (PRO, C.P.25(2)/228/Hilary 44 Elizabeth/Surrey).

21. PRO, C.24/305/1, Emerson's deposition, item 7; PRO, C.2.Jas I/L.13/62, Browker's answer.

22. PRO, K.B.27/1370, memb. 375d; /1376, memb. 279d.

23. PRO, C.24/304/27. C. J. Sisson (*The Boar's Head Theatre*, London, Routledge and Kegan Paul, 1972, p. 57), by misreading this document, has placed the events it describes at least a year too early. He also furnishes an incorrect reference.

24. PRO, C.24/304/27. In *The Boar's Head Theatre*, Sisson claims that the players capitulated to Langley's demands because "they were aware that he had friends at Court and was a dangerous man" (p. 57). This puzzling statement is glossed elsewhere: "It is plain that Langley, thanks to his relationship by marriage with Asheley [*sic*], had the resources of the Marshalsea Court and to some extent of the Privy Council behind him" (p. 60). This supposition can hardly be accepted. Langley was in disgrace at this time because of the alnager affair, and Ashley had no influence whatever with Cecil or the Council. The players capitulated to Langley's demands no doubt simply because to have done otherwise would jeopardize their playing and therefore their livelihood, as Mago the carpenter saw quite clearly. But Sisson prefers to speak (p. 52) of the "undue influence" Langley was able to exert, "the influence of his sinister brother-in-law Sir Anthony Asheley, brother of his wife Jane, and a Clerk to the Privy Council." Ashley had of course not been attached to the Council since the Cadiz fiasco, and the reader may judge for himself whether "sinister" is an appropriate adjective. It has been traditional, however, to view Ashley with respect. Fifty years earlier, C. W. Wallace spoke admiringly of Langley's "official position as one of the alneagers of the City, to which he had been recommended by the Queen's Privy Council, supported as it was by powerful Court influence, among which was his brother-in-law Sir Anthony Ashley, for many years before and after (until 1610) the potent Clerk of the Privy Council," and concluded that such an alliance of powerful supporters made Langley and his playhouse, the Swan, "impregnable against any attack from the Mayor and Corporation" ("The Swan Theatre and the Earl of Pembroke's Servants," *Englische Studien* 43 [1911], p. 356). But we have seen that the Privy Council's support of Langley in the matter of his appointment as alnager was for ends quite unrelated to Langley's own welfare or prosperity; that *potent* is hardly the word to describe Ashley in his function as clerk to the Council; and that Langley's perform-

ance as alnager was scandalous. Langley's love of rowdyism, however, provides a common thread. Earlier in the summer he was apparently involved in an affray at the site of the Theater in Shoreditch, a part of the running battle between Giles Allen and Cuthbert Burbage. Allen's Star Chamber plea (PRO, Sta.Cha.5/A.33/37) claims that "about the sixteenth day of May last past" [1601], Langley and his cohorts John Knapp, John Lewis, Roger Amis, and John Jobson "did . . . riotously assemble themselves together and then armed themselves with divers and many unlawful and offensive weapons, as namely swords, daggers, bills, axes, and such like," after which they "in very riotous outrageous and forcible manner" seized and held a portion of "your subject's ground," ground which had formerly been "in the quiet possession of one Cuthbert Burbage, then your subject's farmer thereof." There is, unfortunately, no further information about this escapade.

25. PRO, C.2.Jas I/L.13/62, Browker's answer. "Roomths" means open spaces, not rooms.

26. The final concord, Langley to Browker, is dated February 3, 1602; PRO, C.P.25(2)/228/Hilary 44 Elizabeth/memb. 4.

XVII Cardigan

1. For Lee's purchase of the Cheapside properties, see PRO, C.24/307/29.

2. There is no detailed study of the life of Meyrick. An article appears in the *Dictionary of National Biography*; other details may be found in G. B. Harrison, *The Life and Death of Robert Devereux Earl of Essex* (New York, Henry Holt and Company, 1937).

3. Inquisitions might be held in various places if one's holdings were scattered; the relevant inquisition for the Welsh mines was held at Treheden, Cardiganshire, on May 7, 1601, before Sir Thomas Jones and other commissioners. See PRO, E.112/145/71.

4. For mining in general, see T. A. Rickard, *Man and Metals: A History of Mining* (New York, McGraw Hill, 1932). For sixteenth century mining, especially in Wales, see William Rees, *Industry before the Industrial Revolution*, 2 vols. (Cardiff, University of Wales Press, 1968). For further details on Cardigan, see *A Just and True Remonstrance of His Majesty's Mines-Royal in the Principality of Wales, Presented by Thomas Bushell Esquire, Farmer of the said Mines-Royal to his Majesty* (London, 1642); and *Fodinae Regales, Or the History, Laws, and Places of the Chief Mines and Mineral Works in England, Wales, and the English Pale in Ireland, By Sir John Pettus, Knight* (London, 1670). For Potosí as a synonym for wealth, see Hist. Mss. Comm., *Salisbury Papers* vii, 138.

5. Mr. Customer Smythe, like Gelly Meyrick, has been neglected by modern researchers. A. L. Rowse reports a thesis on Smythe by

his student at Oxford L. L. S. Lowe, in *The England of Elizabeth* (London, Macmillan, 1964, p. 331).

6. For the Lewkenor family, see the Harleian Society *Visitation of Sussex* (London, Harleian Society, 1905). For Richard Lewkenor, see W. R. Williams, *The History of the Great Sessions in Wales* (Brecknock, 1899). For Lewis Lewkenor, see *Notes and Queries* 209 (1964), p. 123ff.

7. These and the subsequent details lie in various places in the Public Record Office. See C.3/279/18, Langley vs. Lewkenor, the bill and answer; E.112/145/5 Hide and Hancock vs. Lewkenor; E.112/145/71, Lewkenor vs. Meyrick; Prob.11/127, the will of Sir Richard Lewkenor.

8. Sir Richard's recollections are from PRO, C.3/279/18, the answer.

9. PRO, C.3/279/18, the answer.

10. Still C.3/279/18; Langley's assertions are from the bill, Sir Richard's statements from the answer.

11. Still C.3/279/18; Jane's recollections from the bill, Sir Richard's from the answer.

12. The details are still from C.3/279/18.

13. Jane's comments about the Gresham suit are from PRO, C.2.Eliz/G.2/28, the answer; the other quotations are, as before, from C.3/279/18.

14. Sisson, like Wallace before him, was persuaded that Langley had died in the summer or autumn of 1601, though neither man offered any evidence to support this date. In a document that Sisson himself cites (PRO, C.24/305/1; see Sisson, *The Boar's Head Theatre*, p. 48), there is clear evidence that Langley was still alive in February 1602, though Sisson seems not to have noted this. No one, apparently, bothered to look in the parish register of St. Saviour's church to see when Langley was buried.

XVIII   Exit Langley

1. Jane's description of herself is from the bill in her suit against Hugh Browker, PRO, C.2.Jas I/L.13/62. Ashley's suit is PRO, K.B.27/1376, memb. 279d. I have found no bills or replies in the suit of Hannibal Gammon and Richard Langley vs. Jane Langley, but see PRO, C.24/307/29, deposition of Sir Robert Lee on behalf of Jane; PRO, C.38/5, a stay of action enabled by Ashley; and various Chancery decrees (all PRO), as C.33/105 fols. 925, 989; /107 fols. 14d, 62, 126d, 287d, 791d (for Bacon), 796; /108 fols. 292, 791; /109 fol. 598; /111 fol. 244; /113 fol. 101d. Grace Darrell's suit, for debt, is PRO, C.P.40/1693, memb. 1514.

2. The quotation is from PRO, C.3/279/18, the bill. Ashley's suit against Lewkenor is PRO, E.112/145/57; the depositions are PRO, E.134/Hilary 14 James I/no. 16. Sir Richard Lewkenor, in his own

will in April 1616 (PCC 62 Cope, now PRO, Prob.11/127), directed his executor "to satisfy and pay a hundred and fifty pounds unto the executors or administrators of . . . Francis Langley." Sir Richard added that "by law I think myself no way compellable to do" this, yet he undertook the repayment "for clearing, satisfying and discharge of my own conscience." The mines came into Hugh Myddelton's hands in the 1620s, and he worked them with vigor, extracting thousands of pounds worth of silver. In the eighteenth century, Cwm Ystwyth alone produced a clear profit of about a thousand pounds a year. See J. W. Gough, *Sir Hugh Myddelton* (Oxford, Clarendon Press, 1964), and, more particularly, Samuel Rush Meyrick, *The History and Antiquities of the County of Cardigan* (London, Longmans, 1808, reissued at Brecon in 1907), p. 108. For the antiquity of the mine, see O. Davies, "Cwm Ystwyth Mines," in *Archaeologia Cambrensis* xcix (1947), pp. 57–63.

3. The 1605 token book is GLRO, P92/SAV/254/23. For the sewer commission entries, see GLRO, SKCS 18, fols. 422v, 426v, 427, 432v. The 1616 token book is GLRO, P92/SAV/255/27. George Delahaye's will is PCC 51 Dorset, now PRO, Prob.11/113. In it he styles himself "esquire, of Reigate, Surrey," and names Jane Delahaye his well-beloved wife and Robert Ashley his brother-in-law. The marriage is entered in the St. Saviour's parish register.

4. The relevant token books are GLRO, P92/SAV/256/12, /257/31, and /258/34, for 1607, 1608, and 1610.

5. Details of the wedding are in the Shaftesbury Collection in the PRO (PRO.30/24/2/14). Ashley's will is PCC 17 Barrington, now PRO, Prob.11/153.

6. Browker's will is PCC 15 Windebank, now PRO, Prob.11/111. The burial is recorded in the St. Saviour's parish register.

7. For Alleyn's election, see GLRO, P92/SAV/450 p. 414. For the later career of the Swan, see G. E. Bentley, *The Jacobean and Caroline Stage*, vol. 6 (Oxford, Clarendon Press, 1968).

Index

329

PN   Ingram:
2598   A London life
.L22   in the Brazen age
I5

PN   Ingram:
2598   A London life
.L22   in the Brazen age
I5

DEMCO